BEYOND BELIEF

POLITICS, HISTORY, AND CULTURE

A series from the International Institute
at the University of Michigan

Series Editors
George Steinmetz and Julia Adams

Series Editorial Advisory Board
Fernando Coronil, Mamadou Diouf,
Michael Dutton, Geoff Eley,
Fatma Müge Göcek, Nancy Rose Hunt,
Andreas Kalyvas, Webb Keane, David Laitin,
Lydia Liu, Julie Skurski, Margaret Somers,
Ann Laura Stoler, Katherine Verdery,
Elizabeth Wingrove

Sponsored by the International Institute at the University of Michigan and published by Duke University Press, this series is centered around cultural and historical studies of power, politics, and the state—a field that cuts across the disciplines of history, sociology, anthropology, political science, and cultural studies. The focus on the relationship between state and culture refers both to a methodological approach—the study of politics and the state using culturalist methods—and a substantive one that treats signifying practices as an essential dimension of politics. The dialectic of politics, culture, and history figures prominently in all the books selected for the series.

Beyond Belief

India and the Politics of

Postcolonial Nationalism

SRIRUPA ROY

∷

DUKE UNIVERSITY PRESS
Durham and London
2007

© 2007 DUKE UNIVERSITY PRESS
All rights reserved

Designed by Amy Ruth Buchanan
Typeset in Quadraat by Keystone
Typesetting, Inc.
Library of Congress Cataloging-in-
Publication Data appear on the last
printed page of this book.

CONTENTS

PREFACE AND ACKNOWLEDGMENTS ::: VII

INTRODUCTION ::: 1
Imagining Institutions, Instituting Diversity: Toward a Theory of Nation-State Formation

CHAPTER 1 ::: 32
Moving Pictures: The Films Division of India and the Visual Practices of the Nation-State

CHAPTER 2 ::: 66
Marching in Time: Republic Day Parades and the Ritual Practices of the Nation-State

CHAPTER 3 ::: 105
Indian Darkness: Science, Development, and the Needs Discourse of the Nation-State

CHAPTER 4 ::: 133
Cities of Hope: Steel Townships and the Spatial Practices of the Nation-State

CONCLUSION ::: 157
After Midnight

NOTES ::: 171

BIBLIOGRAPHY ::: 219

INDEX ::: 237

PREFACE AND

ACKNOWLEDGMENTS

:::

This is a book about history "from above." The narrative unfolds in the center of a capital city. Its protagonists are powerful elites and dominant institutions. Its inspirations are boredom and dust; the boredom that is associated with listening to official speeches, signing forms in triplicate, reading ponderous slogans and incomprehensible bureaucratic jargon, and wondering why anyone bothers in the first place. The dust that, months after a trip to the National Archives of India, spills out of my notebook in a sleepy Massachusetts town and reminds me of all the files that I eagerly waited for, only to receive a crumpled slip of paper with the terse notation "NT": not transferred.

This is a decidedly unfashionable book to write at a time when we know that if history is made from above, then it is undone from below; that for every dominating center, there is a subversive margin. It is written with the conviction that if we want to breathe new life into these tired clichés, then we cannot look away from the how and why of the making and the centering. And so this book is an exploration of the project of nation-state formation in postcolonial India; about how the state worked to define the meaning of India and Indianness, and in the process constituted a distinctive and authoritative identity for itself; about how, why, and if it succeeded; and about how it is only through understanding the complex modalities of this past making that we can begin to understand the present unmaking and envision a future remaking.

The historical institutional questions of nation-state formation were far from my mind when I began the field research for my doctoral dissertation in 1997. Rather, I was interested in understanding the contemporary rise of Hindu nationalism and in evaluating the nature and significance of its challenge to established patterns of political authority, social structure, and national identity in India. What did the ascendancy of an ethnic nationalist movement that sought to recast national identity along religious majoritarian and monocultural lines mean for the future of Indian secularism and democracy? The research questions reflected my disciplinary location in political science, where the task of the researcher is to find causal explanations for novel and disjunctive sets of "current events."

The research questions also reflected a personal curiosity. Although I grew up in India I had been living in the United States since 1988. The significant political, economic, and social transformations that had taken place in India over the decade of the 1990s—the liberalization of the socialist economy, the shift from a one-party dominant political system to an era of unstable coalition governments, the increasing assertiveness of lower-caste and regional political parties, and of course the emergence of new vocabularies and practices of national identity—had for me occurred at a distance, and I was eager to make sense of the unfamiliar now of India.

Although my research focused on one particular aspect of change, namely the replacement of the secular and pluralist formulation of nationhood by a new understanding of India as a Hindu nation, I was equally interested in the broader political, social, and economic realignments that had variously played a role in the emergence and consolidation of Hindu nationalism over the past decade. The theorization of national disjuncture and transformation was thus the central concern of my research project: as I initially understood it, to explain how we got from "there" to "here" would be the primary burden of my fieldwork.

I soon ran up against a problem of benchmarking. To substantiate the thesis of Hindu nationalism (and the "new India" in a more general sense) as disjuncture, an engagement with the preexisting national project was in order. The inquiry into national identity transformation in late-twentieth-century India begged a prior question: transformation of and from what? The answers to this question were surprisingly elusive. There is a rich body of historical scholarship on the Indian nationalist movement in the colonial period. However, most studies end at or around the moment of Indian independence in 1947, and thus do not take forward the story of nationalism "after midnight"—the production of national identity in the newly sovereign nation-state of India. Although many other aspects of order and change in postcolonial India have received sustained attention, the realignments of national identity and the transformations of nationalist discourses and practices that attended the imagination of India as a sovereign nation-state after 1947 are conspicuously understudied. There is a profusion of sharply defined and fiercely defended normative opinions on Indian nationalism in the postcolonial period: the "Nehruvian national project" as it is commonly glossed in reference to the distinctive ideological vision of the first prime minister of the independent nation-state (1947–1964). The existing discussions reproduce either a nostalgic lament for a prelapsarian, "golden age" of pluralist and inclusive national identity, or its polar opposite of a sweeping condemnation of the state-dominated, centralized, and "top down" project of nation building that took place during this period. In both cases, normative evaluations take precedence over a systematic exploration of the project itself.

For the most part, questions of nationhood, nationalism, and national identity have emerged as topics of sustained scholarship only in the 1980s and after, as scholars have turned their attention to the Hindu nationalist movement. There are several reasons for this gap in knowledge. Arguably the main reason why the story of nationalism after midnight resists analytical telling has to do with the perception that it is a story that is only too well known and understood; that is, simply put, the view that there is nothing new or interesting that can be said about the Nehruvian national project, except as the contrastive backdrop or "lineage" of the present.

The timeliness of such an inquiry is another concern. In India, as in other parts of the world, the authoritative role of the nation-state as a determinant and coordinate of individual and group identity is presently being called into question by ongoing global transformations in economic and political structures and relations. In such a context, a study of the mid-twentieth-century project of state-centric nationalism runs the risk of irrelevance: scholarly attention is mostly directed to the unmaking rather than the making of nation and state.

The problem of conceptual fit is another deterrent. Like its counterparts in other national contexts, accounts of Indian nationalism focus primarily on the mobilizational energies and impact of mass-popular social movements that have contested the state such as the anticolonial nationalist movement prior to 1947 or Sikh nationalism, Tamil nationalism, and Hindu nationalism in the postcolonial period. The study of the postcolonial national identity project, where state institutions, structures, and agents played a key role in elaborating and consolidating the understandings and practices of nationhood, cannot easily or readily be accommodated within this conceptual terrain of nationalism qua social movement.

Finally, there are also the significant empirical obstacles to this line of inquiry. Although the postcolonial state exhibits the same frenzy for record keeping as did its colonial predecessor, it is another matter altogether when it comes to the actual practice of collection, preservation, systematization, and archiving. Official secrecy, bureaucratic neglect, the lack of a centralized record-transfer policy, and scarce resources have all combined to ensure that the experience of archival research on postcolonial state policies is a particularly bewildering and frustrating experience. From this perspective, the reason why the project of postcolonial national identity has been understudied has to do with the paucity of systematic records and information available to the contemporary researcher.

The missing archives soon became the main preoccupation of my research. I found myself spending most of my time devising elaborate strategies to prise records out of the steely grip of the state. I defined a successful day of research by physical rather than cognitive discovery: Would I be able to get my hands on that file? Apart from these pragmatic concerns, the information that I did locate on the processes and practices of the Nehruvian national project gave me considerable room for pause. The postcolonial imagination of nationhood in pluralist and state-centric terms—the distinctive means by which it was reproduced along with the political costs and opportunities of the pluralist, state-centric national imagination—pushed to be considered not as a causal prehistory of the present but as an active making in its own right. What had started out as a temporary detour to collect background information thus took on a life of its own. The result is the book that follows, the story of what happened to Indian nationalism after midnight.

In telling this story I engage with several questions of general theoretical and practical importance. First, what distinguishes the world of nation-states from other possible worlds? The nation-state has been the primary and constitutive unit of the "world polity" for more than half a century, ever since the international system was reconstituted under the sign of the United Nations (and its economic counterpart of the Bretton Woods system) in the aftermath of World War II. The normative exemplar of this age was the discretely bounded nation-state, the territorially delimited expression of the coincidence of political authority and cultural essence. I take seriously this issue of coincidence or the hyphenated structure of the nation-state; accordingly, I answer the question about the nation-state's distinctiveness by delineating the practices of "nationalizing the state" and "institutionalizing the nation" through which nation and state have been conjoined: practices that entail placing the state at the center of definitions of the nation and that emphasize the intrinsic diversity rather than the homogeneity of the nation.

Second, what makes this manifestly produced entity stick? That is, what are the means by which the made world of nation-states comes to be seen as a found or a natural world? I answer this question not through the familiar route of investigating the internalization and reception of nationalist meaning but instead by documenting how nation-statist practices frame or structure the political and cultural domain. As I establish in this book, the investments and belief of people in the nation-state are less important than how their lived environments and interested actions draw upon and reproduce its categories and logic.

Finally, what does it mean to speak of domination and resistance; the freedom and the unfreedom of identity practices in the world of nation-states? I answer this question by moving beyond the state versus society dichotomy that addresses such questions through determinations of who or what is exercising power and according to which the state is invariably the agent of domination, while resistance can stem only from spaces outside the state's reach. I argue that the state is not as monolithic or coherent as accounts of its omnipotent reach make it out to be. The dominant ideologies of nationhood are reproduced and sustained not just by state officials and institutional fiat but also through the "coproductions," strategic appropriations, and contestations of nonstate actors. Moreover, as I endeavor here to establish, the inclusive embrace of cultural diversity—through policies of multiculturalism and other institutionalist attempts at recognizing and tolerating the differences of group identity—can equally perpetuate inequities in relations and structures of power.

Although the intellectual enterprise is usually characterized as a long and lonely individual effort, in the case of this book only the former holds true. I have had the luxury of writing this book in amazingly good company, and I have benefited from the unstinting intellectual generosity, friendship, and inspiration of many individuals.

I have also received generous institutional support during the long course of my research and writing. I am grateful to the Social Science Research Council–MacArthur Foundation's International Peace and Security Program and the University of Pennsylvania's Penfeld Fellowship for enabling my doctoral field research and writing between 1996 and 1998. Tom Bender and the International Center of Advanced Studies at New York University gave me an invaluable postdoctoral opportunity in 1999–2000 that pushed me to rework many of my existing assumptions about the politics of nationalism and citizenship. The University of Massachusetts Faculty Research Grant program enabled several extended field research trips between 2000 and 2004. Finally, a grant in 2003–2005 from Seteney Shami and the Social

Science Research Council's Middle East and North Africa program for international collaborative research allowed me to engage with questions of nationalism and state formation in a comparative framework and complete the manuscript while in discussion and dialogue with scholars of the Middle East.

To my teachers David Ludden, Tom Callaghy, Sumathi Ramaswamy, Anne Norton, and Ian Lustick my debts are infinite. Sumathi Ramaswamy's intellectual passion, rigor, and breadth inspires by example. Anne Norton opened up for me an entirely new world of ideas with her writing and teaching. She has pushed me to recognize that the science of politics does not illuminate the political and that "theory" comes in multiple guises. Ian Lustick's encouragement and intensive engagement with my work, ranging from an undergraduate seminar on Gramsci seventeen years ago to my dissertation and beyond, has been formative in more ways than he may know or recognize. His injunction to question not just the answers but the questions themselves has made me aware of the considerable theoretical, political, and ethical stakes and responsibilities of academic writing.

This book has greatly benefited from discussions with numerous individuals over the years. For their critical insights and intellectual generosity, I am deeply grateful to Sankaran Krishna, Amrita Basu, Thomas Hansen, Dipesh Chakrabarty, Alev Cinar, Manu Goswami, Ravina Aggarwal, Paula Chakravartty, Vijay Prashad, Itty Abraham, Radhika Mongia, Lisa Wedeen, Rudra Sil, Christophe Jaffrelot, Sudipta Kaviraj, Zoya Hasan, Kanti Bajpai, Patricia Uberoi, Gurpreet Mahajan, Ashis Nandy, Atul Kohli, Ashutosh Varshney, Lloyd Rudolph, Susanne Rudolph, Leela Fernandes, Pratap Mehta, Raphael Allen, Jason Weidemann, and Muthiah Alagappa.

Thanks also are due to my colleagues and friends in the Department of Political Science at the University of Massachusetts, Amherst—Barbara Cruikshank, Laura Jensen, Craig Thomas, and especially Nicholas Xenos—for their advice on matters both intellectual and strategic and for their commitment to a multidisciplinary, nonparochial, and ecumenical understanding of political science.

I thank Julia Adams for her early and continued encouragement of this project, and for agreeing to house my work in her wonderful series. Very grateful thanks are also due to my editors at Duke University Press—Reynolds Smith and Sharon Torian—for their cheerful tolerance of an endless stream of questions and their superb ability to transform an unwieldy manuscript into a more coherent book.

In India, the resourceful librarians and staff at the Nehru Memorial Museum and Library; the National Archives; and the Central Secretariat Library helped me to locate essential research material in 1997–1998 and again in the summers of 2001, 2002, and 2003. Mr. Thakur at the Research Reference and Training Library of the Ministry of Information and Broadcasting literally opened the doors to a vast (and dusty) treasure trove of files just when I thought that all hope and all documents were lost. Guliz Dinc provided timely research assistance in summer 2003, and Anand Vivek Taneja tracked down vital references in summer 2004 and greatly improved chapter 4 with his incisive suggestions.

My friends sustain me in ways too numerous to list. My conversations with Teja Ganti, Usha Zacharias, Gianpaolo Baiocchi, Biju Mathew, Vijay Prashad, Radhika Mongia, Maha Yahya, Banu Subramaniam, Anita Roy, and Nagaraj Adve have been a direct and constant source of ideas, encouragement, and inspiration. And Kai Friese, Alev Cinar, Hilary Appel, Zeynep Aksin, Buju Dasgupta, Paula Chakravartty, Malini Ghose, Brinda Dutt, Vandana Kapur, Ravina Aggarwal, Sangeeta Kamat, Manu Goswami, and Annie Mathews have raised to an impossible level the bar of friendship.

Finally, my families continue to make just about everything possible: Rahoul Roy, Lakshmi Roy, Shonali Bose, Radhika Roy, Prannoy Roy, Mira Vachani, Nand Vachani, Debraj Ray, Nilita Vachani, Brinda Karat, Prakash Karat, Atiya Bose, Borun Chanda, and above and beyond all, my mother Indrani Roy. Lalit Vachani has gamely juggled homes and careers over two continents for a decade. The words and ideas that follow have been shaped by his imagination, companionship, and love.

It is my deepest regret that my words will not be read by Nirmal Roy, my grandfather, and Siddhartha Roy, my father. This book is for Dadu and Baba, who lived the history that I tell.

INTRODUCTION

Imagining Institutions, Instituting Diversity

Toward a Theory of Nation-State

Formation

::::

In March 2002 the western Indian state of Gujarat was the site of an organized pogrom against the Muslim residents of the state.[1] Following the news reports about how a group of "Muslim miscreants" had set fire to a train carriage filled with sympathizers of Hindu nationalism—the ascendant political-cultural movement in India that seeks to reconstitute the nation along Hindu majoritarian lines—a wave of "revenge killings" against Muslims engulfed the state. Approximately two thousand people lost their lives; women were subjected to unimaginable acts of sexual brutality; nearly two hundred thousand were displaced from their homes; and the loss to property has since been estimated to be in the range of 280 million dollars.[2] Despite the efforts of the state and national governments to depict this event as a spontaneous popular upsurge of Hindus seeking revenge, there is overwhelming evidence that government agencies, law enforcement officials, and political leaders from the ruling Hindu nationalist Bharatiya Janata Party (BJP) were directly involved in enabling and perpetuating the violence. The unforgettable photograph of the terror-stricken face of a Muslim man looking directly into the camera, his hands folded in a desperate gesture of pleading for his life, conveyed to the world beyond Gujarat the intensity of the violence and the fear that defined the experience of being Muslim in twenty-first-century India.

At the time of this writing, four years and one general election after the events of 2002, it would appear that the juggernaut of Hindu nationalism has been halted, or at the very least that attempts to foster and exacerbate ethno-religious divisions among the citizenry—what in India is referred to as the "communalization" of the body politic—have not reaped any electoral dividends. The Hindu-nationalist dominated coalition government was voted out of power in the elections of 2004.[3] The new regime, the United Progressive Alliance coalition government formed by the Congress Party, has explicitly committed itself to a restoration of India's secular ethos and the "composite culture" of ethnic diversity, promising to "detoxify" educational curricula and replace the Hindu nationalist ideologues who currently occupy leadership positions in a range of state agencies.[4] Qutubuddin Ansari, the man whose face haunted newspaper headlines four years ago, is today alive and well and living in Calcutta, two thousand kilometers away from Gujarat.

Since summer 2004 a new Kodachrome representation of Indian life has structured the media imaginary. As the exuberant opinion-editorial commentaries accompanying the photograph repeatedly tell us, it signifies the restoration of the "real" idea of India. The photograph is of the swearing-in ceremony of the new national government. A Muslim president from the southern state of Tamil Nadu administers the oath of office to a Sikh prime minister from Punjab, as the leader of his party, an Italian-born Catholic woman, looks on with a gracious smile. The rainbow of diversity couldn't shine any brighter.

How do we tell the story of the conceptual—and also the political and ethical—distance between these two Indian images and the larger social-ideological formations that they index?[5] Two opposing explanations have been proposed in recent years, which transpose to the Indian context a general and long-standing debate about the management and accommodation of ethnic diversity by nation-states. The first explanation is an optimistic tale of how the institutional and ideational configuration of India's "unity in diversity" is strong enough to withstand wear and tear. The argument is that the patchwork of subnational identities that make up Indian culture and society cannot quite so easily be transformed by majoritarian ideological maneuvers. Although the violence of Gujarat constituted a significant rupture in the existing pattern of ethnocultural accommodation in India, the temporal and spatial isolation of the events—the fact that the violence did not spill over beyond the confines of March 2002 and Gujarat—is taken as evidence of the resilience of the institutional and cultural commitments to religious diversity in India, and of the exceptionalism of the Gujarat violence.[6]

Similar observations about the "holding together" of India have been applied to other instances of ethnic mobilization that have challenged the existing configuration of India as a multiethnic nation-state.[7] For instance, over the six decades of its existence, the postcolonial polity has witnessed the emergence of numerous ethnonationalist movements, whose demands have ranged from augmenting the exercise of subnational autonomy within the existing federal structure to outright secession as in the case of the Khalistan movement in the late 1980s.[8] Nevertheless, the territorial-national integrity of India still survives. Moreover, the Indian polity continues to exist as an active and functioning democracy, held together by mechanisms other than force or authoritarian dominance. From this perspective, India represents a success story of diversity management. The complex mosaic of subnational identities constituted along a multiplicity of axes—region, religion, language, caste—has been granted constitutional and ideational recognition without compromising the authority and effectiveness of the centralized state system, and without abrogating democratic rules and practices.

In sharp contrast, the second explanation dispenses with the cyclical logic of the suspension and subsequent restoration of the idea of secular-diverse India, or the view that the violence of Gujarat was an aberrant moment in postcolonial history. The argument here, resembling those offered by Zygmunt Baumann and others in the context of the Jewish holocaust,[9] is that such events of unspeakable horror do not represent a departure from the norm but instead a confirmation of it. The quick return of the rainbow spectrum attests not to the strength but rather the hollowness of the unity-in-diversity formula of nationhood. In simpler terms, the argument is that India has always been a proto-Hindu nation constituted around an ethno-majoritarian core,[10] and that it uses the rhetoric of diversity as a window dressing. Needless to say, the diversity mosaic presently on display leaves these commentators cold.[11]

Despite their many differences, both perspectives are grounded in a common set of assumptions—namely that of the endurance of the diversity-embracing idea of India and the considerable influence that it has had on the field of postcolonial culture and politics. Equally, both perspectives share a common silence about the means or mechanisms for the reproduction of such an imagination. For the most part, they assert the contemporary existence of the national imagination without offering any insights into its origins and spread. The proposition that unity in diversity is a central organizing principle of the Indian national imagination is the "negative heuristic" of both sets of explanations;[12] that is, the unquestioned starting point from which assessments of India's "mosaic nationalism" develop their positive programmatic agendas. The reasons why this imagination has been successful in promoting a tolerant cultural ethos and serving as a bulwark against monocultural nationalist projects—or alternatively, why it has failed to secure substantive equality for individuals and groups and has in fact laid the groundwork for the emergence of Hindu nationalism—are not addressed.

It is this uncharted terrain that I seek to explore by investigating the nation-state formation project in postcolonial India, notably the ways in which the distinctive entity of the nation-state assumed its form, authority, and meaning through the "imagination of institutions" and the "institution of diversity." The story I tell moves beyond the rigid dichotomies of the "success" and "failure" narratives of the Indian national imagination described above, or the assertion of an absolute difference versus an absolute identity between the secular-diverse and the monocultural imagination of India. I engage instead with the dynamic and fissured political field—along with the political openings as well as the closures, and the structures of domination as well as the emancipatory possibilities—that has been constituted by the postcolonial imagination of India as a diverse nation unified by the labors of a transcendent state.

Things Do Not Fall Apart: Divided Societies and Durable Polities

How, and why, has the ethnically diverse society of India been able to endure as a unitary polity for more than half a century? This question is of considerable relevance in the present global context, where discussions on how best to accommodate, recognize, tolerate, and otherwise manage subnational diversity have assumed renewed urgency.[13] One strand of scholarship seeks answers in institutional arrangements by focusing on the kinds of institutional-legal-constitutional mechanisms that can best respond to ethnic and cultural diversity without destabilizing the political order. Measures that are seen to protect and nurture the intricate mosaic of subnational diversity with which all nation-states are endowed include constitutional commitments to individual rights along with substantive provisions for the protection of minority rights; the institution of consociational, federal, and other power-sharing mechanisms; electoral-system designs that facilitate the political representation of different subnational groups; and policies of affirmative action or "compensatory discrimination" that redress economic inequalities experienced by members of historically discriminated groups. At the same time, the argument goes, institutional safeguards have to be in place to ensure that an "excess" of subnational identity does not disintegrate the political system, whether through secession or civil war, and that a center can be preserved even as diversity is accommodated.[14]

Institutional-procedural arguments, premised as they are on an interest-based view of individual and group behavior, do not take into account issues of subjectivity, history, and lived meaning: that is, the very stuff of ethnic identity.[15] Instead, they reproduce a thin and hollow understanding of institutions as procedural mechanisms or policy complexes that respond to social and cultural identities. Moreover, the recipe for success appears to be longevity, or the fact that it is only through long-standing and iterated patterns of interaction with these institutional-legal mechanisms that ethnic identities can be "tamed." Given this conclusion, it would appear that nation-states of recent provenance are condemned to living with endemic conflict and instability. This conclusion seems especially bleak when we add up the numbers of "new" nation-states in the world (those that were established in the mid-twentieth century and beyond): a category that includes vast areas of the Asian and African continents, along with significant areas of Europe that were constituted as sovereign nation-states following the disintegration of the Soviet Union and the reconfiguration of the cold war geopolitical map in the 1990s.[16]

Moreover, the thesis of habituation meets its limits in the context of India. The institutional-legal mechanisms for the accommodation of diversity have been in place for only fifty-odd years, and have been so with a considerable gap between "paper-truths" and lived realities, or between procedural commitments and their actual implementation. And in a further repudiation of the requirement of historical distance between episodes of violence and peace that enables the institutional embrace of diversity to function as the taken-for-granted status quo,[17] memories of the protracted religious violence of partition—the "communal frenzy" that accompanied the imperial division of territory along religious lines to create the two sovereign states of India and Pakistan in 1947 that led to the loss of almost a million lives—live on in public culture, albeit in displaced or disguised forms.[18] In short, the case of India poses an empirical anomaly for institutionalist-proceduralist arguments. The question of why things have not fallen apart in India cannot be explained by accounts that focus on constitutional provisions, legal instruments, and institutional innovations alone.

An alternative line of inquiry addresses issues of ideology and belief in recognition of the fact that instrumental rationality and cost-benefit calculations do not determine expressions of group identity. In terms of the "diversity yet durability" puzzle, or the question of how it is that ethnically and culturally fragmented societies are able to generate resilient political orders, the answer is seen to lie in the ideological lineaments of social formations. Instead of the mechanical workings of institutional structures, the "thick" motivations of human belief, desire, and sentiment are here the focus of analytical attention. The explanatory task at hand becomes one of how an appropriate national identity framework that is inclusive of diversity can be fostered, or what Juan Linz and Alfred Stepan, following Habermas, have described as the successful inculcation of a "we-feeling" or a "constitutional patriotism" at the level of the general polis rather than a particular ethnos.[19]

However, once again the Indian case presents a significant anomaly. The postcolonial Indian state does not appear to have undertaken a national identity project comparable to the deliberate and centralized project of nationalization undertaken in France that effected the transformation of "peasants into Frenchmen";[20] the concerted propaganda around the figure of the "New Soviet Man" in the USSR;[21] the heavy investment in ideological resources by the National Socialist regime in Germany;[22] or the orchestration of national leadership cults in Syria and Iraq.[23]

In India, educational curricula are determined by regional state governments rather than by a centralized national agency. Although until the late 1980s the state monopolized radio and television broadcasts, the pervasive socio-economic inequalities limited considerably their national reach or coverage. Low levels of literacy have militated against the dissemination of national ideologies through "print capitalism."[24] Mostly absent in India is the proliferation of civic-republican images and icons along the lines of those in the United States, where the ubiquitous presence of the Stars and Stripes reproduces "banal nationalism" through everyday encounters with "unmindful flagging,"[25] or those in Turkey, where statues of the founding father Kemal Ataturk abound in public spaces.[26] Thus it was only as recently as 2002 that the fifty-year-old Flag Code of India was amended to allow citizens the right to display their national flag.[27] And while most Indian cities have a statue of Gandhi somewhere in their midst, it is instead the stone testimonies to imperial pasts and regional histories (Victoria in Calcutta; Chhatrapati Shivaji in Bombay) and the giant billboard representations of individual and collective desire (posters of Tamil film stars in Chennai; billboards advertising Nokia cellular phones in Chandigarh) that define the urban landscape.

What, then, explains the cohesiveness of India? What enables the Indian nation-state to endure as a single political unit despite the persistence, and even the proliferation, of subnational diversity? Answering these questions requires a critical engagement with the existing terms of inquiry. To ask about "durability despite diversity" is to reproduce a depoliticized and static understanding of diversity as a pregiven natural reality to which a state can respond in better or worse ways: a ready-at-hand, self-evident problem that requires a solution. But a problem for whom, and how and why? And whose solution is it anyway? Such questions remain unanswered within the naturalizing paradigm of "diversity accommodation." Moreover, the modular and isomorphic terms of the paradigm are limiting as well. The problem of racial diversity in Brazil is regarded as a serial replica of the problem of racial diversity in the United States;[28] the Indian state's recognition of religious difference and its recognition of linguistic identity are treated as equivalent, even identical, cases.[29] In this manner, the complex, dynamic, and often-incommensurable experiences of identity and difference are relocated within a singular and aggregated matrix of "natural" diversity. The interested origins and power effects of this matrix—the fact that diversity is as much of a "made" as it is a "found" formation—are removed from our line of sight.

Taking a different approach, in this book I advance the hypothesis of durability *because of or through diversity*.[30] I show how the *naturalization of diversity*—the reproduction of a particular imagination of India as naturally diverse—has consolidated state authority in postcolonial India. Ranging from the annual pageantry of Republic Day parades to the documentary films produced by the state-owned Films Division of India, and from the constitutional decision to adopt a particular design for the Indian national flag and a particular song as the national anthem to the texts, speeches, and policy frameworks addressing various aspects of national existence, India since its foundation as a sovereign nation-state in 1947 has been represented in terms of its intrinsic and inalienable subnational diversity—nationhood called up as a mosaic of ethnocultural fragments.

This embrace of diversity was not just a reflection of or a response to a natural or preexisting order. Instead, it entailed the active production of an "institutional pluralism" or the selective inclusion and transformation of group identities into a particular state-supporting matrix of diversity in which only certain kinds of group identities were recognized.[31] Accompanying this depiction of Indian diversity was the presentation of the state as the successful manager of diversity—the legitimate institutional authority under whose helpful guidance individuals could enjoy security, groups could enjoy freedoms and recognition, and the nation as a whole could enjoy unity and stability. My primary task in this book is to explore the contours of this institutional pluralist imagination in postcolonial India whereby subnational diversity and state authority exist not in opposition but instead as complementary and co-constituted formations.[32]

To address this task I document the distinctive modes of reproduction of the institutional pluralist imagination, or the symbolic, discursive, and material processes through which these understandings of the nation's essential and inalienable diversity, and of the state as the problem solver of the diverse nation, have been consolidated. As noted earlier, many of the familiar techniques and strategies of nationalization are less prevalent in the Indian context, and yet the institutional pluralist, unity-in-diversity imagination has an enduring presence. Explaining this paradox calls for a fresh look at the distinctive project of nation-state formation, or the ways in which a *nation-statist* identity, as opposed to a national identity, is produced. In fact, an explanation entails supplementing the "national identity" paradigm,[33] and the understanding of the internalized psychological and cognitive workings of ideology that it endorses, with an examination of the externalized effects of nation-statist ideologies—the ways in which presumptive understandings about state, nation, and citizen are reproduced through routine or everyday as well as momentous or extraordinary forms of political discourse and practice on the part of a wide range of state as well as nonstate actors. As Étienne Balibar has argued, "a social formation only reproduces itself as a nation to the extent that through a network of apparatuses and daily practices, the individual is instituted as *homo nationalis* from cradle to grave, at the same time that he or she is instituted as homo oeconomicus, politicus, religious."[34] In the chapters that follow, I draw attention to the constitution and working of these networks and practices, and I argue that it is their iteration rather than their credibility, their ability to elicit recognition rather than inspire passion, that consolidate the dominant ideologies of the postcolonial nation-state. In sum, this volume, as its title indicates, is an attempt to retheorize the formation and consolidation of nation-statist ideologies without making the (impossible) claim to know the content and workings of individual belief, or "what is actually going on inside people's heads"; that is, the unstated assumption that informs much of the existing literature on nations and nationalism. To illuminate this issue, in the following section I look at this body of work in closer detail.

Nation, State, and Nation-State

There are varied accounts of the origins of the nation as a distinctive socialpolitical and cultural formation. While some locate the nation in a premodern era, others place causal emphasis on modernity, variously defined as a set of social, political, economic, cultural, or ideational changes that took place in Europe between the sixteenth and the nineteenth centuries. Each of these perspectives is anchored in a different understanding of national ontology. For those who locate nations in the mists of antiquity, the mythopsychic character of the nation is key. Thus, for Anthony Smith the nation is primarily an expression of the human need to "bond and cleave," interwoven with the equally basic and universal human propensity toward desire, fantasy, and emotion.[35] The existence of premodern *ethnies*—human groups cemented together by emotions and experiences of shared kinship—laid the groundwork for modern nations, which are seen to represent a reworking and recasting of these premodern formations rather than an entirely new invention.

In Smith's account, while the difference between the premodern ethnie and the modern nation does indeed amount to a significant transformation, it is one of degree rather than of kind. In other less-nuanced accounts, such as those offered by socio-biologists, the nation is similarly conceptualized as an expression or outcome of human psychic and biological urges and drives.[36] Although political structure and agency are accorded a role to play,[37] the "primordialist" derivation of nations in human biological and psychological impulses (i.e., the formation of kin groups as a response to natural selection, or the deep attachment that kinship and maternal metaphors invariably evoke in all human beings) remains the primary explanation for national provenance, with the nation itself defined in similarly essentialist terms as a basic form of human communal expression.

In marked contrast to this portrait of the ineluctable mytho-psychic or socio-biological nation is the view of the nation as a structural shell that dominates the work of "modernist" scholars, or those who argue for a distinctively modern provenance for the nation. For Ernest Gellner, one of the most well-known proponents of this argument, the emergence of nationalism is best understood as a functionalist response to macrosociological changes set in motion in and through the transformation of agrarian societies into industrial societies.[38] In the Parsonian terms of this classic transition narrative of *gemeinschaft* into *gesellschaft*, the nation is a structural-functionalist byproduct of industrialization, encapsulating a distinctive set of modern "pattern variables." Its emotive content and affective impact—the nation as a community of feeling, or a "crucible of emotion"[39]—is of less interest than its formal or structural features, as the means and also the outcome of the cultural homogenization "required" by an industrial polity. Moreover, Gellner's nation is an entity marked by the conspicuous absence of politics and power. In his account, the formation of the nation is unmoored from any conscious or deliberate acts of political agency, and is theorized instead as an ineluctable and unintended byproduct of structural transformations. The alignment between political and cultural units that is at the core of Gellner's definition of the nation takes place not as a result of the concerted efforts by state elites to create a homogenous national culture, but as a cumulative effect of changes in modes of production, social relations, and political organization.

Other modernist accounts make political agency more causally efficacious. Thus, for instance, Miroslav Hroch's discussion of European nation formation accords an integral role to political entrepreneurship, with the mobilizational strategies of different circles of political agents enabling the diffusion of nationalist ideology from the rarefied confines of the intelligentsia to a mass population.[40] In a similar vein, Tom Nairn and Michael Hechter, although upholding a structural-systemic account of the nation's origins in the transformative impact of capitalist development, place central emphasis on how the experience of uneven development by political elites in the periphery led them to undertake deliberate projects of nation building and state building.[41] In all of these instances, the sociopolitical and materialist determinants of nation formation rather than its emotional or psychic lineaments receive emphasis. The ideological and identitarian aspects of nationhood and the impact of the nation form on subjectivity and lived experience—what it means to *be* or to *become* national—do not occasion sustained analytical attention. Even as modernist scholars partake of a "constructivist" view of the nation,[42] conceptualizing it as a "made" and historically contingent rather than an essentialist, "found" community, the constructive labors that constitute the nation are for the most part seen to stem from external structural sources rather than from the desires, fantasies, and imagination of individual human subjects.

It is in this context that Benedict Anderson's account of nations as "imagined communities" breaks new theoretical ground. In combining the structuralist-materialist accounts of nation formation with a sustained focus on the ideational-subjective constitution of nationhood, Anderson defines the nation as an "imagined political community—and imagined as both limited and sovereign."[43] At one level the emergence of the nation is explained in terms of social and economic transformations such as the advent of "print capitalism,"[44] or as the formation and consolidation of a new form of human solidarity—a bounded community that perceives itself to exist in the simultaneity of "homogenous empty time"—as a result of the widespread circulation of print-capitalist commodities such as the newspaper and the novel. Anderson also turns his attention to the structuring effect of political formations and modes of governance, theorizing the emergence of "creole nationalism" in the eighteenth-century Americas in relation to the particular modalities of colonial government. He argues that the "blocked mobility" experienced by creole elites born in the colonies, where positions of power were invariably occupied by *peninsulares* (those born in Spain), triggered movements for national autonomy—an experience that would be replicated several centuries later in the context of the Asian and African anticolonial nationalist movements. Anderson's explanation for the advent of "official nationalism" also incorporates a similar discussion of political exigencies, with the nationalizing campaigns undertaken by imperial formations such as the Hapsburg empire or Tsarist Russia described as politically strategic efforts of state elites to counter and co-opt popular linguistic nationalist movements.

At another level, however, the emotional and affective aspects of nation formation and the work of the "imagination" in bringing the national community into being are integral to Anderson's argument. The "dawn" of nations during the "dusk" of religious belief is enabled not solely by the technological innovations of print capitalism, nor by the (deliberate or unintended) effects of political structures and the interested maneuvers of political agents, but by the universal human need to believe in a higher, trans-individual purpose in a post-Enlightenment world where unquestioned faith in divine providence is no longer a possibility. As Anderson observes, "With the ebbing of religious belief, the suffering which belief in part composed did not disappear . . . What then was required was a secular transformation of fatality into continuity, contingency into meaning . . . few things were better suited to this end than the idea of a nation."[45]

When the death of God and the "disintegration of paradise" are seen to enable the birth of the nation, the workings of human belief become integral to the definition of a nation. In this sense, even though Anderson's account of nations and nationalism draws upon historical materialist epistemologies, it bears more than a passing resemblance to the psycho-mythic discussions of nationhood examined earlier. As in these discussions, Anderson places causal emphasis on individual, "ineffable"[46] psychological drives and desires without exploring the actual mechanisms that are involved.[47] What were the means by which the individual "need" for belief was transformed into a collective belief in the existence of a national community? Equally, what are the means by which scholars can ascertain the existence of such a collective belief—that is, how do we know that an increase in the number of readers of the modern novel meant that the "imagined community" of the nation had assumed material reality? Such questions move beyond the consideration of "what" a nation is to an engagement with the "how" of nation formation, an issue that remains mostly obscured in Anderson's otherwise comprehensive investigation. As Michael Herzfeld has rightly observed, Anderson's argument consequently has "a tinge of psychological reductionism—we are never really told how we know how and what people imagine."[48] If socio-biological and psycho-mythic accounts of nationhood overlook the enabling role played by political and social structural transformations in the emergence of nations, and if structural-functionalist accounts err in the opposite direction by neglecting to discuss the role of human emotion and affect, then Anderson's attempt to combine these two approaches constitutes an equivalent omission.[49] Although he sets out to explore the structural as well as the affective conditions of possibility for nation formation, he shies away from a sustained examination of the *relationship* between structures and sentiment and then ends up asserting rather than explaining the joint role played by institutions and the imagination in bringing the modern nation into being and ensuring its continued existence.[50]

Such an explanation would entail grappling with one of the central (and in some respects the most curious or inexplicable) silences that haunts scholarship on nations and nationalism—namely, the silence around the figure of the state. Although modernist and perennialist accounts of the nation's origins differ over the extent to which nations are new or old, or are artifactual or natural phenomena respectively, the nation is commonly acknowledged to be a formation that is substantially different from other configurations of human sociality, such as families, religious orders, or interest groups. This difference turns on the unique conjunction of politics and culture in the nation, or the fact that the nation is simultaneously a political as well as a cultural expression of sovereign community.

The distinctive hallmark of the "age of nations" is widely considered to be the alignment of political and cultural units either through structural transformations in capitalist relations or through more agent-centric means—that is, by nationalist movements that contest existing political structures in order to build a state of their own (state-building nationalism) or by state elites that undertake projects of homogenization and nationalization within the territory over which they rule (state-built nationalism). Nationalist attempts to establish a representative relation between nation and state such that the state is the sovereign "gauge and emblem" of the nation, and the resulting centrality of the "state idea" to the idea of the nation, are notions with which few would disagree. Thus, in Anderson's famous definition of the nation, it is both an "imagined community" and one that is imagined as a "sovereign" and a "political" community. Gellner's definition similarly brings together cultural and political attributes, explicitly making the state the sine qua non of the nation's existence: "Nationalism's core tenet is the belief that the 'national state, identified with a national culture and committed to its protection, is the natural political unit.'"[51]

However, despite this tacit consensus on the state-centric nature of nations and nationalism, this aspect of nationalist thought and practice has received sparse attention. For the most part, the scholarship on nationalism focuses on the project of community making rather than on institution making. The formation of a nation is understood to entail the imagination of community through the inculcation of a homogenous sense of cultural identity. And while the state does enter the picture, it does so either as *telos* in the case of state-building nationalism, or as a given institutional reality in the case of state-built nationalism. In neither case is the formation of the state theorized as an active and ongoing project or a form of cultural making in its own right that is as intrinsic to the production of nationhood as is the construction of a homogenous cultural identity. Yet, while the nation is formed and sustained through the inculcation of a sense of "horizontal solidarity" among individuals, the specification of hierarchical relations of authority between nation and state—what John Kelly and Martha Kaplan have described as the "organized" and "instituted" aspects of "popular will"—are of equal importance in constituting the nation as a *political* community.[52] As I will demonstrate, the "imagination of the state" and that of state-nation relations take their place alongside the "imagination of community" as the central concerns of nationalist discourse and practice.

This is especially the case when it comes to the building of new cultural-political sovereignties in the aftermath of World War II in the context of imperial withdrawal and decolonization. In a repudiation of the diffusionist thesis of the "modular transfer" of nationalism, whereby later nationalisms imitate, adopt, or otherwise reference earlier nationalist templates, the mid-twentieth-century project of nation-state formation was informed by a very different set of political imperatives than those that had structured the "creole nationalisms" of the eighteenth-century Americas; the "linguistic-popular nationalisms" of nineteenth-century Europe; and even the "last wave" of anticolonial nationalisms in Asia and Africa.[53] Unlike these instances of nationalism qua social movement, the production of a nation-state entailed not just community-building or popular mobilization around a "national cause," but the identification of institutional authority and, in many cases, a defusion of mobilizational energies as the anticolonial nationalists who had confronted the colonial state were sought to be transformed into obedient national subjects of the postcolonial state. Equally, nation-state formation broke the mold of "official nationalism" pursued by nineteenth- and twentieth-century states, such as the "Russification" campaigns in Tsarist Russia,[54] or the efforts to convert "peasants into Frenchmen" in nineteenth- and twentieth-century France. Unlike these cases, the imperatives of democracy and popular sovereignty, even if expressed at the level of rhetoric alone, inflected most postcolonial projects of nationalization: the constitution of state authority and the institutional relations of power had now to be represented in autonomous, voluntarist, and consensual terms.

Perhaps the most substantial difference between nation-state formation and the projects of popular and official nationalism was the dual production of stateness and nationhood that the establishment of the compound entity of the nation-state entailed. Engaging with nation-state formation in its own right consequently calls for an exploration of how the "myth of the state" is produced and fostered by representations of nationhood—how along with the elaboration of affective bonds that enable individuals to believe in and identify with their nation is the specification of institutional identity and hierarchical relations of power.[55]

In what follows, I highlight the specific modalities, rationalities, or techniques that enable nation-state formation and I argue that the reproduction of the nation-state rests not on the existence of individuals who identify with the nation but rather on their ability to *identify the state* as the nation's authoritative representative. This effort in turn calls for a revised understanding of how nation-statist ideologies work and for a shift from the paradigm of "internalized" identity and belief to a consideration of external effects and public practices—the public actions, performative displays, spatial interventions, and political discourses of consent and dissent that repeatedly accord recognition to the existence of the state and its claim of representing the nation.

Beyond Belief: Nation-Statist Encounters

Lisa Wedeen, in her discussion of the operations of political power in Syria, argues that the analytical category of belief is quite limited when it comes to explaining the formation and reproduction of dominant ideologies.[56] For instance, she notes that the claim to a perfect knowledge of the inner workings of individual minds, which the notion of belief is predicated upon, amounts to a leap of faith in its own right. Further, her investigation of Syrian politics reveals that although the public expressions and behaviors of citizens appear to conform to the requirements of the "cult of Assad" that structures the political arena, such outward expressions of obedience coexist with high levels of cynicism, incredulity, and other forms of active *disbelief*. In Wedeen's account, it is the civilian strategies of dissimulation in the face of power (the ability to "act as if"), rather than the cognitive state of belief, that enable the perpetuation of dominant power structures (and the resistances that they engender). In extending this insight to the particular puzzle that frames this book of the Indian nation-state's continued existence, or the more general question of how and why nation-states endure, I argue for a similar move beyond discussions of national identity as an internalized belief, and of effective nationalizing practices as those that engender unisonant sentiments of love, loyalty, and belonging, to an exploration of the political-cultural action context; that is, the ways in which discourses, practices, and visual-symbolic effects structure political action to reaffirm the authoritative existence of the nation-state.[57] It is through repeatedly encountering rather than believing in the official imagination of nationhood, through recognizing the sights and sounds of the state rather than "buying into" its mythologies, that the nation-state is formed and reproduced.

I work with an understanding of the nation-state that is quite different from the notion of the nation as a tangible, anthropological "community," or from the view of the state as a given and discrete institutional complex that is self-evidently separated (and separable) from society. Extending the insights of Rogers Brubaker, Katherine Verdery, and others who have argued for the reconceptualization of the nation as a "practical category" rather than a substantive entity,[58] and of state theorists who conceive of the state as a set of ongoing practices, discourses, processes, and "effects" rather than a given object, I define the nation-state as a publicly articulated discursive and material field, a series of, in the words of Peter van der Veer, "projects and arrangements through which society is organized," to create a structure of opportunities and obstacles for the conduct of politics.[59] To borrow from Philip Abrams, the nation-state is a "structuration within political practice."[60] Both state and nonstate actors draw upon the vocabularies, stances, or positions that are constituted by (and that in turn constitute) this field, which is reproduced not only by expressions of consent and affirmation but equally by expressions of dissent and criticism.

The conception of the nation-state as a field of political discourse and practice rather than a concrete entity has several theoretical and methodological implications. For example, this view calls for a sustained exploration of the structures and patterns of political discourse and the logic of political practice.[61] If "to have a national identity is to possess ways of talking about nationhood,"[62] an exploration of the terms and conditions that govern such "nation-talk" in any given context can shed light on the existence and the workings of nation-statist ideology. Are there constant themes, refrains, or conceptual clusters that recur in public deliberations on "national issues"? What are the terms in which state and nonstate actors articulate their interests? What are the issues around which national debates take place—the complex of "nationally relevant" issues on which we agree to disagree? Such questions reconfigure the terrain of enquiry of nationalism scholarship in three significant ways.

First, the investigation of the politics of culture—the invention of cultural traditions, the production of a national symbology, and the harnessing of cultural technologies such as poetry, music, art, and literature in the project of national construction—is supplemented by an exploration of the culture of politics. Debates and interventions on "noncultural" issues, such as economic development, science and technology, international relations, social welfare, and law and order, are seen to form and transform the framework of nationhood and to contribute to the "routine deixis of the homeland"[63] by repeatedly referencing the reality of the nation-state as much as interventions that are explicitly cultural and identitarian in their impulse. As has been widely observed, movements of nationalist mobilization in India, such as the anticolonial nationalist movement launched by the Indian National Congress in the colonial period, or the efforts to produce and disseminate Hindu nationalist identity that began to take center stage in the 1980s and beyond, relied upon affective or sentiment-laden campaigns and events to inculcate a sense of "political love" and national fraternity. Thus the project of inculcating a sense of national identity was addressed through the production of national songs, rituals, and feminized iconography that represented the nation as an enchanted object of veneration and desire, an expression of collective longing and belonging. The reproduction and the naturalization of the postcolonial nation-state as the authoritative "master code"[64] of political life, however, harnesses very different techniques and registers, taking shape through ponderous slogans, the minutiae of bureaucratic paperwork, the instrumental bargains struck in the political marketplace, and the articulation of distinctly nonresonant or estranging and noncredulous cultural expressions. These are the stuff of nationhood as well, and it is through their examination that the search for the "success story" of the Indian nation-state's endurance must proceed.

Second, the debates, disagreements, and dissent as much as the consensual, unisonant affirmations are seen to constitute the nation-statist field. As the chapters in this book will illustrate, over the half century of the Indian nation-state's existence the discourses of state failure and inadequacy, the contestations over the "real meaning" of the nation, and the expression of doubts about the present existence and future viability of India have variously played a role in consolidating the taken-for-granted status of the nation-state.

Third, the conception of the nation-state as a field and the attendant focus on the action context of politics as the means as well as the site for nation-state formation and transformation requires that we take seriously the materiality of discourse. Discourses *about* the nation-state are constitutive *of* the nation-state. They structure not just the contours of the national imagination qua idea, but also the terrain of lived experience. In locating the nation-state in and as political discourses and practices, I am stressing the constitutive and material aspects of discourse and the corresponding rejection of the discourse versus "real politics" dichotomy, or the presumption that discourses are but reflections of real social, political, and economic processes.

The debates on the nation-state that I identify in this book go on to affect real lives and bodies in all too tangible ways. For instance, the discourse of "nation-building" in post-independence India and the attendant prescription for an interventionist state to build and develop a backward nation informed and legitimized the many developmentalist schemes of modernization that had a direct impact on the conduct and experience of everyday life, from dam building and heavy industrial projects to the effort undertaken between the 1950s and the 1980s to scientifically plan the economy. In a similar vein, the imagination of cultural diversity in regionally territorialized, material or visible, and linguistic terms authorized the distribution of resources and the granting of political recognition to groups that could lay claim to a territorially circumscribed and visibly distinctive culture or to a language of their own, while religious groups were addressed by institutional and legislative gestures of "minority protection" rather than redistribution or political recognition.[65] In both cases, it is the nation-statist discourses that constitute or produce the choices, strategies, agents, structures, and stakes of politics. In sum, the conceptualization of the nation-state as a field of discourse is not a dematerializing stance but one that is centrally engaged with the question of material effects.

This brings me to the final set of theoretical and methodological revisions proposed by this study, namely the understanding of nation-state formation as a project of enabling the recognition for and of the state and its preferred representation of nationhood rather than a project of fostering a new form of community consciousness. The mechanisms and practices that attend such a project of "state identification" are different from those conventionally associated with the formation of national identity. For instance, as discussed above, certain forms of critique or dissent can work alongside unisonant affirmation and consensual expressions of loyalty and belonging to shore up the understanding of the state as a discrete institutional entity located "outside" and "above" society and politics.[66] In another departure, as noted by Timothy Mitchell, the nation-state is not a "subjective belief, incorporated in the thinking and action of individuals, but . . . a representation reproduced in visible and everyday forms."[67] It is through the habitual experiences of "encountering" the nation-state that the identification of the state and its idioms of nationhood takes place.[68] The sights and sounds of the nation-state "clutter public space,"[69] and it is their familiarity or pervasiveness rather than their persuasiveness[70] that engenders public recognition.[71] As Thomas Hansen and Finn Stepputat have argued in a related discussion of the cultural practices of state-formation, the "continuous state spectacle[s] asserting and affirming the authority of the state . . . *only occasionally succeed in producing the specific social effects they aim at, but always reproduce the imagination of the state as the great enframer of our lives.*"[72]

These encounters take place in a variety of ways, and the venues, audiences, and agents involved are equally varied.[73] Although they enable the formation and dissemination of the official national imagination, they do not derive from a singular and centralized institutional authority, but are "coproduced" by a diverse range of state and nonstate actors, institutions, and practices.[74] At times they take spectacular and mediated forms, such as the cultural pageants that are staged at the heart of the capital city and witnessed on television screens across the nation during the annual commemoration of Republic Day. Other kinds of encounters are more immediate and everyday: filling out forms in triplicate; pondering how best to go about submitting a passport application when the "Form Giving" counter at the Passport Authority of India office opens two hours after the "Form Accepting" counter has closed; experiencing traffic grinding to a halt to allow the passage of a "VVIP" motorcade of white Hindustan Ambassador cars with flashing lights.[75]

Some encounters are visual and verbal, such as seeing a documentary film produced by the Films Division of India or listening to the president's annual broadcast to the nation on Republic Eve. Others are viscerally felt by bodies in pain: the "shoot at sight" orders given to the riot police; the judicial order authorizing the continued construction of a giant dam and the resulting displacement of thousands of people; and the passage of the Terrorist and Disruptive Activities Prevention Act (1987) to allow the preventive detention of any person suspected of being a terrorist.[76] In sum, the reproduction of the nation-state in and through such diversely constituted encounters draws upon the rhetorics and practices of violence (the state as an object of fear), bureaucratic reason (the state as rules, laws, policies, and paperwork), and spectacular displays (the state as an object of awe). Each encounter is attended by different modes of affective address, including both the "magic" of spectacular displays of state authority and also boredom, estrangement, and fear.[77] The effect that the encounters all have in common is that of eliciting recognition for and of the state as the authoritative representative of the nation: an effect that is achieved through iteration and ubiquity.

Nation, State, and Citizen in Nehruvian India

Encounters are also occasions or sites that perpetuate a distinctive set of organizing principles, prescriptions, and prohibitions that structure the field of political discourse and practice. They endorse particular ways of seeing and comprehending state, nation, and citizen, although the actual experience and form of each encounter may be very different, as I note above. Thus in the Nehruvian era of postcolonial India the encounters both everyday and momentous, informal and organized, political and cultural, and individual and collective all drew upon and reproduced a common set of normative understandings.[78]

India's profusion of subnational diversity was one such thematic. Its counterpart was the understanding of the state as the unifier of the fragmented nation—of national unity as an outcome that is state facilitated and "manufactured" rather than natural-organic. The repeated encounters with the unity-in-diversity master code took place in a variety of ways, such as the regional cultural performances during the annual pageantry of commemorative rituals and the images of spear-bearing Naga tribals, fez-wearing Muslims, and masked Kathakali dancers that invariably graced the People of

India wall charts in school classrooms, as well as the allocation of state resources and political recognition to groups that could successfully demonstrate their possession of a territorialized and materially distinctive cultural heritage or ethno-linguistic identity.

Along with these many affirmative gestures of celebrating, displaying, and otherwise according recognition to subnational diversity were the proliferation of discourses and institutional interventions that addressed the dangers of "diversity gone wrong": whether the parliamentary, media, and civil society debates on the "mob passion" and "irrational frenzy" of inter-religious riots and the attendant pleas to be steadfast against the machinations of political entrepreneurs and to restore the natural and apolitical ethos of tolerance that "really" defined Indian life; or the use of state violence to counter the "anti-national" activities of militants whose demands for increased regional autonomy in different parts of the nation threatened the federal balance of power. Where the celebratory performances of India's natural cultural diversity put positive norms of nationhood in place, these negative exemplars of "untamed" and "politicized" expressions of group identity drew attention to the dire consequences of deviating from the norm of diversity as an ethnocultural, nonpolitical matrix organized and maintained by the state.[79]

The ideals of citizenship were also articulated in similar, state-centered terms. Nehruvian India's most frequently invoked figure was that of the "infantile citizen" and his need for state tutelage and protection in order to realize the potentials of citizenship, itself conceptualized as an infinitely receding horizon rather than an existing bundle of rights.[80] Indeed, and in marked contrast to the liberal-democratic norm of the autonomous citizen, the ideal citizen of postcolonial India was defined in terms of his dependence upon, and intimate relationship with, the lineaments of state authority, with individual freedom seen to derive from rather than precede and make possible the sovereignty of the nation-state.

Finally, the idealization of apolitical behavior was another ubiquitous refrain, with state elites and social movement activists alike expressing a common distaste for the corrupting, petty, messy, and otherwise "profane" nature of political action,[81] and invoking a contrasting ideal of a world unmarked by conflict, inequality, and political struggle.

Together these themes organized the political field in postcolonial India around the presence and actions of the state, imagined as a neutral institutional entity located at a safe distance from the rough and tumble of politics, and imbued with the unique ability to address the many needs and problems of citizens, subnational groups, and the nation as a whole. This constitution of the state as the definitive problem solver in turn meant the continued problematization of nation and citizen. India and Indians were repeatedly defined in terms of their constitutive deficiencies, lack, and incompleteness —as the fragmented nation and the backward citizen with an inherent need for the state. Equally, the state-centric national imagination also entailed repeated admissions of state failure, with the urgency and constancy of the national need for the state established through highlighting the unmet goals, failed journeys, and unimplemented policies that marked the present. In other words, if nation-statist discourses and practices placed the state at the heart of individual and national life, so that encounters with citizenship and nationhood were inevitably encounters with the munificence of state power, they also illuminated the inherent limitations of such power. The state that was generated was thus simultaneously all encompassing and limited, omnipresent and nontotalizing.

Moreover, even as all such encounters commonly served as occasions for the elaboration of a distinctive "stated" understanding of nationhood and citizenship, there were significant variations in state authority in each case. In a reflection of the multiple and contending structures, actors, relationships, and networks that make up the modern state, different encounters revealed different "faces of the state" and put very different "languages of stateness" in circulation.[82] Thus, as the following chapters illustrate, the imagination of the state and of the state-nation relation that the organizational efforts of the defense agencies of the central state brought to light in the annual Republic Day parade, both mirrored and departed from the nation-statist imagination that emerged in the context of localized projects of township development, the documentary films that were produced by the Films Division of India, or the techno-scientific schemes introduced by the five-year plans.[83] As a result, the political field consolidated by all of these different nation-statist encounters was uneven and dissonant. It legitimized the reign of statist reason even as it inflected the substance of this rationality with multiple, and contending, meanings—equally endorsing the imagination of the "ruling state" and the "serving state"; bringing into being the state as an entity simultaneously invincible and fragile, grand and humble, timeless and new.[84]

In sum, while the burden of this book is to document how the endurance of the Indian nation-state is linked to the successful establishment of the state as the raison d'être of nationhood and citizenship, the narrative that unfolds is a fissured and contradictory one. Even though the chief protagonists are official institutions, agents, and ideologies, and the focus is on the production rather than the reception of nation-statist discourses and practices, it is the uneven "ambiguities of domination,"[85] rather than the seamless omnipotence and uniform application of state power, that assumes center stage.

Reconsidering Postcolonialism

What explains the emergence of this particular constellation of "ideas of India?"[86] What are the reasons why the "style" of Indian nationhood was structured along these lines?[87] To raise such questions is to recognize the historical contingency and contextual specificity of nation-state formation—the fact that the "enframing effect"[88] of the nation-state results from the interplay of political structures and processes, social relations, historical trajectories, and cultural repertoires that vary significantly across temporal and spatial contexts.[89] Equally variable are the techniques that produce this effect, as citizens encounter the logic of the nation-state in markedly different ways. Here it is instructive to look at the difference between the "magical" mode of nation-state making in South America, the "coercive" mode in Syria, and the "banal" mode in India. For instance, the "spectacular dramaturgies" of nation-state making in Venezuela that form the subject of Fernando Coronil's *The Magical State*, and the magisterial state-formation projects in the "unnamed Latin American elsewhere" discussed by Michael Taussig in *The Magic of the State*, draw upon representational strategies, affective registers, and power relations that are very different from those that inform the "shabbiness" of Assad's cult documented in Lisa Wedeen's political ethnography.[90] Similarly, the conjunction of habit and obedience in Syria—the fact that coercion, compulsion, and enforced participation are as critical to the reproduction of political power in Syria as are noncoercive, iterative techniques—is absent from the postcolonial Indian context, where two sets of (potentially contradictory) normative compulsions influenced the direction of nation-state formation, namely the commitment to democracy as well as to centralized state authority.

Understanding how and why the diverse nation, the infantile citizen, the transcendent state, and the fear of politics came to be the principal themes of the postcolonial political field in India, and why the dominant mode of the nation-state encounter in India took the specific form that it did, requires an exploration of the processes and practices of building a sovereign nation-state in the specific world-historical conjuncture of the mid-twentieth century. This in turn calls for a critical engagement with the notion of the postcolonial, the term that is most commonly used to describe India in the period following the formal transfer of power from British to Indian hands at midnight on August 14, 1947. To echo David Scott's powerful and provocative declaration, the time has come to interrogate—and set aside—the existing "problem-space" of postcolonial studies.[91] While Scott bases his argument on the political-ethical limits of postcolonial theory, or its failure to advance an active or engaged and meaningful political criticism,[92] my reservations address its analytical limits, or its inattention to the political and institutional dynamics of postcolonialism as a historically specific, and contextually located, project of establishing a sovereign nation-state.

Much of the scholarly work on postcolonialism treats it exclusively in epistemological terms as a particular stance of theoretical critique. It is the name for a position from which we can interrogate colonialism and its forms of power and knowledge, rather than a descriptor for temporally and spatially located processes of institution and identity formation (for instance, Algeria after 1962 or Pakistan after 1947) that had a direct impact on human lives. Even when postcolonial theory takes an empirical turn, it often fails to grapple with the historical contingencies of nation-state formation. Thus, for instance, some scholars exclude this completely by defining postcolonialism as an intrinsically oppositional, "subaltern" phenomenon: "The discourse of oppositionality that colonialism brings into being."[93] Finally, even those who set out to explain the emergence of new state forms and relations of power perpetuate a similar exclusion through their portrayal of a decontextualized "postcolonial condition" that apparently manifested itself in more or less equal measure throughout the globe, from Casablanca to Kuala Lumpur, Colombo to Accra.[94] For the most part, the promise of illuminating the practices, subjectivities, and structures and relations of power constituted by the process of postcolonial transformation remains unfulfilled, and we are urged instead to contemplate a templated, agentless, and invariant experience of "postcoloniality."[95]

These views of a modular postcolonialism are overstated. While the production and naturalization of the nation-state in India mirrored and foreshadowed projects of nation-state formation that had been undertaken in other parts of the world, it was also shaped by imperatives and factors that were distinctive to "our modernity," to use Partha Chatterjee's leading phrase. For instance, the commonsensical understanding of India as a constellation of discrete ethnocultural communities was linked to the workings of "colonialism and its forms of knowledge,"[96] as well as to the mobilizational strategies and ideological practices of subcontinental nationalisms in the colonial period. As Bernard Cohn and Kenneth Jones have shown, the "dynamic nominalism" of the colonial census in British India shored up the salience of religious identity.[97] With the introduction of this new institutional matrix of identity and difference in 1871, dichotomous and enumerated formations of religious community began to replace the earlier more fluid and porous formations.[98] This transformation was furthered and consolidated by the constitutional and legislative measures undertaken in later years—such as the introduction of separate electorates for Hindus and Muslims; the differential application and constitution of the law to reflect the "natural" religious divisions of Indian society; and the proliferation of official discourses about the "ancient and intractable" hatreds that Hindus and Muslims harbored toward each other—that translated every instance of group conflict into the master narrative of religious communalism.[99]

Other sets of colonial laws and policies emphasized other kinds of natural ethnic differences, such as those forged around the axes of caste, regional culture, or tribal origin. This logic of ethnicization was reproduced in almost all arenas of governance, ranging from military recruitment, law and order, and electoral system design to education and marriage.[100] In all of these instances, the ethnic community was upheld as the primary social unit and, in the case of religious community, the primary unit of political representation as well. Both the colonial state and its nationalist interlocutors made the representation of ethnic diversity (and the protection of ethno-religious minorities in particular) one of the defining pillars of state legitimacy. In colonial India, the question of the state's ethnic representativeness served as the means and ground for differentiating legitimate from illegitimate forms of rule. Thus for the colonial rulers, only a colonial state standing "outside" the chaotic diversity of India could represent the interests of all communities. In contrast, for the Indian National Congress ethnic representativeness required a sovereign national state form whose secular-democratic constitution could represent "each and all"—diversity as well as unity. And for the Muslim League, the representation of ethno-religious minorities required the establishment of two sovereign national states: a Muslim state to represent the Muslim nation, and a Hindu state to represent the Hindu nation.[101]

The historical legacy of colonial-nationalist interactions in India was thus to establish institutional structures and governmental techniques that reaffirmed the reality of ethnic identity, and to make diversity recognition and minority protection central idioms of state legitimization. Moreover, as noted above, both generalizable as well as particular imperatives and dynamics contributed to this outcome. Thus, while the common presumption of a colonial civilizing mission would lead to similar patterns of ethnicization in Rwanda and Nigeria, the specific configuration of the ethnic landscape in India and the *way* in which state, nation, and ethnicity were conjoined were the products of several localized and conjunctural developments. For instance, the creation of the Indian National Congress provincial committees on the basis of language zones in 1920 was a measure that granted recognition to the political claims of linguistic communities.[102] The tension between the mainstream nationalist movement and the many movements of subaltern resistance destabilized the universalizing claims of the former and ensured that proclamations of "national unity" would always be accompanied by gestures toward subnational diversity.[103] The political interventions of Bhimrao Ambedkar and other leaders of the Dalit/Untouchable (lower-caste) movement in the bipolar field of Hindu-Muslim relations pluralized the category of ethnicity to include considerations of caste identity,[104] while the long shadow of partition reframed the question of interreligious coexistence into one specifically about the protection of Muslim minorities by a secular state.

In this sense we can say that the formation of the nation-state in India was an experience simultaneously generalizable and incommensurable, with the dominant status of unity in diversity secured by the structured determinations of history as well as its fortuitous accidents and events.[105] A social-historical exploration of the postcolonial nation-state formation must consequently encompass macro-institutionalist processes such as census taking as well as the contingencies of sudden deaths; the generalizable, modular technologies of colonial rule as well as their realization and application in a specific time and space;[106] and the complex maneuvers of political agents as well as the determining effects of social and economic structures.[107]

If the *longue durée* of colonialism is integral to its discussion, so too are the events and exigencies that emerged during the "long transition" from colonial rule, or the years between 1947 and 1950.[108] The transfer of power from British to Indian hands was ceremonially staged at the "stroke of the midnight hour"[109] in a function that symbolized the predominantly constitutionalist and negotiated means by which Indian independence was secured. However, the formal establishment of India as a sovereign democratic republic took place more than three years later, when the Constituent Assembly adopted the new constitution on January 26, 1950. At one level, the intervening years were marked by tumultuous changes and uncertainties. The steady streams of refugees into the capital city of Delhi and the makeshift refugee camps that were hastily established to accommodate the thousands of people displaced by the partition of India and Pakistan served as daily and all-too-visible reminders to the delegates of the Constituent Assembly that the present of the nation whose future they were deliberating was unsettled and indeterminate.

The territorial reach of state sovereignty was another open question during most of this period, as separate "instruments of accession" had to be negotiated with the 562 "princely states" that had not been subject to the direct colonial rule experienced by the provinces of British India.[110] In a few cases accession was a particularly contentious process; in Hyderabad and Junagadh it would entail the application of armed force, and in Kashmir it would occasion international conflict and intervention as well.

The discourse of "nation building" and the related emphasis on the inadequacies and incompleteness of nation and citizen emerged out of this context of uncertainty and flux. Instead of triumphant, celebratory declarations about the "victory" of independence, the political rhetoric of this period consisted of somber, even stern, reminders of the distance between "independence" and "real freedom" and the sacrifices and hard labor that were required to narrow the gap. As Maulana Azad, the education minister in the interim government would announce in his radio broadcast to the "children of India" on the first anniversary of independence: "Adversity is part of this independence package . . . we have to lift burdens like strong real men. Colonization meant that we weren't burdened, this was part of being enslaved. We can no longer sit back on a bed of flowers. We need to run on thorns."[111]

The tumult of transformation is not, however, the only characteristic of this transitional period. There were significant institutional continuities as well, and in this sense the interregnum is better understood not as a moment of radical rupture but as a process of translating—in its literal sense of "carrying over"—colonial governmental structures and technologies into a nation-statist order. The factors that put the "post" of postcolonialism in abeyance, or the idea that India after 1947 was a time and a place after and beyond colonialism, include the colonial provenances of the constituent assembly as a body authorized by the provisions of the Government of India Act of 1935;[112] the plethora of legislation enacted by an "interim government" with similar roots in the ancien régime;[113] the endurance of a common bureaucratic "steel frame" across the "great divide" of 1947; and finally, the use of vocabularies and techniques of nation-state legitimization that previously had been deployed in the service of the colonial state.

In terms of nation-statist ideologies and practices, there were continuities in many of the ideas of India that had been endorsed by the colonial state, such as the emphasis on India's natural diversity, the state-centrism of the political-cultural field, and the imagination of the state as an impartial, apolitical, and transcendent institutional entity.[114] There were continuities as well in how these ideas were articulated and disseminated. As I will show, the encounters with the nation-state in Nehruvian India were sites and moments for the reproduction of idioms of "high bureaucracy," and the generation of copious paper trails and other techniques of state rationality associated with colonial governance. The effect of state recognition that is critical to the endurance of the nation-state was thus secured not through the creation of new "postcolonial" practices but rather the renewed application of old colonial ones.

However, even as colonial techniques and vocabularies were reproduced in Nehruvian India, they were inflected with meanings that reflected the transformed political-social context of a free India. For instance, the reconfiguration of the political field under the sign of democracy and federalism meant that state power after 1947 was imagined in layered terms as both autonomous and constrained. Admissions of state failure and indictments of the multiple inadequacies and the inherent limits of the state now emerged as familiar themes of official discourse, thus marking a significant shift from the triumphant certitudes of colonial authority.

The presumed understandings of India and Indians were also reshaped in the context of several distinctive events. Thus in the wake of the "language unrest" of the 1950s or the popular struggles that were launched in several states to demand a reorganization of the federal system along ethnolinguistic lines, territorialized language communities were entrenched as the primary unit of the diversity mosaic, and as the only kinds of subnational groups that could legitimately advance claims for political recognition and the redistribution of power.[115] The war with China in 1962 was another such "structuring event" that put new idioms of nationhood in circulation, and the unitary vision of the nation-state and the militarist conception of the ideal citizen that had emerged in the context of India's first "national emergency" were subsequently carried over into the prosaic practices of politics as usual after the immediate emergency situation had passed.[116] These and other examples of continuity yet change attest to the dynamic constitution of the Nehruvian nation-state; that is, to the fact that the "imagination of institutions" and the "institution of diversity" were determined as well as conjunctural outcomes. The themes of stability, endurance, repetition, habituation, and familiarity that drive this book do not preclude an attention to historical contingency and to the varied and unexpected ways in which nation-state identity is reproduced and transformed.

The arguments in this volume are developed and substantiated in four chapters that concern four different kinds of encounters with the nation-state in Nehruvian India and the range of cultural-symbolic, visual, spatial, and policy practices that produced and consolidated presumptive understandings of India and Indians. My work in these chapters draws upon three years of field research that involved a diverse range of techniques—from archival research and interviews with state officials on policy formulation to participant observation of cultural practices and the critical reading of visual texts. In my effort to convey the processual or ongoing character of nation-state formation, I do not restrict my discussion to a single and fixed time period. Thus, while my primary focus in each chapter is the period spanning the first two decades after independence and the varied institutional and ideational efforts that were undertaken to realize the goal of "nation building," all of the chapters include several forays into later times.

Reflecting the multiple facets and often contradictory imperatives of the nation-state building project, the specific examples discussed in this book are deliberately broad ranging: from the production of visual symbols of the nation-state to policies on science and technology; from the planned development of model industrial townships to public ceremonials of ritual commemoration that take place on January 26 every year to mark the anniversary of the Indian constitution. While I show how all of the examples contributed to the "imagination of institutions" and the "institution of diversity," their divergences and contradictions are also addressed; the spectacular commemorations, the didactic documentary films, the inauguration of industrial research laboratories, and the constitution of commissions of inquiry to investigate the outbreak of religious conflict in industrial townships are all shown to have played a distinctive role in advancing the logic and practice of the nation-state.

If the story that emerges in these pages is more fragmented than seamless and linear, so too was the experience of the nation-state encounter, as ordinary citizens were addressed concomitantly by all of these contemporaneous projects. The resident of a steel township, for instance, could in the context of her everyday life encounter the "diverse nation," the "transcendent state," and the "fear of politics" in all of the four different ways that I describe in this book: the annual spectacle of national celebrations; the ponderous address of state-produced documentaries; the institutional schemes of technoscientific modernization; and the urban planning and development of the steel township as a model national space.

All of these encounters may well have been "beyond belief"—that is, they may have failed to resonate with the township resident's practical, lived experiences. The luminous facades of the new steel township that the Films Division brought into focus were possibly as estranging as the colorful float of *Chhau* dancers from Orissa that stood in for her identity at the Republic Day parade in Delhi. My task here, however, is not to establish the credulity of the nation-state encounter, or the fact that ordinary subjects "believed," "accepted," or were "convinced by" the rhetoric and imagery of nation and state at hand, but rather to document the iteration and material manifestation of certain sets of presumptive, and authoritative, understandings.

The first two chapters engage with the materialization of the nation-state in the most literal sense: the production of visual images and representations of India and Indians. In chapter 1, I examine the "moving pictures" of Indianness that were produced by the Films Division of India, a documentary and newsreel production agency that was established by the Ministry of Information and Broadcasting in 1948. I show how the Films Division enabled the constitution of a distinct identity for the state as an authoritative representative of the Indian nation—an identity that could be recognized both by nonstate audiences and by the state elites themselves. In this project of state identification, the content of the visual representations produced by the Films Division was of considerable importance; that is, the ways in which the Films Division quite literally allowed national audiences to "see the state" and the concrete activities that it was undertaking "on behalf of" the nation. Of equal importance, however, was the distinctive filmic idiom that it deployed. It was through the elaboration of a particular filmic genre of the "state documentary"—through the formal differentiation that resulted from audience experiences of "boredom," "disenchantment," and "nonresonance"—that the authorial flourish of the state's signature was secured.

Chapter 2, "Marching in Time," is an examination of the public rituals of commemoration on India's annual Republic Day; notably the ways in which visual practices and ritual performances have consolidated the "unity in diversity" formation of nationhood. Establishing the argument of this book, I show how this annual event has been concerned with celebrating the state in the name of the nation; with "imagining institutions" rather than "imagining community"; and with defining Indian identity in terms of cultural diversity rather than homogeneity. In this chapter I engage with both the formation and the transformation of the visual vocabularies and performances of nationhood by tracking the ritual repertoires of Republic Day ranging from the ceremonial commemoration organized in 1951 to mark the first anniversary of the adoption of the Indian constitution to the choreographed pageantry that awaited audiences attending the fiftieth anniversary celebrations in 2001.

In chapters 3 and 4 I focus on the discursive and material effects of what are arguably the two most distinctive and familiar enterprises of the Nehruvian political arena—namely, the state-led projects of scientific and technological modernization and economic planning that were undertaken in the 1950s and 1960s, the decades of "high developmentalism" in India. Chapter 3, "Indian Darkness," is an examination of the "needs discourse" of Nehruvian India or the ways in which India was defined as a collection of persistent and unfulfilled problems, failures, and needs by development policy discourses. I focus specifically on the discourse of science policy and the "need for science" that was presented as the ultimate national need and the most pressing priority for the state to address. I show how the understanding of the nation-state as a homogenous space populated by identical individuals was enabled in the Indian context by the discourse of needs rather than the discourse of rights or of cultural commonalities. What was distinctive about this was not so much the negative definition of the nation in terms of its inherent lack or deficiency, but rather that the omissions and weaknesses of the state were also highlighted, and that this charge of state failure was a state-produced discourse. In such a context, criticisms of state policies reproduced rather than subverted the existing structures of power and further consolidated the link between nation and state.

In chapter 4, "Cities of Hope" I turn my attention to state-led plans for rapid industrial growth. Specifically, I examine the spatial practices associated with the Nehruvian state's push toward "nation building" through rapid industrial development, and the ways in which the dream of a "new India" was realized through the building of carefully designed new urban spaces. By focusing on the formation and transformation of one such type of new urban space—the steel towns, or the industrial townships that were built to house the workers of the nationalized steel plants—I document the concrete, localized practices that enabled the abstraction of the nation-state to take shape. Steel towns were upheld as the exemplary national spaces of the new India—spaces that would enable the birth of new, "nationally integrated" producer-citizens and bring forth the future of national time; spaces in which the state could foreground activities undertaken on behalf of the nation and thereby render visible its representative character. I trace the journey of the steel town from its original establishment as the exemplary national "dreamworld" in the late 1950s to its reconceptualization a decade later as the exemplary national "catastrophe" in the wake of the religious riots that erupted in the steel town of Rourkela. I argue that this shift tapped into and fostered a significant and structuring theme of political rhetoric in India—namely, the "fear of politics" and the attendant distinction between the nonpartisan, neutral, or disinterested operations of state rationality and the selfish, unruly, and misguided maneuvers of mass politics. I also document the "problematization of diversity," or how, through the repeated presentation of "unmanaged" and "untamed" diversity as a perennial danger that plagues the nation, the identity and authority of the state as the definitive national problem solver was secured.

In the conclusion, "After Midnight," I revisit the theoretical and historical arguments of this book from the perspective of the political present. What does it mean to highlight the symbolic limits of institutionalized diversity in Nehruvian India when the ascendancy of monocultural nationalism has led to the real death of at least two thousand Muslims in the recent past? What does it mean to critically evaluate discourses of multicultural tolerance when new global regimes of discrimination are being entrenched with renewed vigor? The conclusion is meant neither to be an exercise in validation through falsification nor a search for generalizable grand theory; instead, it is an interrogation of the limits and possibilities of the answers provided in this book, and an evaluation of whether the questions I have addressed are the ones worth raising in the first place.

CHAPTER 1

Moving Pictures

The Films Division of

India and the Visual

Practices of the

Nation-State

: : :

> It is no good my complaining, because it is our fault if we cannot put across to our people the magnitude of the work that is being done in India at present . . . I am anxious that we should reach our people in the villages as well as in the towns with some kind of a record of the work that has been done and that is going to be done . . . It is not enough to give just a glimpse of something being done. It should be a longer and more educative picture.
> —Jawaharlal Nehru, 1963

> The Films Division has been interpreting India to Indians and to the world. Through its films it has shown the multi-racial; multi-lingual; the multi-costumed and multi-faceted India in its glory and wretchedness, in its gay and sad moments, in its diversity and depth . . . In the storage vaults of the Films Division is the memory of the nation.
> —Jag Mohan, *Two Decades of the Films Division*

The vast body of scholarship on nations and nationalism is fissured by a series of sharply etched methodological, epistemological, and political and ideological cleavages. Should we conceptualize the nation as an expression of a primordial, prepolitical, even a socio-biological human urge to "bond and cleave"? Or is it better understood as a formation that is produced and transformed by the strategic instrumentalist calculations of political elites? In recent years several scholars have found a way out of this theoretical impasse of objectivist versus subjectivist approaches to the study of nations and nationalism.[1] Their endorsement of a historical constructivist approach holds out the promise of a middle ground between these two apparently irreconcilable perspectives on the origins and essence of nations, and in so doing directs our attention to the historical dynamics of political change and endurance. Thus, although nations may indeed be emergent social and political constructions that over time are invested with variable cultural meanings, the analytical task here at hand is not so much to unmask their contingency but to explain how, despite their contingent origins and existence, they have come to be seen as real. In the theoretical ground that has been cleared, the pressing issue is to understand the "as if" of nationhood—to investigate the ensemble of practices, processes, and structures that constitute national identity as an immutable given of human existence.

In the spirit of these inquiries, my work in this chapter is motivated by a similar search for the "as if" of postcolonial nationhood, or the mechanisms that have consolidated Indian national identity in the postcolonial period. It is a search that leads through unexpected terrain. It draws attention not to passion, enchantment, and other affective sentiments and emotions of political love that are most commonly associated with our notions of the nation as a community of deep horizontal comradeship,[2] but instead to what may well be regarded as their opposite: experiences of disenchantment and nonresonance. As I establish below, such experiences played an integral role in bringing into being the distinctive hyphenated entity of the nation-state by enabling the identification and recognition of the state as the authoritative representative of the nation. Nationhood in the era of the nation-state has not been solely a work of the "imagination" sustained by the creative energies of poets, artists, novelists, and cultural practitioners; instead, bureaucratic, stilted, and singularly unimaginative labors have also played a constitutive role. If, following Rogers Brubaker, nationhood is better conceptualized as a perspective on the world rather than a substantive entity in the world—a framework that is activated rather than an identity that is possessed—then a critical role has been played by the routinization of the national frame through discourses and practices of familiarization rather than emotional identification.[3]

My specific focus here is on the history, practices, and productions of the Films Division of India, which was established as a branch of the state

Ministry of Information and Broadcasting in 1948—shortly after independence. In the fifty-odd years of its existence, it has produced over eight thousand documentaries, short films, and newsreels, or an average of one new film every three days, making it the single largest producer of documentary films in the world. Until 1994, under the terms of a compulsory exhibition and licensing policy, owners of commercial movie theaters throughout India were required to screen a state-approved documentary film or newsreel before the start of any commercial feature film. In addition, the Films Division supplied prints to several central ministries such as the Ministry of Welfare and the Department of Field Publicity (a branch of the Ministry of Information and Broadcasting that was constituted to generate rural support for the project of economic planning) for free screenings in rural areas. With this framework of distribution in place, the Films Division could claim an average audience strength of eighty million viewers every week.

However, as a review commission noted as early as 1967, the prodigious output of the Films Division and the ambitious scope of its distribution scheme did not necessarily translate into, and may even have militated against, the meaningful reception of its visual texts.[4] The national distribution scheme paid little attention to the specific conditions under which different groups of subnational audiences actually receive or engage with the films. Reflecting this disinterest in questions of effect, most Films Division documentaries are characterized by their ponderous and heavy-handed style; for the most part, they lend themselves all too readily to charges of clumsy propaganda and bureaucratic ineptitude. When we examine the spectacular and enchanted dreamworlds of "Bollywood" or Hindi commercial cinema with which they compete for attention, the credibility of such dismissals is further heightened. What explains this phenomenon of "production for its own sake?" Why are Films Division documentaries so boring?

By way of answering these questions, in this chapter I undertake a close investigation of an apparently paradoxical phenomenon: the "disenchanted imaginary" produced by the Films Division of India in the first two decades after Indian independence. Through a discussion of the origins, governing imperatives, formal treatment, and thematic choices made by the state producers of documentary film during the first few decades after independence, I show how the Films Division enabled the constitution of a distinct identity for the state as an authoritative representative of the Indian nation—an identity that could be recognized both by nonstate audiences and by state elites themselves. In this project of state identification, the content of the visual representations produced by the Films Division were of considerable importance—the ways in which the Films Division quite literally allowed national audiences to "see the state" and the concrete activities that it was undertaking on behalf of the nation. Of equal importance, however, was the distinctive filmic idiom that it deployed. As I demonstrate below, it was through the elaboration of a distinctive filmic genre of the state documentary—through the formal differentiation produced by effects of "boredom," "disenchantment," and "nonresonance"—that the distinctive authorial flourish of the state's signature was secured.

Lineages of Documentary Film

I begin here with a discussion of the origins of the Films Division and of the multiple imperatives and actors that shaped the relationship between state and film in the early years of postcolonial India. Although the Films Division was formally established by the postcolonial state shortly after the transfer of power from imperial to sovereign national hands in 1947, the practice of state involvement in the production of film has an older colonial history. To quote a publicity brochure issued by the Films Division in 1969: "Like the roads and the railways, the posts and telegraphs, the administrative system and the armed services, which the British built up primarily in the interests of Empire and secondarily in the interests of the ruled, the Documentary film and the Newsreel too were brought in. And in the transplanted soil, both seemed to have thrived well."[5]

Both state and nonstate actors were involved in this exercise of transplantation. If documentary film played a key role in disseminating visual representations of nation and state in India, this was not so much an outcome engineered by state propaganda agencies as it was a "coproduction" authored by a motley crew of bureaucrats, independent filmmakers, civil society associations such as the Documentary Unit of India and the Independent Documentary Producers Association that were established as production consortiums and lobby groups for documentary filmmakers, and international organizations such as UNESCO and the Ford Foundation that played a critical role in encouraging the use of audiovisual technologies in the "new nations" of the third world.[6]

The term "documentary" was first used by the filmmaker John Grierson to describe Robert Flaherty's film *Moana* (1926). For Grierson, a documentary film was one that entailed "a creative treatment of actuality,"[7] and it is this notion of portraying "actuality" or accurately depicting reality that informed the earliest efforts at documentary filmmaking in India. The existing tradition of filmmaking in India already included "topicals," or short films on real events,[8] but these were nonreflexive, "random filmings of scenes" devoid of any overarching structure or message.[9] The return to India of three Indian filmmakers—P. V. Pathy, K. S. Hirlekar, and D. G. Tendulkar, from Paris, Berlin, and Moscow, respectively—led to the initiation of the Indian documentary movement in the 1930s.[10] Inspired by the example of German *kultur* films; by Soviet cinema (primarily the work of Sergei Eisenstein); and by the work of John Grierson and Paul Rotha in England and Robert Flaherty and Pare Lorentz in the United States, these Indian filmmakers felt that film should have a definite social purpose of instruction, information, and motivation. The choice of appropriate "topics" and their "creative treatment" therefore required careful attention. Accordingly, the earliest Indian documentaries were films made for "the education and enlightenment of the people."[11] These included films on the Indian nationalist movement (*The Haripura Congress Session*, 1938), films appealing for funds for earthquake victims (the Imperial Film Company's film on the Quetta earthquake), films publicizing the railway system in India (the travelogues of K. Subramaniam), and films that focused on a specific cultural or historical aspect of Indian reality (including works such as Mohan Bhavnani's *Mysore—Gem of India*; as well as the film *Keddah*, on elephant trapping, and *Wrestling*, on "the various peculiarly Indian techniques of this popular sport").[12]

For the practitioners of documentary making in India in the 1930s, the medium could be an agent and instrument of social change, with filmmakers emulating the documentarian Paul Rotha's self-description as a "legislator of mankind" or a builder of a new social order.[13] However, this impulse of social reform did not interrogate the authority of the colonial state, and the aim of "educating and enlightening" the people did not disrupt the civilizing presumptions of colonial rule. Thus the universal themes of modernization (the railways; the notion of voluntary civilian donations to help the underprivileged; and even the existence of impulses of political modernity such as the Indian National Congress) were showcased in an effort to trace the movement of the Indian people in the direction of development and progress under the guidance of the colonial state. India itself found particularist meaning as a conglomeration of culturally diverse and custom-bound groups.

The colonial state had similar views on the instructive nature and social function of the documentary film, and it was the state's utilization of the documentary genre as part of its "war effort" during World War II that gave the Indian documentary movement its first institutional support structure. With the onset of the war in Europe, the state turned to its subjects for crucial assistance in the form of manpower and strategic supplies. In 1940 the Imperial Department of Information, through its chief bureaucrat, Desmond Young, authorized the creation of a Film Advisory Board (FAB). The FAB's mission was to produce films that would publicize the urgency and the requirements of the war situation, as well as appeal for popular support.[14] Despite its explicitly imperial concerns, the FAB was supported by a number of individuals sympathetic to the nationalist cause, for whom the importance of engaging in an immediate battle against fascist forces in the international arena overshadowed more localized concerns. The films produced by the FAB include war-related documentaries on topics such as military recruitment (*He's in the Navy*) and military technology (*The Planes of Hindustan*), as well as nonstrategic documentaries on general themes that would both be of interest to and inform the Indian public (*Women of India; Industrial India*). However, even the latter category of "nonpropagandist" films linked the representations of India to the presence and activities of the British state, which was presented in both *Women of India* and *Industrial India* as the central protagonist—that is, as the progressive and developmentalist institutional authority that enabled India and Indians to move forward.

Further, the particular filmic form favored by FAB officials was one that underscored a vertical or hierarchical relation of authority between filmmaker and film viewer and, by implication, between state and society. The company Time-Life Inc. sponsored the documentary series *The March of Time* (produced by Louis de Rochemont in 1938), and its authoritative conventions such as the use of "voice-of-God" interpretive narrations, the tendency to summarize personal interviews with explanatory comments, diagrams, and charts, and the focus on "important people" had a strong impact on the FAB chairman, Ezra Mir, who actively encouraged the production of similar films for an Indian audience. The FAB was eventually replaced by a set of three specialized organizations: the Information Films of India (IFI), Indian News Parade (INP), and the Army Film Centre (AFC). While newsreels and films related to war propaganda were those most frequently produced, the occasional creative and nonpropaganda ventures were also supported by the British state (e.g., Mohan Bhavnani's *The Private Life of a Silkworm*, and Paul Zil's *Bombay: The Story of Seven Isles*). These films attempted to portray some aspect of Indian life to domestic audiences, and education and information were once again the primary motivations. The state also turned its attention to the distribution of films and enforced rule 44A of the Defence of India Rules to mandate compulsory exhibition of state-produced films by private exhibitors all over India.

The colonial state's documentary production and distribution efforts ceased in 1946 because there was no longer a need for war propaganda. Moreover, in the particular conjuncture of the "endgame of empire," the state increasingly resorted to coercive measures, thereby abandoning its project of persuasion and the quest to secure the normative compliance of the subject population. Nevertheless, as the film historian Sanjit Narwekar notes, many Indian nationalists continued to view with suspicion the FAB and the IFI, and by association, the broader enterprise of the official documentary film, accusing these organizations of "try[ing] to dragoon an unwilling nation into the war."[15]

The task of reinventing the documentary film as the handmaid of a national rather than a colonial state was part and parcel of a larger enterprise of reimagining the new, postcolonial India. The redefinition of the state as national rather than colonial, of the relation between the state and its people in terms of citizenship rather than subjecthood, and even of the national community itself (given the geographical and demographic reconfiguration of India after the partition in 1947) were pressing tasks confronted by the postcolonial polity. Several scholars have commented on the "postcolonial anxiety" or "insecurities" that haunted this practice of reinvention, as political elites worked to create a distinctive meaning for the Indian nation-state in a world in which the templates of nationhood and of statehood had been hammered out long ago. The imperatives of "modulation" or the "constitut[ion] of certain national experiences as originals and [the definition of] the task for latecomers as replicating the experience of such originals" produced in postcolonial polities a nagging sense of having arrived just a little too late.[16] Sankaran Krishna has described what resulted as a logic of endless temporal and spatial "deferrence,"[17] where political elites defined national identity in terms of a "becoming" rather than a "being": a dynamic, future-oriented, ever-unfolding process. Moreover, the state was presented as the key agent in this process of national becoming; a new, sovereign state, that, unlike its colonial predecessor, could be visibly shown to undertake activities that were "truly representative" of the Indian people.

In postcolonial India, this imperative of visibility was served through the adoption of a "monumental"[18] style of state making, or the undertaking of large-scale technological and industrial projects. India after 1950 was a nation that was defined through the big dreams of its state. On the domestic front, this view translated into a commitment to planned development through the construction of institutions, expertise, and material artifacts that could quite literally be seen to command the economy from a transcendent, directorial vantage point. Science and technology also enabled the dreams of greatness to be literalized: the new India could, and did, build big dams, big bridges, big railway coach factories, big power plants, and big atomic reactors. And these projects were all proclaimed to exist because of the representative labors of the sovereign state. In official public discourse as well as in the contemporary media landscape, the state facilitation of big development, big science, and big technology received maximum emphasis and was upheld as visible evidence of the representative commitments of Indian independence. But this logic of visible representation could make sense only in the eyes of a viewer; only if a particular way of seeing could be presumed. From April 1948 onward, the Films Division and its documentary films and newsreels were harnessed in the task of consolidating this gaze. With this, the national value of the documentary film no longer needed to be the subject of impassioned pleas put forth by documentary filmmakers. They could now be nation builders, and the state could now be a documentary filmmaker.

In sum, the decision to establish the Films Division in 1948 was shaped by the interplay of varied imperatives and stakes that structured the political field of decolonization. The emulation of colonial governance practices; the particular exigencies of "postcolonial anxiety" in India; contemporaneous inspiration from the use of documentary film by other nation-states such as Britain, the United States, Canada, and the Soviet Union;[19] and pragmatic calculations about the value of audiovisual pedagogy in a country characterized by a high level of illiteracy all played a role in authorizing the state's use of documentary film.

As noted above, a discussion of the complex origins of the Films Division would not be complete without considering the significant role played by nonstate actors in shaping the relationship between state and film. Thus, the genesis of the Films Division and the authorization of the state's pedagogical mission of producing documentary film also has to be located in the initial years after independence at the intersection of debates between independent filmmakers and the state on the "utility of film"; that is, whether there is something "educational" (and therefore redeeming) about cinema, or whether it is mere "entertainment" and therefore a "luxury" ill-suited for developing nations like India.

Documentary filmmakers as well as representatives from the commercial film industry were involved in these discussions, with both eventually corroborating the state's understanding of filmmaking as a utilitarian instrument of nation building. In this sense, we can say that the state's use of documentary film was socially sanctioned by actors located outside of official circles of power. They appropriated and reproduced the discourse about the national utility of film, choosing to describe their work in terms of its functionalist rather than aesthetic value. The discussions at the Film Seminar of February-March 1955 organized by the newly established Sangeet Natak Akademi (the Academy of Music and Dance, modeled along the lines of the French academies) are a case in point. As the presiding officer, Rajamannar, noted in his opening address by drawing an explicit parallel between filmmaking and nation building: "I welcome you, Sir, [Prime Minister Nehru], as the Director of one of the greatest films in history—the film of New India's destiny. Politicians and statesmen, capitalists and workmen, scientists and technicians, artists and poets and millions of common men and women are participating in this great film of which you are the supreme director."[20]

Other speakers at the seminar also echoed the state's discourse about national priorities—economic development, scientific progress, national unity—in describing the purpose and mission of filmmaking.[21] Similar sentiments were expressed on other occasions as well. Thus in September 1956, at a symposium on "Historical and Biographical Films" organized by the Ministry of Information and Broadcasting,[22] it was the independent filmmakers as much as the state officials who argued, "The industry must give to the nation pictures around our daily life and its social and economic problems. India's history . . . travelogues, documentaries, newsreels and shorts such as they produce in America must now be started here." In the words of another seminar participant, "a new era of people's films, national in form and progressive in content" was at hand.[23]

Seeing India

In terms of its organizational structure, the Films Division resembled all other bureaucratic organizations, with little to distinguish its particular mandate of aesthetic labor. Its headquarters were in Bombay, with three nodal field offices in Delhi, Calcutta, and Bangalore and several branch offices in other metropolitan centers in India.[24] The organization was headed by the chief producer, and while the first few heads were professional filmmakers, in later years the post was filled by generalists drawn from the

Indian Administrative Services who did not necessarily have any prior filmmaking experience.

In its initial years, the Films Division consisted of a production wing and a distribution wing. Film topics were suggested by different ministries, government agencies, and state governments. There was also an annual interministries meeting where coordinated topics were suggested, and on the basis of this meeting an annual production plan was finalized by the Ministry of Information and Broadcasting. The responsibilities for documentary production were shared by three producers: one in charge of documentaries; one in charge of newsreels; and one in charge of commissioning productions by independent filmmakers.[25] With the state as the biggest patron of the short film in the 1950s and 1960s, filmmakers were eager to sign contracts with the Films Division and they viewed its work in very favorable terms. The relation between the Indian state and the independent artist was thus a collaborative and accommodative one in the immediate post-independence period—for the most part, both parties shared common understandings about the nature and purpose of documentary film as a tool that could bring awareness to "ethically incomplete"[26] national audiences. Filmmakers interested in establishing themselves as the creators of serious or intellectual cinema frequently turned to the Films Division for sponsorship and financial support.[27] A list of directors and producers of Films Division documentaries over the past fifty years includes names like Satyajit Ray, Mrinal Sen, Shyam Benegal, K. A. Abbas, Sukhdev, and other pioneers of independent Indian cinema.

The distribution wing coordinated the complicated process by which forty thousand prints were screened in cinema theaters throughout the country every year. A hundred new newsreels and another hundred new documentary prints in the thirteen official languages were released weekly to two hundred different "first-run" cinema houses throughout the country. After one week, the first-run houses that had initially received the documentaries would receive the newsreels, and those initially receiving the newsreels would receive the documentaries. Once this circuit had been completed, the prints would be sent on to the second-run houses and so on until over the course of a year all of the national cinema houses in the country had received the prints. From each cinema house, the Films Division would collect 1 percent of the total box-office earnings as a rental fee for the screening of its documentaries and newsreel films. In addition to this revenue-generating process of film circulation, prints were supplied to the Field Publicity Directorate for free showings to urban and rural audiences.[28] The scope and

Table 1. Categories of Films Division documentaries, 1949–1972

CATEGORY	NUMBER OF FILMS
Art and Culture	139
Archaeology and monuments	30
Arts	55
Crafts	9
Festivals	13
People of India	32
Citizenship and Reform	314
Civic education	35
Government and citizenship	59
Health and hygiene	137
Education and youth activities	78
Coins, weights, and measures	5
Development and Planning	696
Agriculture	137
Community development and cooperation	59
Cottage industries	20
Fisheries	12
Five-year plans and their projects	65
Housing	10
Industry	89
Labor and employment	25
Relief and rehabilitation	27
Savings	43
Science and technology	40
Social welfare	35
Trade and commerce	29
Transport and communications	105
Miscellaneous	304
Biography	50
Children's films	11
Classroom films	15
Current history	28
Experimental films	18
Food	28
Geography and travel	115
Natural resources	13
Sports, pastime, and recreation	26
Defense and International	289
Defense	121
International scene	168
TOTAL	1,742

Source: Pati, *Films Division Catalogue of Films, 1949–1972*.

ambition of this distribution scheme led at least one critic to estimate that the Films Division films had an "audience potential" of over ten million individuals every week.[29]

To what extent did this audience potential translate into lived experience? Further, what did the viewing of a Films Division documentary entail—that is, what was illuminated and what in turn was obscured? Finally, who was addressed, by whom, and how? To answer these questions, I turn to the actual films themselves along with the specific choices of form and content, the production practices, and the visual treatment that together enabled the Films Division to chart a distinctive line of sight in postcolonial India.

According to the Films Division's own classificatory scheme, it produced several different kinds of films for the "people of India."[30] These categories include: art and experimental films; biography and personality films; classroom films and children's films; educational and motivational films; Defence Ministry films; export and tourist promotion films; and "the visit" films, or documentaries on official trips taken by Indian state officials to other countries. A somewhat different categorization scheme informs table 1, which is based on thematic distinctions that were endorsed by the Films Division at the time of a comprehensive review of the approximately seventeen hundred documentaries that had been produced by 1972—commemorating twenty years of its establishment. As the table indicates, approximately 8 percent of the documentaries were on topics of art and culture; 18 percent on citizenship and reform; 17 percent on defense and the "international scene"; and 38 percent on development and planning. The remaining films were an assortment of biographical documentaries, children's films, documentaries on "geography and travel," and experimental films. It is useful here to take a closer look at some of these efforts to document different aspects of Indian reality and the visions of India and Indians that were elaborated for audiences across the nation, whether in the plush air-conditioned environments of colonial cinema houses in the major metropolitan centers, or in the open-air *maidans* (fields) in small towns and villages.

The art and culture documentaries portrayed India's natural regional cultural diversity. These films represented culture as a tangible artifact, object, or visible practice that could be located in a specific time and place: for example, Madhubani paintings from Bihar in eastern India, temple carvings from the Ajanta caves in western India, or Kathakali dancers from the southern state of Kerala. On display were the discrete, almost hermetically sealed worlds indexed by each of these distinctive cultural forms and practices. Further, in reflecting the nationalist predilection for the folk, the location of culture was invariably nonurban. The gaze of the Films Division was almost exclusively directed toward prelapsarian vistas of colorful exuberance that constituted Indianness as a collection of exotic others. No matter who the audience was, there was always some "forgotten," "unknown," or "hidden" cultural community that could be presented before it as a result of what Films Division officials described as their painstaking labors of cultural recuperation and excavation.

The depictions of folk cultural diversity created a spatial distance between the audience and the subject of films on painting, music, and dance, contributing to the sense that "real culture" was inevitably located elsewhere. A series of films on architecture created a similar effect of temporal distance, as they located culture in a remote past at considerable remove from the time-space of the contemporaneous viewer. Here, too, the diversity of architectural form was the dominant theme, with Indians urged to contemplate their heritage as a constellation of singular monumental forms scattered throughout national territory, united only by the eye of the statist camera. The state's role as the unifier of the nation, or the fact that only state-sponsored cultural activities could bring forth an undifferentiated sense of being Indian, was underscored through another set of art and culture films—namely, those that turned their lens on the "festivals of India." Here, the only festival that enjoyed the unqualified or uninflected label of Indianness was that of Republic Day. All others were marked by their distinctive religious and regional particularities: a Buddhist commemoration, a Punjabi marriage, or a carnival in Goa, all of which were described as "festivals of India" even as—and in fact because—they belonged to discrete, subnational cultural universes. In a similar vein, alongside the documentaries that highlighted the diversity of regional musical instruments and forms were the films that showcased the efforts of the state-owned All India Radio to promote a genre of "national music," drawing attention to the unique ability of the state to integrate the culturally diverse nation.[31]

A second set of documentaries addressed various aspects of "citizenship and reform." The understanding of citizenship that informed the cinematic imaginary of the Films Division was one that emphasized the proximity, rather than the distance or the autonomy, of the citizen from state institutions. The ideal citizen was characterized by her or his ability to obey, comply with, and otherwise follow the instructions of the state, and the practice of citizenship was depicted in tutelary and pedagogical terms as a learning activity or an ongoing process of acquiring skills and attributes rather than an already-possessed right or claim that could be exercised in the present.[32]

The Films Division imparted a wide range of citizenship lessons. Some documentary films undertook the task of familiarizing audiences with the technologies of citizenship in the most literal sense of the word by providing instructions on how to mark ballot papers and how to use ballot boxes.[33] Others called for various forms of behavioral reform that would invest selfish individuals with a sense of social responsibility and enable them to appreciate and fulfill the manifold duties of citizenship. Individuals were "motivated" to realign their private values with public ones, and to redefine self-interest in terms of the national rather than the individual self. For instance, in *The Case of Mr. Critic* (1954), the ideal citizen was depicted as one who refrained from engaging in "socially unproductive acts" of criticism and was mindful of the "damage caused by loose and irresponsible talk."[34] A similar exhortation informed *Dilly Dallying*, a film produced in 1957 that purported to convey "how the habit of delay can ruin a man" and can cause considerable damage to the larger national project of social and economic advancement.[35]

The political and ideological denouements of Indian decolonization are most often described in terms of the victory of Nehruvian beliefs in modernism, industrialism, and state-centrism, and the corresponding marginalization of Gandhian "antimodernist" ideas about economy, society, and governance.[36] The ascendancy of Nehru's vision was already underway in the last decade of colonial rule, with the Indian National Congress committing itself to a vision of state-led economic planning and modernization in independent India. With the passage of the new Indian constitution, the vision of independent India as a decentralized, non-industrial nation of village republics that had informed Gandhi's political rhetoric from the 1920s onward was relegated to the nonjusticiable section of the constitution. Henceforth, these would serve as noble "directive principles" to which successive governments would pay homage, even as there was no obligation to act upon them.[37]

Indeed, the distance between the laws and policies that were enacted in the years following independence and the Gandhian vision was considerable. A unitary or centralized federal system, a commitment to rapid heavy industrialization, and an unqualified belief in the progressive promises of technology were the constitutive features of the postcolonial polity, and all were far cries from the decentralized, semi-autarkic vision of Ram Rajya that Gandhi had outlined.[38] At the same time, however, the enduring and structuring effect of the Gandhian shadow in Nehruvian India should not be overlooked or underestimated. Whether because of political expediency and instrumental calculations, force of habit, or even commitment to some of Gandhi's ideas on the part of some political actors, nationalist discourse and practice in the postcolonial period drew upon Gandhian idioms and imagery on a regular basis, if only as a rhetorical device. The citizenship imaginary produced by the Films Division, with its emphasis on duty, austerity, the distaste for political machinations, and the sacrifice of individual interests and desires for the greater common good, is but one example of the Gandhian haunting of postcolonial nationhood in India and the contradictory national field to which it gave rise,[39] as citizens were simultaneously exhorted to believe in the promises of state intervention and to develop skills of "self help" in recognition of the inherent limits, fallibilities, and inadequacies of state-sponsored modernity.

The theme of "exemplary Indians" was the explicit focus of another category of films, the "biography and personality" documentaries. Unlike the anonymous address of the citizenship films, this set of documentaries focused on named, individual exemplars. According to the Films Division's own summary, the selection of individuals included "those who fought the British, emancipated the women, unravelled the mysteries of science, expounded the philosophy of Hinduism, and enriched Indian art and culture."[40] Crucial significations of ideal Indians were embedded in these choices, with the individuals deemed worthy of emulation as those who uphold the values of national sovereignty (fighting the British), rationality and science ("unravelling the mysteries of science"), and above all leadership/guidance and instruction (philosophers, artists, emancipators of women). The choice of exemplary individuals also took into account the representation of regional diversity. In portraying the lives of "great men and women," both their contributions to the greater national good as well as their distinct regional origins received equal emphasis—thus the Nobel Laureate Rabindranath Tagore is depicted as both a national poet and a "son of Bengal."[41] In this way different regions were presented with their "own" national hero: the act of exemplification at once totalizing and fragmenting in its effect and import.

While films on art and culture, citizenship and reform, and biography documented "the people of India" and their varied cultural and civic practices, a significant number of films showcased the forms and feats of state institutions and officials. In the "defence films" and the films on "the international scene" (these covered the visits of Indian presidents and prime ministers to other countries and the reciprocal visits of "foreign dignitaries" to India), the protagonists were the office bearers of the state rather than ordinary—or in the case of the biography films, extraordinary—civilians. If the Films Division may be seen to have consolidated a statist vision of nationhood, tying national identity to the presence and actions of the state, then these films advanced this vision in the most explicit way. Armies and prime ministers stood in for the state, which then stood in for, and as, the nation and its citizens.[42]

Finally, the single largest category of Films Division documentaries, representing more than a third of the total output of documentary films in the first two decades after independence, were those that addressed the themes of planned development and various aspects of social and economic modernization. The specific treatment of these themes was realized in a variety of different ways. In some films the abstract ideals of the Nehruvian imaginary of modernization and planned development took concrete visual form and were materialized either as distinct artifacts such as dams, steel plants, locomotive factories, or agricultural equipment, or as specific sets of embodied practices: thus we see farmers using new water pumps in *Partners for Plenty* (1955); women in *salwar kameezes* adeptly handling test tubes in *The Black Gold*, a film made in 1965 about "oil exploration in India"; and engineers engaged in dexterous labors of "flood control" along the embankment of a rapidly rising river in *Fight the Floods* (1955), a film that "dramatically presents the havoc wrought by floods in various parts of the country and highlights the work of the Central Flood Control Board."[43] The accompanying narrative commentary located these images in the contemporaneous time-space of the viewer, with progress, modernity, and development described not as idealized future horizons but as immediate, tangible substances. The monumental edifices of the Bhakra Nangal dam towering over an empty landscape (*A Symbol of Progress*, 1965); the glowing furnaces in steel plants that "took one's breath away";[44] and the smiling farmers steering gigantic tractors with studied ease and nonchalance in *Where the Desert Blooms* (1962), a film on the Central Mechanised Farm in Suratgarh, Rajasthan, were all a part of the Films Division's distinctive elaboration of a modernity that was "spectacular" in both senses of the term—visible as well as grand.

In contrast to this spectacular and "fetishized figuration of modernity,"[45] other Films Division documentaries presented modernity and development as imperceptible phenomena that left no material traces in the present. In films such as *Our Regulated Markets* (1960), a film on the "hardships and losses inflicted on the producer-sellers by the middlemen and efforts made to eradicate them in the form of regulated markets,"[46] or in *Dry Leaves* (1961), on the "dowry system" and how "this age-old custom has ruined many a home,"⁴⁷ the present was characterized not by the concrete achievements of modernity but by backwardness, negation, and loss. Where other films emphasized the successful grasping of modernity in the present—thus India *today* has a steel plant, a dam, a self-sufficient economy—these films elaborated a different vision of a deferred modernity, reproducing images and narratives of problems and obstacles rather than solutions and triumphs. Suggesting that the temporal logic of official developmentalist discourse is more doubled or ambivalent than teleological, this set of films depicted the present as an uncertain "waiting room,"⁴⁸ rather than a definitive and triumphant "moment of arrival."⁴⁹

The question of agency in processes of development and modernization also met with multiple responses in Films Division documentaries. Who or what was the agent of development and modernity—the state or the people? Or did agency and intention not matter at all, and were development and modernity occurrences that were structurally determined and inevitable? The documentary films of the state endorsed all of these positions, and elaborated visions of "assisted progress" as well as "natural progress." Some films focused on the state's essential role in initiating and promoting modernization and development (*Phosphate for Plenty*, 1970). Others emphasized instead the autonomous initiatives of ordinary people (*Your Contribution*, 1954). Still others departed from these agent-centric understandings altogether in their elaboration of the unstoppable and self-propelling dynamics of modernity (*Kisan* ["The Farmer"], 1967).

Of significance is the simultaneity or the coexistence of these differential visions, and the fact that the ambivalent and fissured constitution of modernity ostensibly stemmed from the singular institutional source of the state. Calling into question the monolithic presumptions of James Scott's influential metaphor of "seeing like a state," the contending imaginaries produced by the Films Division drew attention instead to the fragmented nature of the statist vision—to the blurring rather than the "legibility" of "social mapping" practices.⁵⁰ In their representation of development, progress, and modernity as simultaneously achieved and unachievable, material and ephemeral, specified and anonymous, triumphant and anxiety-laden, and assisted and self-generating, these films reflected the complex constellation of competing imperatives, governance levels, policy frameworks, and political actors that constituted the postcolonial Indian state.

Shifting Visions I: Temporal Transformations

With the different chief producers of the Films Division interpreting in different ways the organization's mandate as a documenter of "Indian actuality,"[51] and with individual filmmakers bringing their distinctive creative visions to bear on the filmmaking process, the visual representations of nation, state, and citizen took a variety of forms. The varied ways in which Films Division documentaries represented the state and depicted the bonds between state and nation were also a product of transformations in the political field, with different kinds of "state effects" generated as new sets of political actors, structures, imperatives and legitimization practices emerged over time. Thus in the first decade of the Films Division's existence, when the consolidation of the command economy and its apparatuses of economic planning was the dominant task at hand, most of the films were on planned development—whether documentations of development projects undertaken in different parts of the country; instructional films on specialized topics such as the "correct use of fertilizer" or "how to conserve water"; or "motivational films" that exhorted audiences to believe in and enthusiastically support the various developmental initiatives of the state.

The hegemony of the developmentalist imaginary led to a curious situation where despite the recent experience of interreligious conflict following the partition of the British Indian empire in 1947, and the numerous language struggles and demands for the reorganization of the federal system along ethno-linguistic lines that dominated the political arena in the 1950s, the treatment of such themes was conspicuously absent. Even though the establishment of the Films Division had entailed an express recognition of the persuasive powers of the audio-visual medium, the act of persuasion appeared to be limited to the furthering of developmental goals alone. Issues such as "the need for national integration" and "the evils of communalism" that would become ubiquitous themes in later years were missing from the visual vocabularies of official nationalism in the first decade after independence.[52] The first-order problem that confronted and indeed constituted India and Indians was seen to be their lack of development, and development in turn was presented as the ultimate and only solution to all other "secondary" problems such as caste and ethno-linguistic or religious conflict.

Films from this period were marked by another kind of silence, or rather by an amnesia. There were no attempts to narrate a national history or create a national hagiography. Events, places, and people associated with the anticolonial movement were all missing from the films from the 1950s: the genre of the "freedom struggle" film was yet to be born.⁵³ To see India through the lens of the Films Division in the first decade after independence was to gaze exclusively on the promises of the future and to overlook the many ways in which the present had failed to live up to the promises of the past.⁵⁴ At one level, the futurist tilt of the early postcolonial nationalist imagination has a pragmatic explanation: there was no necessity to remind Indians about a past that was all too recent. Moreover, the project of national memory work, or the attempt to produce a unitary collective memory for the nation, was difficult to undertake when the history that was sought to be captured by and for the nation was something that individuals could claim as personal, lived experience. To Ernest Renan's famous description of nation formation as a dialectic of "remembering and forgetting," we can add the following qualification: the viability of this dialectic rests upon the absence of counterstrategies of popular remembrance. The injunction to forget loses its compulsion when everyone still remembers only too vividly and too well. Like the American narratives of the revolutionary war,⁵⁵ the narrative of the "national movement" in India would achieve full-blown expression not at the founding moment of the new nation-state but rather after sufficient time had lapsed for the uncontested reworking of the personal memory as a seamless and linear narrative of national history.

At another level, the diversion of the Films Division's focus from the colonial and anticolonial past speaks of the preoccupation with newness and the faith in the redemptive possibilities that structured the national imagination of Nehruvian India, as indeed that of other contemporaneous new nations across the globe.⁵⁶ In drawing attention to the fact that the nation is a dynamically constituted political field—a process or a stance rather than a thing or a substance—the historical preoccupations that had structured the discourse of nationalists in the colonial period were now superseded by longings for the future. If *Discovery of India*, Nehru's famous account of Indian history was an emblematic text of the anticolonial nationalist movement, then *New Pastures*, a Films Division documentary from 1949 on how the reclamation of wastelands by the state would usher in a brighter future for Indian peasants, was its postcolonial counterpart.

The decade of the 1960s saw the emergence of a new set of visual vocabularies. Even as Films Division documentaries continued to imagine India in terms of the constitutive and indissoluble link between nation and state, the representations of nation and state registered several significant shifts. For instance, the specific conjuncture of India's war with China in 1962 led to the production of films in which martial strength was the defining attribute of the state; vulnerability the distinguishing characteristic of the nation; and sacrifice and bravery the constitutive features of the ideal citizen.[57] A trailer with the no-nonsense title of *National Anthem-cum-Flag* was produced by the Films Division in 1963 at the behest of the Committee for Emergency Publicity (in existence from 1962 until 1968) and the National Defence Council, a multipartisan group constituted to coordinate civilian defense efforts. All commercial film screenings were required to conclude with an exhibition of this one-minute film. The national sound waves were also harnessed by the new requirement of increasing the visibility of official emblems, and a new practice of playing a recording of the national anthem at the conclusion of the daily broadcast of All India Radio was introduced in March 1963 at the same time as the mandatory screening of the anthem/flag film.[58]

Other films undertook the task of meaning making. It was not enough simply to disseminate the sights and sounds of the state, but their correct national significance also had to be specified. As the annual report of the Ministry of Information and Broadcasting (the parent organization of the Films Division) noted in 1965, it was imperative to produce films that could effectively communicate and explain "the necessity of maintaining decorum whenever the national anthem is sung."[59] If in the documentary films from the 1950s a dam, a laboratory, or a census survey stood in for the relationship between nation and state, the entry of a new discourse of "national security" in the 1960s occasioned an additional set of signifying practices. The feats of the armed forces, the chords of the national anthem, and the fluttering tricolor flag now became familiar presences in Films Division documentaries, with Indians urged to contemplate not what the state could do for them but what they could do for the state.

Amid these many transformations in the cinematic vision of the state that reflected the dynamic, processual character of the nation-statist project in postcolonial India, certain representational themes and devices remained unchanged over time. In particular, and despite the significant changes in political, economic, and social structure and practice that took place between the Films Division's founding in 1948 and the major retrospective organized in 1972 to celebrate two decades of its existence, the cinematic representations of "the Indian Muslim"—or rather, the aporias and elisions of these representations—remained remarkably constant. The catalogue of films produced by the Films Division in 1972, covering twenty-two years of documentary film production, describes in detail an impressive total of

Table 2. Representations of Muslims in Films Division documentaries, 1949–1972

TITLE	YEAR	DESCRIPTION
Magnificent Memory	1950	Kathak dance and the courtly culture of the Mughal emperor Shah Jahan
A Page from History	1952	Mosques of Bijapur
Do You Know	1958	Monuments of Qutb, Gol Gumbaz, and the Taj Mahal
Taj Mahal	1958	Monument built by the Mughal emperor Shah Jahan
Bound for Haj	1959	How the state provides financial and logistical assistance for Bombay-based Muslims to visit Mecca
Family of Faiths	1961	Religions of India
A Muslim Festival in Secular India	1965	Celebration of id-ul-fitr at the house of Dr. Zakir Hussain, president of India
Music of India (Classical)	1966	Hindustani classical music and the Mughal era
Akbar	1967	Miniature paintings and Mughal culture
Baba	1969	The contemporary musician Allaudin Khan
Dr. Zakir Hussain	1969	President of India
Tribute to a Scholar	1969	Dr. Zakir Hussain, president of India
Ghalib	1969	Poet from the nineteenth century
An Article of Faith	1969	Explaining constitutional provisions on secularism
Kathak	1970	Kathak dance and the courtly culture of the Mughal emperor Shah Jahan
Amir Khan	1970	Contemporary musician
Ustad Allah Rakha	1970	Contemporary musician

Source: Pati, Films Division Catalogue of Films, 1949–1972.

1,742 documentaries. As table 2 indicates, only seventeen of these films, or less than 1 percent, had anything to do with the presence of Muslims in India.

Moreover, although these films differed in terms of their subject matter, they all contributed to a common understanding of the status of Muslims as special minorities set apart from the national mainstream in one way or another. The Films Division documentaries from the 1950s and 1960s invariably constituted "Muslimness" as a special or qualified national presence. Some films celebrated the lives of exemplary, famous, and "good Muslims" —for example, the Mughal emperor Akbar, the poet Ghalib, and the musicians Zakir Hussain, Allah Rakha, and Allaudin Khan. In another instance, *Bound for Haj* (1959), the visibility of Muslims served to illustrate the protective beneficence of the state in facilitating the sacred pilgrimage to Mecca. The theme of select Muslims as ideal citizens was furthered as well in *A Muslim Festival in Secular India* (1965), a film depicting the Id festivities at the official residence of then-president Zakir Hussain. *A Muslim Festival* stood in marked contrast to the unqualified and generalized address of *The Faith* (1967), a film about the Hindu pilgrims at the Kumbh Mela festival along the banks of the river Ganges in Allahabad. A final set of films evacuated contemporaneous subjectivity and agency from Muslims altogether, with architectural monuments (the Taj Mahal, the Qutb Minar) and "cultural heritage" (Hindustani music, Kathak dance) standing in for Muslims in India. In this manner, and to use the agency's own words as quoted at the opening of this chapter, the "memory of the nation" encapsulated within the "storage vaults" of the Films Division attests to the graded hierarchies of diversity displays in postcolonial India. Even in the "golden age" of Nehruvian secularism, then, the light of Indianness shone in a selective and partial manner, as encounters with the nation-state consistently illuminated some experiences of national belonging and obscured others.[60]

Shifting Visions II: Contending Imperatives

Not all variations in the documentaries produced by the Films Division could be explained by temporal shifts in the political field. As noted in the previous section, the Films Division also produced significantly different representations of state and nation within the same time period. With the postcolonial state itself constituted as a multi-layered arena informed by different, even contending, imperatives, the Films Division played several different roles at any given point in time. For instance, while the Films Division embodied a productive or positive relationship between the state and film—that is, the state as filmmaker—a significant set of negative restrictions and prohibitions were also put in place at the same time, from the rationing of film stock and the activation of colonial censorship laws to the state control of venues and channels of film distribution. Engaged in the work of film production at a time when the access of filmmakers to raw film stock was severely restricted,[61] the Films Division was charged with the responsibility of presenting the "right" cinematic vision, and of working in tandem with the censorship agencies of the state and their mandate of preventing the "wrong" visions from gaining public exposure.[62] In supplementing the negative or prohibitory impulses of state power, the Films Division was assigned a role in the postcolonial project of producing an interventionist state that was at the same time accountable and limited: one that would not be characterized by the heavy hand of coercion alone.

Thus on the one hand the documentary films produced by the Films Division addressed themselves to the pedagogical mandate of the state by upholding exemplary visions of India and Indianness before an infantile nation in need of reform and development. On the other hand, the structuring influence of a "democracy mandate" undercut such assumptions about national backwardness, emphasizing instead autonomous choices made by ordinary citizens to watch and appreciate these documentaries. In the initial years after independence, the official descriptions of documentary film deployed economic metaphors of monopolistic domination as well as those of free-market competition in discussing the role and significance of state-produced film;[63] descriptions that in turn drew upon and reproduced substantially different understandings of the "maximalist" and "minimalist" state respectively.[64]

In another duality that reflected the varied imperatives of nation-state formation in postcolonial India, the Films Division was required to engage in acts of neutral observation as well as exhortation and advocacy. Thus, one of its chief tasks was that of providing information through the production and dissemination of documentary films and newsreels. Through such nonfictional "realistic" depictions of the ongoing activities of the state, as well as the goals of the nation-building project and the current social, political, economic, and cultural aspects of national life, the Films Division served the goal of "state publicity," which the state elites described as a key component of the process of democratization. As the Films Division's parent organization, the Ministry of Information and Broadcasting, noted in its annual report of 1950–51: "Under a democratic set-up, in addition to publicity for government activities or explanations of policies and decisions, the importance of a positive approach and of publicity as an instrument of popular education cannot be underestimated."[65]

In its role as an agent of publicity, the Films Division worked alongside several other state agencies, such as All India Radio, the Press Information Bureau, the Research and Reference Division, the Publications Division, the Directorate of Advertising and Visual Publicity, and in later years the Department of Field Publicity, which was entrusted with the specific task of providing information about the economic planning activities undertaken by the state. In all of these cases, the fact that the state agencies of publicity alone could guarantee the neutrality of information, and hence its objectivity, was repeatedly emphasized. Through its self-description as a nonpartisan truth teller, the Films Division located itself, and by implication the state, in a transcendent domain that Thomas Hansen has aptly termed "sublime politics," as insulated from the "profane politics" that characterized the messy workings of political democracy in India.[66]

In highlighting its work as a nonpartisan publicist and information provider, the Films Division endorsed a limited vision of its own agency as a mere vehicle for communicating preexisting truths, with its role restricted to the passive reflection of exogenously determined realities alone. Discussions about the state's work of publicity and information provision in fact invested agency in the people rather than in the state through the repeated assertions of how, once they were in possession of the truth about the national projects being undertaken by the state, ordinary Indians would be galvanized into action and become nation builders on their own accord. At the same time, however, and in what amounted to a direct refutation of the "limited messenger" role described above, the Films Division was also authorized as an agent of social education, transformation, and motivation. In fulfilling these tasks, documentary films were required to play an active role in the project of nation building, instead of merely reflecting or communicating the details of the project. As a review commission would note in a 1967 report on the workings of the Films Division, "mere publicity" alone was not enough: persuasion was another, and key, task at hand.[67]

Recognizing the State

If the content and themes of Films Division films consolidated a particular, if ambivalent, vision of India around the sights and sounds of the state, it was the form of these films that definitively established the state as the author of the national vision. Despite their varied choices of content, topic, and exposition, Films Division documentaries and newsreels were instantly recognizable as Films Division documentaries and newsreels. It was precisely their unmistakably state-produced style that played a key and constitutive role in the project of state identification, enabling as they did the public recognition of the state's distinctive vision and register of address. The practices of "state reification" that produce the state as a distinctive social actor as well as the authorized representative of the nation are not exhausted by microlevel, disaggregated, and invisible or "interiorized" interventions.[68] In Ann Anagnost's words, the "hypervisibility of the apparatus of power and its operations on the social body,"[69] that is, the continual and visible demonstrations of the state's ability to make claims on behalf of the nation, are equally important.

Beginning with their introductory sequences, the Films Division documentaries addressed this imperative of state recognition in a variety of ways. Just as the familiar sight of the torch-bearing figure of Columbia or the roaring lion of MGM serves as a particular visual cue for audiences of Hollywood films about the nature of the film-viewing experience that awaits them, so too did the logo of the Ashokan pillar with its four-headed lion motif (designated as the official emblem of the Indian state in 1950) and the accompanying legend "Films Division of India presents" frame the expectations of spectatorship through repeated exposure. In a similar vein, the distinctive aural address of Films Division documentaries established the films as "official texts," where a disembodied exegetical voice-over explained, contextualized, summarized, and otherwise narrativized the visual events unfolding on the screen—an effect that was once again secured through iteration.

Although the content differed from film to film, most Films Division documentaries were characterized by a common narrative style. An introductory statement usually predicated at the highest level of generality would open the film once the title credits had faded to black, with the voice-over either unfolding in tandem with the visual sequences or coming in as an explanatory interjection after a silent montage had quickly flashed across the screen. "The glory that was India attracted people from different lands," declared *The Road to Freedom*, as the solid colors of a two-dimensional standard-issue map of India gradually faded away until the outline of the map was all that was discernible—a boundary around the grainy images of kings, pilgrims, horses, ships, and marching soldiers that now filled the interiors of the map. In the opening sequences of *Destination India* the pithy announcement "Welcome to India" followed a rapid montage of Hindu pilgrims bathing in the Ganges at Benaras, a panoramic shot of the Taj Mahal, a near shot of the Buddha's face, and a tight close-up on an elaborate stone trellis that panned out to a wider view of the inner walls of St. Paul's Cathedral in Calcutta. The commentary continued throughout these films, interrupting the flow of images at times with a laconic description ("India became free at the stroke of midnight"), at others with a detailed exegesis that cast the images in an explicitly pedagogical light ("There is a diversity and freedom of expression in our democracy, freedom we must cherish if democracy is to have any meaning"). While the visual representations embodied and materialized the meaning of nationhood in specific and localized terms, the accompanying commentary invariably addressed its audience as an undifferentiated and abstract collectivity, alternating between a collective first-person and a third-person mode of address: thus "we are" and "India is."

In its early years, the Films Division would rely on the same individuals to record voice-overs for as many of its films as possible. As a result, the "sound" of the state came to acquire a distinctive and recognizable quality: the distinctive tone and enunciations of the Anglicized baritones of Romesh Thapar and Sam Berkeley-Hill or the modulations of a Sanskritized Hindi.[70] The effort to establish a regionally unmarked "voice from nowhere" had the effect of constituting a "voice from somewhere," enabling as it did the identification of how "the state states."[71]

In this regard, the specific idiom of state speech is of note—the fact that Films Division commentaries consistently drew upon the registers of "policyspeak" that informed official discourse and practice in a wide range of arenas—from the commentary broadcast on Rajpath during the annual Republic Day parades and the programs on All India Radio to the voluminous texts produced by the Planning Commission. Like these other statist articulations, the commentaries of the Films Division were characterized by their use of specialized terminology, neologisms, and acronyms; hyperbolic pronouncements; and ponderousness.

If the Films Division played a significant role in establishing a distinctive sound for the state through its use of a specific style of commentary, its development of a familiar visual repertoire facilitated the social recognition of the gaze of the state, so that over time a particular set of images came to be identified with an official envisioning of nationhood. The same images appeared over and over again in state-produced documentary films and newsreels, and filmmakers drew upon a common archive of stock shots despite the fact that there were significant variations in the actual topic of the films being made. The familiar montages of India's natural and cultural diversity —from turbaned men on camels against a desert backdrop to fisherwomen on the coconut palm–fringed shores of Kerala's backwaters; the recurrent image of a "simple peasant"; the teeming "crowd shot" that stood in for the Indian masses—all established a specific way of seeing India, one that could be unambiguously identified as the vision of the state.

The State as Critic

Just two decades into the Film's Division's existence, the state itself noted that its envisioning of nationhood was more ponderous and disenchanted than resonant and believable. In 1967, the Ministry of Information and Broadcasting, the parent organization of the Films Division, convened an investigative commission, referred to as the Chanda committee, to evaluate the various "publicity wings" of the Indian state: the Films Division, the Directorate of Advertising and Visual Publicity, and the Press Information Bureau. In its mission statement, the committee described its task as one of explaining the paradox of state attempts to monopolize and regulate public information in a democratic polity. In reflecting its central concern with the contradictions of an "official information agency in a democratic society," the indictment of "propaganda" dominated the committee's review of the Films Division, and the call to produce nonpropagandist films was among its chief recommendations. The understanding of what constituted propaganda drew upon the familiar dichotomy between political and nonpolitical activities and expressions. According to the Chanda committee report, the portrayal of "*questions above public dispute* such as literacy, agricultural production, sanitation etc." did not constitute propaganda—a statement that recast contested policy formations that were mired in partisan contests as transcendent and consensual expressions of the national interest.[72] On the basis of this distinction, films that advanced partisan perspectives, showcasing the achievements of particular political leaders and political parties, were denounced as examples of political propaganda, while films that depicted the "neutral" activities of the state were upheld as examples to emulate: "In a developing country the raison d'etre of the Films Division is to propagate the aims and portray the activities and achievements of a welfare state. But this does not imply that the films should depict largely the activities of the political leaders and the meetings and projects in which they participate."[73]

Along with the recommendation to produce documentary films on impartial themes, the Chanda committee called for a transformation in cinematic style, and also deliberated on the question of effect and reception. It was not enough to passively depict "the activities and achievements of a welfare state," but also the goal of "provok[ing] constructive thinking" had to be addressed. In the words of the committee: "It is necessary that the objectives of the planning effort should be presented with subtlety, [and be] able to hold the attention and make an impact on the viewing public. They should be provocative and pose a challenge to the community . . . they should portray the realities of life, pose the problems boldly."[74]

Several factors were held to be responsible for the palpable lack of resonance of Films Division documentaries, or their failure to "hold the attention and make an impact on the viewing public." First, there were significant flaws in the organizational structure of the Films Division and in its mode of operation. It lacked organizational autonomy and thus produced the bulk of its documentaries in response to the requests it received from different ministries instead of being able to chart out an independent cinematic vision. Related to this issue was the problem of personnel. Decision making within the Films Division was undertaken primarily by bureaucrats instead of by trained filmmakers. At the time of the review, the practice of hiring graduates from the Film and Television Institute of India had been discontinued for over five years, and the directorial positions within the organization were occupied by nonspecialist civil servants who were impervious to aesthetic concerns.

Another factor was related to problems in the production practices of the organization. Not only was the availability of technological infrastructure inadequate, leading to the production of films that the committee described as "stuck in the 1930s," but the existing system of commissioning films actually provided incentives to make films that failed to hold the attention of audiences. Filmmakers were paid according to the footage of film they produced, which meant that it was in their interests to produce films that were as long as possible. Moreover, the practice of commissioning films according to a "lowest-tender" system meant that thriftiness or the ability to generate the lowest-budget figures rather than considerations of aesthetic skill informed the selection of filmmakers, and thus further contributed to the low quality of Films Division films.[75] The Chanda committee cited specific examples of this aesthetic lack: the penchant for spoken commentary at the expense of visual content; the absence of "human interest" stories in newsreels; and the absence of humor, satire, suspense, and drama in documentaries.

Finally, the distribution scheme of the Films Division also occasioned extended criticism. According to the Chanda committee, the compulsory distribution policy did not advance, and in fact obstructed, the meaningful reception of films. Instead of allowing exhibitors (the owners of film theaters) to choose documentaries and newsreels that were appropriate for their audiences, the centralized process of distribution allocated films on an arbitrary basis that did not take the specific local context into account. This led to situations that, far from eliciting support and loyalty for the "disinterested" state, might in fact have fostered disaffection and anger for the indifferent state. The incident of a film on floods being screened before audiences in Orissa at a time of extended drought was one such example cited by the committee. A parallel example, though less extreme, was the screening for elite audiences in urban theaters of instructional films on the application of fertilizers, or films demonstrating the superior performance of the latest tractors made in India.[76]

In this regard even the scheme of distributing free film prints to rural areas had significant flaws. For example, the small number of free prints produced was not commensurate with the size of the rural population.[77] Moreover, with the absence in many Indian villages of film-screening equipment, and the even more basic lack of electricity, films could only be screened in rural areas through the use of mobile cinema vans. This in turn was possible only if "motorable roads" were in existence, a requirement that, according to the Chanda committee's calculations, effectively reduced the rural outreach of the Films Division to a mere 500,000 people.

Language was another limitation for rural distribution. The films were dubbed in the thirteen official languages of India, which meant that they were not easily understood among India's many "dialect communities."[78] In sum, twenty years after its existence, at approximately the same time that the Films Division published a catalog listing its "impressive achievements" of producing almost two thousand documentary films, another state agency issued an emphatic and scathing indictment of the limited reach, the dullness and unimaginativeness, the heavy-handed bureaucracy, and the singular lack of resonance of the "moving pictures" of nationhood in Nehruvian India. If the state was an autoenthusiast, it was also its own biggest critic.

In itself, the existence of an official committee report that is critical of the state is hardly remarkable. In fact, the ability to produce and circulate such critical commentaries is widely regarded to be the distinctive feature of an accountable, democratic regime and an "open society." What is of interest here is the ways in which the Chanda committee, like the countless other review commissions that have been convened in India, drew upon and reproduced a distinctive set of repertoires or rituals that furthered the "myth of the [nation]-state."[79] The committee was a theater of state power where, through the proliferation of discourses about the manifest failures of the state to further the interests of the nation, the abstractions of state and nation assumed concrete form and the link between state and nation—the idea that the nation "needs" a state—was consolidated and secured. Here, the nonresonance of the Films Division documentary—the fact that it was boring, heavy-handed, and disenchanted—played a constitutive role, enabling as it did the looping or recursive exercises of review, recommendation, failure, and review again.

Several years after the Chanda committee issued its report and its recommendations for institutional change, another evaluation exercise took place. In 1973, at a seminar organized by the Indian Institute of Mass Communication, a group of academics, filmmakers, bureaucrats, and ministers convened to discuss "the role of film in development."[80] Their findings were almost identical to those of the Chanda committee, as speaker after speaker deplored the many failings of Films Division documentaries. Once again, the major findings were the bureaucratic domination of the Films Division, the limited reach of its films as a result of a poorly conceived distribution scheme, its failure to create the right "social mood," and the tendentious quality of its documentaries that "talked down to people."

As in the case of the earlier report, the seminar participants harnessed the discourse of state failure to call for more, and better, forms and techniques of state intervention, such as the establishment of more regional units of the Films Division across the country. Moreover, in an echo of earlier methodologies, the charge of nonresonance and the failure to communicate was not based on the experiences and perspectives of audience members. Neither of the reports made even a rudimentary attempt to engage with the actual experience of reception. Instead, the failure was expressed in circular terms in relation to the state's own goal of development and modernization: the inability of the Films Division to engender "social change" in India.

How could the documentary films produced by the Films Division most effectively transform the "resigned, dissatisfied and escapist" mindset that apparently pervaded India, and engender instead feelings of enthusiasm and the commitment to hard work?[81] When the representational devices of documentary film rather than inequities of power are cited as the cause of resignation, dissatisfaction, and escapism, then the solution is also one that does not venture beyond the world of images. And so, the seminar concluded with a call for more moving pictures: films that would both move out to the neglected masses and move or affect them in substantial ways.

Conclusion

James Scott, in his influential study of the modernist state and its attendant forms and techniques of power, has drawn attention to the distinctive practice of "mapping" or the production of what he terms as "state simplifications" of complex social realities through instruments such as censuses, surveys, cartographies, and plans. The significance of these maps derives from their instrumental application, or the fact that "when allied with state power, [they] would enable much of the reality they depicted to be remade."[82] In other words, for Scott, mapping is not an exercise of passive representation or description, but an act of "world-making and refashioning."[83] In his account, the maps of the modernist state are the enabling blueprints for the projects of social engineering that have had devastating consequences on millions of ordinary lives.

In this chapter, I have confirmed but also departed from Scott's discussion of "map making" or "seeing like a state" as a productive exercise of state power. In agreeing with Scott I have drawn attention to the state simplifications that were produced in and through the medium of documentary film, or the ways in which the Indian state produced reductive visual representations of national realities, and presented its fictions and fantasies as fact. At the same time, I have moved away from the discussion of how these statist practices impact society, and the related understanding of "state" and "society" as preformed or given entities. Instead, I have considered the state-constituting effect of such practices, or the ways in which these acts of mapping have actually produced the state as a particular kind of authoritative entity.

For more than fifty years, the Films Division has played a key role in the project of seeing like a state. In the first instance, this entailed the production and circulation of visual representations of the state itself whether as object, idea, or activity, and of the intimate and indissoluble bond between state and nation. A monumental dam; a prosperous farmer; a tricolored flag planted on Mount Everest; the signing of a constitution; the bullet-ridden corpse of a prime minister; the protection of folk art forms; a dream for which thousands of "our ancestors" have laid down their lives—these were just some of the myriad images of state and nation that confronted the audiences of Films Division documentaries and newsreels.

Second, to see like a state was also to see the state as a distinctive viewer. It was to come upon a particular line of sight and to recognize its authoritative provenance. Here, the "boredom effect" of the Films Division documentaries played a constitutive role, securing widespread social recognition of the unmistakable style of the official documentary. With the repetition of stock shots in different films; the use of a common "voice from nowhere" style of exegetical commentary; the unchanging quality of the voice itself; and the familiar doubled narrative of state-led nation-building as a task both achieved and deferred, possible and impossibly arduous, the Films Division established a distinctive genre or style of filmmaking that was immediately recognizable: there was no ambiguity about who or what was doing the seeing and the talking.

Third, seeing like a state was about the obstruction of vision. As the custodian of the largest archive of audiovisual material in India, the Films Division has the discretionary authority to grant or refuse permission for the use of its material.[84] In many instances these comprise the only visual records of significant events that have taken place over the past fifty years. With the official camera as the sole witness to numerous episodes in postcolonial history, it is through the lens of the Films Division that we view Gandhi's assassination, the pageantry of Republic Day, nuclear tests, wars, floods, famines, and dams, even if the film we are watching has been produced by the BBC. If the written record of official history erases all fissures, slippages, and ambiguities from its seamless narration of the past, the visual texts of the state constrict our vision in even tighter ways. The outtakes of the Films Division have long been destroyed, and there was no second-camera unit present at the recording of history.

The constricting effects of the state's tunnel vision are not restricted to the domain of history. As this chapter has shown, the Films Division has also taken culture as its canvas, elaborating vivid visual representations of India's cultural diversity. The stereotypical projections of identity and difference that this vision of Indian diversity reflected and fostered have traveled far beyond the confines of official celluloid to structure the representational worlds of Hindi commercial cinema and of multinational advertising. Although the compulsory screening policy of the Films Division was discontinued in 1994, its distinctive visions continue to proliferate. The colorful montage of India's geographic, historic, cultural, religious, and ethnic diversity—the intercuts and dissolves that link coconut trees to the Himalayas, dancing peasants to praying Brahmins, the Taj Mahal of Mughal Agra to the Victoria Terminus railway station in Bombay—is today reproduced in marketing campaigns for Coca-Cola and a promotional video for the MTV India television channel.[85]

Like their statist counterparts, these images invite us to gaze upon a reality that we do not encounter in our daily lives.[86] All traces of polyester and plastic, violence and inequality, and power and resistance have been airbrushed from their colorful vistas. As the historian Shahid Amin has trenchantly observed in a recent discussion of the representational devices of nationhood in India: "The face on the poster does not match the man on the street."[87] The mismatch that Amin highlights is about the arbitrary logics of visual representation. For instance, in the imagery of the "national integration" poster, a staple of Nehruvian secular nationalism,[88] Muslim identity is invariably symbolized by a fez, even though Indians would be hard pressed to cite a single instance when they have actually seen a person wearing one.[89] As we have already seen, this observation about the "[mis]representation of the Mussalman"[90] can be extended to Films Division documentaries as well, which furthered the understanding of the exceptional presence of Muslims in postcolonial India. In this regard, we can say that to see like a state in Nehruvian India was to see Muslims as permanent minorities marked by an essential difference. Although this difference involved the valorization of Muslim identity rather than its stigmatization—thus the Films Division turned its lens on "good Muslims" rather than "bad Muslims"—the qualified or special nature of Muslims remained a persistent theme.

Finally, to see like a state was to partake of a constitutive fear of politics. Although the vibrancy and density of civic associational life in India and the active engagement of ordinary Indians in innovative forms of political participation have been a staple theme of academic discussions about the health and durability of Indian democracy,[91] the Films Division's imagination of the Indian citizen was eviscerated of any such signs of political vitality. It was instead her or his ability to patiently "stand in queue" instead of milling around in a disorderly fashion; to willingly discard "traditional" techniques of measurement for the universal coordinates of the Metric system; to participate selflessly in the "social uplift" of the "disadvantaged sections"; and to realize the "dignity of manual labour."[92] Like the "naturally diverse nation" and the "transcendent state," the ideal citizen of Nehruvian India would also be imagined along extrapolitical, antipolitical lines.

Were there other ways of seeing India? To answer this question, in the next chapter I map a different line of sight, one constituted by the moving pictures of India and Indianness in the most literal sense—that is, the displays of nation, state, and citizen paraded through the streets of the capital city every year on January 26 to mark the anniversary of the Indian republic. The primary mandate of the Films Division was to integrate the experience of documentary film viewing into the routines and rhythms of everyday life, so that all that citizens had to do to encounter the nation-state was to make a simple—and voluntary—decision to go to the movies. In contrast to such everyday, ongoing, and even "banal" arenas and practices of national reproduction, the following pages explore how the nation-state was reproduced on momentous, one-of-a-kind occasions, in and through the extraordinary practices of ritual commemoration that marked the anniversary of India's republican birth.

CHAPTER 2

Marching in Time

Republic Day Parades

and the Ritual Practices

of the Nation-State

: : :

Rituals of national commemoration play two different but related roles in nationalist projects. First, they serve as an effective means of nationalization. The seamless, linear, and teleological narratives of national time that are generated during national commemorations elaborate and consolidate the idea of the nation as a permanent or timeless and unified community. With the declaration that a particular day is uniformly significant to all individual members of the nation; the repetition of identical rituals of remembrance every year; and the showcasing of a preferred reading and vision of the nation's past, present, and future, commemorative rituals give shape and substance to nationalist pronouncements about communal solidarity across space and time. Moreover, the very notion of a national commemoration, and the attendant claim that the nation can "possess" a memory, anthropomorphizes or personifies the nation and imbues it with a life and personality of its own.[1]

Second, commemorations are also sites and arenas for the performance of nationhood. They stage and enact nationhood as an active "happening" or event; they are moments and spaces where individuals can encounter and perform national identity and belonging, where it is possible for them to be "overcome by nationhood."[2] Such encounters also take place outside the ritualistic space-time of annual commemorations. Cheering crowds at international sports matches, the heady triumph of postwar victory parades, and unique occurrences such as the 1969 televised broadcast to American audiences of Armstrong's walk on the moon or the 1998 announcement to Indian audiences of the "achievement" of nuclear tests are other sites for encountering and expressing the sentiments and practices of nationhood. However, the regularity and assuredness of the commemorative encounter—the fact that it takes place every year—sets it apart from these other, more ephemeral and contingent enactments; in this sense, commemorations are more durable, predictable, and regularized arenas for national performances.

In this chapter I discuss the nationalizing work of commemorative rituals through an examination of how Republic Day—the primary commemorative occasion in the official nationalist calendar—has been celebrated in postcolonial India. What are the understandings of India and Indianness that are produced and disseminated each year on January 26? What is remembered and what is forgotten? What is illuminated and what is erased? I address these questions through a reading of Republic Day as a public ritual of commemoration that was part of the effort to materialize a new form of rule after 1947—an effort that was marked by a contradictory orientation toward the colonial past, such that imperial state structures and norms of social address were both rejected and adopted. At one level, the commemorative practices of Republic Day were structured around a moment of rupture when a new state form came into being: the constitutional proclamation of India as a sovereign, democratic republic on January 26, 1950. At another level, however, the investment of postcolonial state agencies in the production of new "ritual idioms" that performed and symbolized the relation between state and nation was a continuation of a technique of imperial governance: namely, the reliance on the spectacular along with the visual elaboration of hierarchies of power through the organization of grand public events such as the imperial assemblage of 1877 or the imperial durbars of 1903 and 1911.[3]

A particular emphasis on the figure of the postcolonial state as the agent and sign of newness and difference resulted from the effort to manage the contradiction of asserting postcolonial difference through the insistence on a new beginning for the Indian nation, even as significant continuities with the past continued to be underscored—whether through projecting the historical essence of the nation back in time, tracing a direct line of descent between the anticolonial movement and the postcolonial state, or maintaining the "steel frame" of the British Raj and the trappings of imperial state power. In the annual Republic Day celebrations, as in other sites and manifestations of official nationalism in postcolonial India, the difference of the postcolonial nation was proclaimed through an emphasis on the ways in which its "gauge and emblem,"[4] the state, was better than and therefore different from its colonial predecessor. And this claim of "being better than" was shored up through references to the representative nature and function

People of India "pictorial chart" commonly seen in government schools. (Published by the Indian Book Depot, Delhi)

of the postcolonial state, and the ways in which it, unlike the colonial state, truly represented the natural diversity of the nation, thereby enabling the free expression of subnational identities and creating a protective and nurturing environment in which cultural differences could flourish.

As I demonstrate below, the nation displayed during the Republic Day celebrations—from the pageantry of the annual parade on Rajpath to the newspaper advertisements for bargain prices on Republic Day buffets at five-star hotel restaurants "featuring regional cuisines from all over our vast and varied land"—is one that is characterized by its essential, natural, and inalienable diversity. And accompanying this vision of fragmentation are the sights and signs of the state's labor of realizing, protecting, managing, and therefore representing diversity. Like the diversity-promotion impulse of Soviet nationality policies, the official national imaginary in postcolonial India appears to subscribe to "Lenin's paradox" that "the surest way to unity in content [is through the promotion of] diversity in form."[5] The nation as diverse; the state as representative of diversity: these are the constitutive elements of the postcolonial national imagination that are elaborated anew during the Republic Day celebrations each year.

With the shift of political interests, social relations, and structures of power over time—a shift that reflects the movement from the Nehruvian embrace of secularism and socialism to the contemporary moment of Hindu nationalist ascendancy and economic liberalization—this basic syntax of official nationalism has been supplemented, modified, and otherwise transformed in and through successive elaborations. Efforts to map the ritual idioms of Republic Day must take such shifts and transformations into account, thereby understanding political ritual not in terms of a transhistorical and fixed "structure" that is translated into an "event,"[6] but as a historically contingent and variable set of practices that produce new "models and mirrors" of nation and state with each successive iteration, even as old ones are reproduced.[7] In what follows I undertake such a mapping of continuity as well as change in the ritual idioms of nationhood across the two great divides of Indian modernity—tracking the transition from colonialism to postcolonialism and from the Nehruvian making to the Hindu nationalist remaking.

Nationalizing Time: The Significance of January 26

The celebration of Republic Day originated on January 26, 1950, when the final version of the Indian constitution was signed by members of the Constituent Assembly who had labored on the lengthy document for four years.

However, the date of January 26 did not signify solely the moment of republican birth but also gestured back to yet another event in the history of India's independence movement. The framers of the Indian constitution had made a conscious decision to end their task of constitution making on that particular day. It was on January 26, 1930, that the independence pledge, committing nationalists to struggle for the achievement of *purna swaraj*, or complete independence for India, was moved by Jawaharlal Nehru and adopted by the Indian National Congress. The civil disobedience campaign against the British was formally launched on this day, and the following year witnessed a series of tumultuous events, such as Gandhi's salt march and the staging of numerous *satyagrahas* all over the country. Although the formal declaration of Indian independence came in August 1947, the pledge was considered unfulfilled so long as a constitution specifying the contours of state sovereignty remained unwritten. Meaningful independence thus was associated with the emergence of a new state form, the materialization of swaraj in a formal constitution, and the attendant development of rules, laws, rituals, and modes of independent governance. The withdrawal of imperial authority in 1947 might have liberated the nation, but as the official nationalist discourse would continue to insist over the years, being liberated was not the same as being independent. As Deputy Prime Minister Sardar Patel observed in his public address to the nation on January 26, 1950, the day the constitution was adopted:

> Exactly twenty years from today, the people of India took a solemn pledge of complete independence. Behind that pledge was the determination of a whole people and the strength which comes of faith in one's destiny. Although we obtained independence on August 15, 1947, it was not complete in the sense of the pledge that we took. Today, by the grace of God, that pledge has been completely fulfilled.
>
> The day on which India attains republican status will be written in letters of gold in its history. With the disappearance of all traces of foreign rule, we become in law and in fact, our own masters and it will be now for us to make or mar our future.[8]

Thus, the symbolic choice of January 26 as a commemorative occasion condenses within it two separate nationalist moments. As such, it has a dual significance: it is a celebration of nationalist will, intention, or resolve, signifying the event of 1930, and it is a celebration of republicanism and constitutionalism, signifying the event in 1950. Moreover, the republican moment of 1950 is seen as the appropriate counterpart to the independence pledge of 1930, which is "completely fulfilled" only when a state institution representing the sovereign Indian nation is formally constituted. To the extent that January 26 is a day of national commemoration, it is a day that celebrates the state as much as, or even more than, the national community.[9] Through the distinction between "liberation" and "independence," the former tied to popular, movement-based struggles and the latter to state governmentality, and through presenting independence as the completion of liberation, the state narrates itself as the condition of possibility for the independent nation. And so, the premier national day of India is the day of the state's birth.

The Colonial and Anticolonial Lineages of Republican Ritual

The Republic Day celebrations in the postcolonial period draw upon two formally antagonistic sets of historical traditions: the ritual displays of the imperial state and the commemorative practices of the Indian nationalist movement between 1930 and 1947, when, as noted above, January 26 was celebrated throughout the country as the anniversary of the independence pledge. As historians of empire have long observed, along with the deployment of coercive strategies of rule, imperial authority was consolidated through the articulation and dissemination of new knowledges and "ways of seeing" that legitimized the imperial state form and its distinctive modalities of governance.[10] The imperial "state effect"[11] was produced through the development of public rituals, performances, exhibitions, and other representational practices that sought to materialize the distinction of the imperial "theatre of power"[12] in the public sphere. The imperial assemblage of 1877, organized to proclaim Queen Victoria as the empress of India, is an exemplary instance of such efforts. As Bernard Cohn observes in his influential account of the event, this particular public enactment and visualization of imperial authority—through the hosting of a week-long gathering in Delhi that brought together native princes and chiefs from all over India to ceremonially encounter empire—"became the standard by which public ceremony was measured."[13] The assemblage of 1877 was replicated in the imperial durbars of 1903 and 1911, where Edward VII and George V respectively were proclaimed Kaiser-I-Hind and King-Emperor of India. The precedent of the imperial assemblage also influenced the ritual practices of Indian nationalism during its initial stages, such as the annual gatherings of the Indian National Congress at the end of the nineteenth century and the beginning of the twentieth. The "derivative discourse" of early nationalism articulated its criticism of empire through the replication or emulation of imperial ritual idioms and practices; organizing the annual durbar-style processions and gatherings in which the "centrality of leaders and their speeches" were emphasized,[14] and reproducing imperial rhetoric about how the legitimacy of rule hinged on the recognition and representation of India's irreducible diversity.

The effort to develop ritual practices for the sovereign nation-state in the postcolonial period would also, ironically, return to the imperial exemplar for inspiration. Thus, just as the plans for the imperial assemblage were developed through the combined efforts of the military and political branches of the imperial state, the postcolonial Ministry of Defence would organize the Republic Day ceremonials in concert with its civil counterpart, the Ministry of Education. Like the imperial assemblage, which consisted not only of the central gathering in Delhi but also three hundred gatherings in other parts of India, the celebration of Republic Day in the postcolonial period would entail spatial practices of centralization as well as dispersal, the scripted celebrations in the capital city replicated throughout the nation through the hosting of similar (though not identical) commemorations in state capitals, district headquarters, villages, towns, and neighborhoods. Finally, like the imperial assemblage of 1878, the postcolonial Republic Day celebrations would stage a meeting or an exchange of gazes between the state and its diverse subjects by assembling representatives from all over the nation to participate in common public rituals of re-pledging allegiance to "their" state.

The Republic Day celebrations also draw upon the distinctive ritual register created by Indian nationalists after the 1920s, when the Gandhian strategies of mass mobilization introduced new kinds of spatial and visual practices, such as *padyatras*, or marches, and public meetings that resembled prayer meetings rather than durbars. In the period between 1930 and 1947, the annual remembrance of January 26, the predecessor of Republic Day, was directly informed by these ritual idioms. The day would be marked by early-morning processions and gatherings organized by schools, factories, and citizens' groups. While the Indian National Congress was solely responsible for the orchestration of the independence day commemorations between 1930 and 1935, other political groups also began to mobilize nationalist sentiment on this day, and by 1945 the date of January 26 was commemorated in separate meetings organized by the communist movement, Muslim groups, and students' and workers' organizations.[15] Despite the wide variety of participating organizations, a common commemorative pattern or repertoire was evident on January 26. Jim Masselos's detailed description of this repertoire is worth reproducing here in full, both to establish the continuities between the rituals of January 26 before and after independence, and to note the differences between practices marking the anniversary of a pledge toward independence and those commemorating the anniversary of the arrival of the independent republic:

> The day would begin with groups of young people wandering about the streets of towns, cities, or in some cases even villages, singing national songs . . . they would march to a central point, usually the local Congress headquarters where they joined other Congress personnel, volunteers, leaders, and supporters. There the national song Bande Mataram was sung; the national flag was hoisted and the independence pledge reaffirmed. Proceedings would finish by about eight or nine in the morning.
>
> In the late afternoon and early evening, there were more ceremonies. Processions formed and proceeded to meeting places, open spaces able to hold large numbers of people. The assembly would again listen to the national song, salute the national flag, and re-affirm the independence pledge . . . During the day, volunteers went around the city, selling flag buttons, Congress literature and otherwise collected money for Congress. In some places attempts were made to raise the national flag over important buildings, municipal corporations, government offices, schools and the like. The government usually forbade such attempts and inevitably the confrontations were dramatic.[16]

Thus, prior to 1947, January 26 was an occasion to mobilize support for the nationalist movement. The emphasis was on participation, activity, and movement, instead of on the enactment and presentation of a fixed script before an immobile audience in a given location—that is, a street performance rather than proscenium theater. The commemorative ceremonies worked to forge and consolidate sentiments of horizontal nationalist solidarity, with individuals brought together in a group around a common symbol (the flag), and participating in similar activities (songs, flag salutes, pledge taking) at the same time: familiar practices of forging national community through an emphasis on unisonance and simultaneity. However, this performance of national unity was simultaneously a recognition and a naming of subnational diversity—the visible presence of heterogeneity at the meetings, processions, and assemblies upheld as proof of the popularity and the wide reach of the nationalist movement.

Moreover, similar to the dual recognition of both "inherited" identity and "made" identity in the rituals of the imperial assemblage, independence day rituals took cognizance of individual as well as group difference, of primordial communities constituted around language, religion, race, and caste, as well as of occupational groups such as peasants and workers. Contemporary newspaper reports drew attention to the gathering of different bodies at independence day events, "stress[ing] the presence of women at the meetings, not[ing] a harijan's ["Untouchable" caste] presence, or that of a Sikh or Muslim, or peasants, labourers, and workers."[17] National solidarity was thus enacted on January 26 as a voluntary coming together of difference, calling for an affirmation rather than an erasure of subnational specificity. And in this "diversity vision" of India, the ritual idioms of imperialism and nationalism found common ground. The classificatory schemas of colonial sociology that understood Indianness in terms of irreducible heterogeneity realized themselves anew in and through the discourses and practices of anticolonial resistance.

Before 1947, January 26 was a day on which national identity was formulated as an oppositional or antagonistic force, when to declare one's sense of Indianness on the day of independence was to challenge and then refuse the authority and the legitimacy of imperial rule. However, this oppositional discourse was directed against the particular imperial state rather than against statist power and authority as such. The use of constitutional-legislative discourse was in fact integral to the commemorative ceremonies, with the battle cry of independence—the Independence Pledge—phrased in formal, rational, and institutionalist terms:

> We believe that it is the inalienable right of the Indian people, as of any other people, to have freedom and to enjoy the fruits of their toil and have the necessities of life, so that they may have full opportunities of growth. We believe also that if any government deprives a people of these rights and oppresses them, the people have a further right to alter it or abolish it. The British Government in India has not only deprived the Indian people of their freedom but has based itself on the exploitation of the masses, and has ruined India economically, politically, culturally, and spiritually. We believe therefore that India must sever the British connection and attain Purna Swaraj or complete independence . . .
>
> We hold it to be a crime against man and God to submit any longer to a rule that has caused this fourfold disaster to our country. We recognise, however, that the most effective way of gaining our freedom is not through violence. We will therefore prepare ourselves by withdrawing, so far as we can, all voluntary association from the British Government, and will prepare for civil disobedience, including non-payment of taxes.[18]

Here, the declaration of national sovereignty or freedom is one that ties the nation-people to an appropriate state form that will refrain from "ruin[ing] India economically, politically, culturally, and spiritually." In the terms of the pledge, the Indian nation will exist as a sovereign entity when the institution of rule—the state—does not cause a "fourfold disaster" but enables its people to grow and prosper. The movement to establish a sovereign nation was thus a movement to establish a sovereign state, which would exercise legitimate authority because it was "truly" a representative organization, unlike its imperial counterpart. The establishment of horizontal bonds of national solidarity proceeded alongside, and even through, the establishment of vertical bonds of authority linking nation and state. Individuals were constituted as members of a national community who would serve the state—to be national was to undertake the responsibilities of service and duty. As Masselos observes in the context of the independence day celebrations between 1937 and 1947: "It was no longer the right to freedom that speakers emphasized but the duties freedom would impose in creating an independent utopia. Even after the former masters departed, India would still need to be made really free and could only be made so by the collective efforts of its citizens."[19] In sum, the legacy of commemorative practices inherited by the postcolonial Indian polity defined the nation in terms of its constitutive diversity, tied national independence to the presence and activities of the state, and understood citizenship as duty.

Founding Moments: Republic Day Celebrations, 1951–1952

The first Republic Day celebrations of the postcolonial period were held at the Irwin Stadium in Delhi on January 26, 1951, to mark the first anniversary of the Indian republic. The aim of this first commemoration was to establish a new ritual idiom of identity and authority for the new polity, albeit one that drew upon earlier presumptions and practices of both the nationalist movement and of the imperial state. The day was marked by flag-raising ceremonies and by the singing of the national song.[20] In the main celebration held in the capital city of New Delhi, processions by the armed forces and flypasts by planes of the Indian Air Force were integrated into the ceremonial procedures, and the climactic moment of celebrations all over the nation occurred when an official representative of the state (the president and prime minister in New Delhi, and the regional governor in different state capitals) unfurled and saluted the flag. The state's authoritative presence on Republic Day was further underscored by the declaration of a paid holiday, the release of specially designed commemorative postage stamps, and the announcement of an amnesty for prisoners—gestures of state command that resonated with the imperial proclamations of the past.

The following year the Republic Day celebrations in Delhi began with a morning parade on Rajpath. The parade consisted of a military display of forces and weapons, as well as a cultural pageant. This military-cultural blend was the product of a deliberate decision taken by the state. As Ashfaque Husain, the joint-secretary of the department of education, stated: "Whereas other countries, on similar occasions, hold impressive military parades which are calculated to give to the whole world an idea of the armed might of the country, we have combined the ceremonial military parade with the cultural pageant, which signifies that this young Republic values cultural progress no less than military strength."[21] While the depiction of the "armed might of the country" was considered to be a relatively unproblematic task to be undertaken by specialists in the Ministry of Defence, the design of an appropriate cultural display necessitated careful and nuanced attention from the Indian prime minister, Jawaharlal Nehru. Nehru's conception of culture was as a national and natural resource—available in abundance but requiring careful monitoring, management, and harvesting by the state. Accordingly, the vision of culture that emerged in his directives to the pageant organizers was one that emphasized the rationalized, managed, or statist aspect of Indian culture as much as its natural, timeless, or popular-spontaneous aspects. Thus, the cultural displays and programs organized on Republic Day highlighted the role of the state in protecting and promoting culture, and the state's "cultural concern" was emphasized in the commemorative functions on January 26.

Nehru suggested that the cultural pageant on Republic Day should be preceded by a cultural festival in various locations throughout the country, with "performances, displays and exhibitions showing something not only of our cultural heritage but also of our cultural progress in the widest sense of the term."[22] Special attention was given to displaying and promoting the culture of what Nehru understood as neglected groups, such as folk performers from the nation's peripheries along with tribal artistes. The focus on folk culture was not just part of an effort to invent a common cultural tradition for postindependence India but also one that enabled the state to present itself as the guardian and the benefactor of all minority groups. In the Nehruvian vision, determinations about the authenticity of folk culture were to be made by the state. As Nehru noted in 1952: "In regard to folk dancing, we can hardly hope to get folk dances from all over India. That would be too expensive a business. We might, therefore, select some areas from which they will be invited. The next year other areas can be invited. It should be clearly understood that we have no amateur dancing. We must have the original stuff."[23]

The Nehruvian vision of culture for the Republic Day celebrations was also a functionalist one in which the utility of cultural identity to the goals and activities of nation building was constantly underscored. For instance, Nehru suggested that cultural displays could depict different groups engaged in the pursuit of "topical" activities, such as the "Grow More Food" campaign. Accompanying the floats depicting the "arts and crafts of each state" would be a procession of "peasants and farmers who have won in the campaign . . . and a tableau could represent in various ways this idea of an abundance of food growing to feed this hungry land."[24] This suggestion was carried forward and in fact modified in future parades so as to interweave the separate elements of "culture" and "nation building" into the visual display of a single float. In subsequent years, cultural floats would move past the viewing stands of Rajpath carrying farmers and workers dressed in brightly colored ethnic garb, with some playing musical instruments and others holding ploughs, scythes, hammers, or saws.

Finally, Nehru viewed the cultural pageant as an occasion to display the cultural diversity of India. As he stated, "The concept of this procession and exhibition and everything else should be to demonstrate both the unity and great variety and diversity of India . . . Each State could represent some distinctive feature of its own in the tableaux or in the exhibition or both. Thus the procession would be a moving pageant of India in its rich diversity."[25] In 1952, the cultural pageant consisted of a series of tableaux representing the cultural diversity of India, where each tableau depicted the inhabitants of a particular state engaged in a distinctive cultural practice indigenous to a specific area, such as a religious festival, a dance, or a wedding ceremony. By allowing each state to design its own cultural float and to choose its own marker of cultural identity, this diversity pageant functioned as a Renanist "plebisicitary practice"[26] of nation building, with the unified nation shown to exist only because its constituent diverse subgroups had freely consented to come together. In sum, by defining Indian culture in terms of its intrinsic diversity rather than its homogeneity, the cultural pageant on Republic Day presented the Indian nation as truly sovereign, as an expression of collective free will.

The Diverse Nation and the Magnificent State

Nehru's proposals for the cultural pageant were incorporated into the Republic Day parade of the following year, 1953, and the cultural displays subsequently became a familiar feature of the ritual repertoire of January 26. Other set pieces of commemorative practice were similarly fixed through such processes of annual iteration, and the descriptions of the parade that appeared on the front pages of national dailies each year on January 27 exhibited a similar kind of routinized conformity in the narrative frames used to convey the parade experience to a reading public. The article's accompanying photographs of floats on Rajpath—in close-up perspective and in long-shots that showed the marching columns of the military receding into the distance, flanked on either side by tightly packed crowds of spectators—were repeated assertions of solemnity and "gay abandon" as the dominant sentiments of the day.[27]

The solemnity of the occasion was conveyed through quasi-reverential accounts of the "dignitaries" who presided over the occasion: the president, the prime minister and members of his cabinet, visiting chief guests specially invited for the occasion, and others singled out as leaders and distinguished personages. The parade was structured around their presence; it began with a thirty-one gun salute announcing to the amassed crowds that the president and his entourage was approaching the viewing platform at the center of Rajpath. Similarly, the departure of the state's representatives announced the formal conclusion of the ritual event. Contemporary newspaper accounts of the day emphasized the labors of the state, variously depicting it as the prime organizer, chief participant, and also the main audience of Republic Day commemorations. In each of these roles, it was described as doing something "for the people," whether through highlighting the "months of preparation and hard work" that it had undertaken in the planning and implementation of the parade, the "grand and majestic" sight that it offered to its audience as it marched past in impressive military formation, or the graciousness and appreciation with which its representatives witnessed the cultural performances of citizens from their vantage point on the viewing platform. Materialized as an objectified and unchanging entity disconnected from the flux and messiness of human and social relations, the postcolonial state emerged as a fetish with multiple "faces"—those of the traffic policemen, tanks, aircrafts, cadets, floats, and president and parliamentarians—that could be gazed upon with awe and respect and that, in turn, could train its gaze back on its people.[28]

Republic Day parade, Rajpath (1951 or 1953). (Courtesy of Nehru Memorial Museum and Library, New Delhi)

Republic Day parade, 1952 (Courtesy: Nehru Memorial Museum and Library, New Delhi)

The parallel description of the visible expressions of excitement and awe with which ordinary spectators witnessed the parade further secured this impression of the state as a distinct object of contemplation that is located outside the field of social relations. Every year, accounts of the parade detailed the enjoyment of the crowds and emphasized how the spectacle of the parade was ample compensation for the myriad inconveniences that they had "braved" in order to be present at the event, such as inclement weather and chaotic traffic. In this regard, the theater of postcolonial state ritual was significantly different from that of its imperial predecessor, the durbar or assemblage. Now the emphasis was not just on the ability of the state to display itself before its subjects, but also on the voluntary attendance and the enjoyment of audience members who had made an active choice to witness such a performance.

Contemporary accounts of the parade also made repeated references to the extraordinary character of ritual time or the ways in which January 26 interrupted the quotidian flow of time as usual. Feature articles in special issues about Republic Day noted how several participants in the parade were visiting the capital city of New Delhi for the first time in their lives, thereby both literally and figuratively charting unexplored territory in the course of their journey from "remote hamlets" to the "center of the nation." The journalist Amita Malik's account of her interactions with folk dancers who had traveled to Delhi to participate in the Republic Day celebrations of 1960 is just one such example of how the meaning of the day was conveyed in terms of its singular, life-changing quality, especially as it pertained to those located outside the national mainstream:

> "And how do you like Delhi" I asked the leader of the Hyderabad dance party, as he pulled his blanket more closely round his shivering shoulders . . . "Oh, it is big, very big," he replied with awe in his soft South Indian voice. "That boy," he said, pointing to a confident-looking youngster, "has been to Hyderabad, and he says it is very big. But not as big as Delhi. Our village is very small," he apologized, "and this is the first time we have left it."
> "We shall tell the people in our village," said a shriveled old man with a white enormous turban, "that Delhi is so big that you need four eyes to see it . . . They will never believe us when we tell them that Delhi is so big."
> "They will never believe us," added the young boy, "when we tell them that we saw Panditji [Jawaharlal Nehru] too."[29]

Through such stories of transformation and incommensurability, journalists communicated to their readers the momentousness of Republic Day. In Malik's account, the sense of unfamiliarity, bewilderment, and estrangement experienced by the folk dancers is what made Republic Day the ultimate national ritual: an event in and through which Indians could encounter their nation for the first time, materialized in the "big" spaces of the capital and the prime minister's body.

Not only was Republic Day unlike any other day in the rest of the year, each parade was also unlike any other and each was deemed "better than ever before." Every year the crowd grew "even bigger," the marching military columns "even more awesome," the performances of the folk dancers "even more colorful," the floats "even more creative." These amplified and hyperbolic descriptions of each parade as a singular event contributed once again to the effect of separation or distinction, underscoring the unmistakable and visible uniqueness of the day of the state's birth, and ensuring that even though this day returned with predictable regularity every year, it was always a day with a difference, even when measured by its own ritual standards.

By 1960, the parade on Rajpath had become the most important public function on January 26. Even though other kinds of commemorative activities continued to be organized by both state and nonstate groups in Delhi and in other parts of the nation, the "national parade" received the maximum press coverage, and All India Radio broadcast a live audio commentary of the parade every year.[30] A formal committee structure and fixed organizational procedures were now associated with the parade, and an interministerial committee comprised of representatives from the Ministry of Defence and the Department of Culture began its preparatory work six months prior to the date. The duration of the parade had been increased, now lasting approximately two and a half hours. In contrast to the relatively free-form and evolving structure of the initial parades, the celebrations were now formally scripted. Like three separate acts in a play that are related to each other but also stand on their own, the festivities were divided into three distinct sections: a military display, a cultural display, and a display by and of schoolchildren.

There was, however, room for variation within this fixed ritual structure; an examination of annual parades over time shows that successive iterations introduce innovations as much as they reproduce familiar and longstanding patterns. As Nicholas Dirks has observed in his discussion of ritual practice as a dynamic process that continually reconstitutes relations of power, "each ritual event is patterned activity, to be sure, but it is also invented anew as it happens."[31] In the specific context of Republic Day rituals, the exercise of historical mapping shows that despite the dominant effect of transhistorical permanence and immutability, the ritual practices of the parade are also contextually specific as changing signs of their changing times. In the period between 1951 and the present, numerous new practices were introduced in response to the particular social and political exigencies of the moment, whether the outbreak of war (the war with China in 1962; with Pakistan in 1965, 1971, and most recently, the "limited engagement" in Kargil in 1999), the suspension of democratic rights and constitutional guarantees (the period of the national emergency between 1975 and 1977), or the assassination of prime ministers (Indira Gandhi's assassination in 1984 and Rajiv Gandhi's assassination in 1991).

The parade has been reconfigured during each of these moments of exception, and these changes have subsequently been normalized through the recursive workings of bureaucratic logic, serving as precedents that go on to pattern ritual practices in future years. The examples in the pages following illustrate this claim and suggest that the "invention of the Republic Day tradition" is best understood as an ongoing, dynamic process rather than a discrete event that occurs at a single point in time, with ritual practices emerging fully formed at some original moment of creation. The vision of historical change that emerges in the following discussion is of small and imperceptible lurches rather than tectonic upheavals. The commemorative rituals of the postcolonial nation, and by extension, the official nationalist imaginary are subject to continuous adjustments over time, that collectively cumulate in significant change.

In 1963, the changed configuration of the Republic Day parade was obvious to all onlookers. As the front-page report in the *Times of India* dramatically announced in its banner headline: "No Cultural Pageant." The report then went on to explain that "the occasion lacked the usual air of gay abandon... There was less of a spirit of joyful celebration in evidence than a dutiful observation of the national day. This restrained mood [was] induced by the treacherous breach of trust by a neighbor."[32] The specific incident in question was the ongoing war with China that had commenced in October 1962. As the first time since independence that the republic was at war,[33] its first effect on the ritual practices of Republic Day was to replace familiar components of the parade with new ones. The military section of the parade was canceled, as was the fly-past by the Indian Air Force planes. The cultural pageant also was canceled; in its place was a solemn procession consisting of members of parliament, Prime Minister Nehru and members of his cabinet, political representatives from the different Indian states, chancellors, deans, professors, and students from Delhi University, one thousand members of various national trade unions, a contingent of two thousand women, and a group of four thousand schoolchildren trained under the National Discipline Scheme.[34] Although this parade undoubtedly was different, contemporary media accounts did not see this as a deficiency or a lack. Even though the highly popular military section of the parade was missing, as was the "gay abandon" of the cultural pageant, other aspects of the new ritual apparently made for an enhanced viewing experience. To quote the editorial observations of the *Times of India*, "The bulk of the civilian groups more than made up for a lack of military precision in their earnestness and resoluteness."[35]

At a moment of national crisis, then, representations of national culture gave way to a visible show of solidarity by recognized and authorized representatives of political and social groups: the nation revealing itself in its hour of peril as willed social contract rather than as timeless cultural essence. This dispensability of culture—the ability to put it aside and present another face of the nation—was a counterpart of the Nehruvian understanding of culture as a purposive resource "for use" by the state on behalf of the nation. If, as we saw earlier, the usefulness of culture to the project of nation building was the prime motivation for including a cultural pageant in the parade in the first place, now the uselessness of culture allowed it to be set aside so that a more germane and relevant representation of the nation could take center stage. In both versions of culture's use-value, we see at work what Aimé Césaire has evocatively described as the process of "thingification," or the production of culture as a discrete, bounded, and possessed object that can either be mined or set aside, as circumstances warrant.[36] Thus, the very next year following the ceasefire between India and China, the dancers and the floats were back on Rajpath, with the normalcy of the situation and the return to business as usual signaled by the restoration of culture to its due place in the annual ritual of the republic—the moment of its bracketing preserved in a few column inches of fast-fading newsprint.

Other sets of wartime changes in the ritual repertoire were retained, however, and they soon became part of the new norm of Republic Day celebrations. Specifically, the rhetoric of militarism and sacrifice was from this point on an intrinsic component of the national imaginary that materialized every January 26. After 1963, a militarist narrative framed descriptions of the parade, reminding the nation that the troops and equipment on display were not just simulacra but the actual stuff of war; the concrete realizations of the state's resolve to protect its people. As described in the *Times of India*, here is Rajpath in 1965: "There was the sound of the footsteps of soldiers, many of whom had defended the country's northern border against the Chinese aggression. There was the drone of jet aircraft underlining the determination of the IAF to keep the skies free of any enemy . . . which mingled with patriotic songs of schoolchildren and the music of folk dancers."[37]

The shot tilts up in 1967, following the cloud trails of the MIGs and Gnats that had, in the words of the *Times of India*, "carved out for themselves a niche in the nation's heart during the 1965 operations against Pakistan."[38] Introduced at a time when the nation was actually at war, but retained subsequently in metaphoric form, the militarist understanding of national subjectivity called for citizens to be just like the valiant soldiers defending the borders, and to replicate in their everyday lives the qualities of sacrifice and fortitude. As if to underscore the point through a visible sign of the rewards earned through acts of courage, the parades after 1967 concluded with a procession of schoolchildren who had won national awards for the "outstanding courage" they had displayed over the year.[39]

Advertisement issued by the biscuit manufacturing company Parle on Republic Day, 1953 (Times of India [Bombay], January 26, 1953)

The rhetoric of war, sacrifice, and fortitude was not limited to the pronouncements of the state alone, but also was reproduced in the advertisements placed in the newspapers by corporations around the time of Republic Day each year, thereby aligning consumption desires with patriotic sentiments—alignments that shifted along with the changing contours of patriotism. Thus in the 1950s, the Indian subsidiary of the Czech shoemaking corporation, Bata, elaborated on its tag line of being "shoemakers to the nation" in Republic Day print ads that tied the manufacture and selling of shoes to the grand national pursuit of economic planning. Visuals and text imbued shoemaking with national significance, presenting the shoemaker as an indispensable partner of the state in the ultimate business of making "plans for the people." As the advertisement announced: "All of them [the people of India] must be provided with adequate shelter, ample food, suitable clothes, and, last but by no means least, durable and comfortable footwear to enable them to advance with confidence over the hard and stony path of exertion to a better tomorrow."[40]

Such semiotic elaborations of national salvation through planning were replaced in 1963 by images and words of war. The Bata ad from that year announces simply, above a stylized rendition of a Madhubani folk painting: "The Mother of Three Jawans Knows No Fear." At the hour of national need, the quest for higher shoe sales is eclipsed by a greater pursuit, as Bata echoes the fervent hope of the state and those it represents of making the Indian jawans "a force no power on earth will conquer."[41] Neither shoes nor economic plans but the need for national defense was the big sale of the day this time around. The next year, with the resumption of Republic Day celebrations as usual in a nation now at peace, the advertisements continued to echo the sentiments of war. As the Punjab National Bank reminded its customer-citizens, "Freedom is *Never Free*"; indeed, the battle is over but the responsibilities of sacrifice and watchfulness persist: "Today while we rejoice in our national freedom our thoughts must turn to the guardians of our frontiers. Their sacrifice must constantly remind us that freedom brings with it responsibilities for every one of us."[42]

Accompanying this annual injunction to sacrifice were the reminders that bravery and "continued vigilance" were ongoing requirements of citizenship —reminders secured through references to the significant threats and dangers that the nation faced at all times. During the Nehruvian era, the imperiled nation had a named, external source of threat and a spatially circumscribed arena for defense and vigilance: the Chinese peril at the borders. Subsequent elaborations of this theme relocated the specter within the national geobody by announcing the proliferation of diffuse internal battlefronts that required the citizen-soldier to be ever on guard against tangible and intangible enemies in a war without end. Thus on January 26, 1972, with Indira Gandhi, Nehru's daughter, serving in office as the third prime minister of independent India, and in the aftermath of the recent military victory over Pakistan (the 1971 "Bangladesh Liberation" war), a "public service" announcement in the newspapers conveyed to the nation this imperative of permanent bellicosity:

> Our unity should not be in the name of war only but for basic ideals. This victory has to be nursed to grow and yield many fruits. The battle the soldier has won on the field has to be resumed on the home front by everyone.
> LET US DECLARE WAR ON PREACHERS OF DIVISION,
> MONOPOLISTS OF PRIVILEGE;
> LET US WAGE A WAR FOR UNITY OF THE NATION, SOCIAL
> JUSTICE FOR ALL."[43]

Hindustan Steel's message for Republic Day from the same year summed up the imperative more succinctly: "We Have Won the War. We Must Win the

Peace."[44] Three years later, the inversionary logic of equating war with peace would be generalized as political practice, as in the case of the declaration of a state of national emergency by Indira Gandhi in which democracy was suspended in order that it be saved.[45] From 1975 until 1977, the emergency years, every day was the day of the republic, as the state marched through the streets of the nation, sorted out good culture from bad, and reproduced the familiar discourses of national security and insecurity, watchfulness and vigilance, that were by now integral components of the official nationalist imagination.

Although the partition of imperial territory into the nation-states of India and Pakistan undoubtedly has cast long and sweeping shadows over the postcolonial landscape, not all aspects of the national imaginary bear the imprint of this original trauma. There are other lineages of the troubled present as well, and we read history anachronistically if we assume that all temporal modulations of Indian nationalism are but attempts to grapple with the vexed question of how to relate to Pakistan. Thus, as the above discussion has shown, the militarist twist to the nationalist tale emerged from India's battlefield encounter with China, not Pakistan. Even though 1962 soon receded in the public imagination and direct references to the Chinese threat were replaced by the more proximate specter of Pakistani aggression, this does not alter the fact that the roots of militarist discourse, and the changes it wrought in the ritual practices of official nationalism, derive from a period in which Pakistan was not (yet) the ultimate public enemy. The scaffolding of the national security state did not emerge from the ruins of empire but instead was laid later on the site of the Chinese "betrayal" in 1962, which was repeatedly interpreted in policy circles as well as in the popular media as a sign that the Nehruvian experiment of charting new trajectories for foreign policy had significant and perhaps even fatal flaws. In this sense, the militarism of the 1960s and the paranoid fantasies of national insecurity that it subsequently generated can be classified unambiguously as postcolonial acts. They are formed in the shadow of the remembered failures of the sovereign state rather than those of its imperial predecessor.

As noted above, the ritual practices of Republic Day registered this change in the national imaginary, incorporating the new dimension of militarism and the attendant imperative of closure into the existing structure and narrative of the parade. This was effected through an emphasis on the military component of the parade as its most important element, and also through the weaving together of the hitherto separate components (the military display, the cultural pageants, and the floats showcasing the state's commitment to planned development and social and economic progress), so that each section also reflected the imperatives and priorities of the other. Thus, in many annual parades the military section served as an occasion to showcase the varied cultural and ethnic composition of the nation's military,[46] and the scientific technology that underwrote the achievements of the armed forces. The military display thus highlighted not just the nation's armed strength but also other desired national attributes, such as cultural diversity and scientific prowess.

Likewise, the cultural floats furthered the message of social and economic advancement by depicting how culture was a vital resource for the national project of achieving social and economic progress. In 1965 this was in fact the explicit theme of the cultural section of the parade. On other occasions, the cultural display reflected the imperatives of national security, imbuing the military discourse of bravery and vigilance with the historical weight—and the normalcy—of culture and custom: bravery is the way of our folk. Thus in 1964 all of the cultural floats of the Republic Day parade had the singular mission of "reminding people for the continued need for vigilance all along the borders." Each float highlighted the diverse ways in which this united purpose was being realized. "Towang back to normal" was inscribed on the float from the North East Frontier Agency (NEFA) states, thereby reclaiming the precise location on which the Great Chinese Betrayal had been enacted a short while ago, when Chinese troops had occupied the border town. The float from the state of Jammu and Kashmir had a similar message of reassurance; with the theme of "Ladakh Today," it depicted the peaceful coexistence of jawans and local communities in the border district of Ladakh.[47] The new emphasis on militarism was thus diffused and incorporated within the cultural spectrum of Indianness. From this point on, the normative worth of culture—what made culture good or valuable—was expressed in terms of national security, just as the necessity of the military was expressed in terms of the cultural regeneration and protection of the nation. In this manner, the culture of the national security state, where the discourse of national security comprises the culture or the distinctive identity of the nation, found expression.

If the genealogical exploration of Republic Day rituals highlights for us unexpected branching points—that is, moments of disjuncture at which new layers of meaning and new articulations of Indianness transformed the given understandings of national identity and of the relation between nation and state—it draws attention as well to the surprise of continuity: the fact that other moments of significant political, social, and cultural change do not reconfigure the official nationalist imagination. Thus, from the republic's first anniversary to its fifty-third, the cultural pageant of the parade has consistently showcased the subnational cultural diversity of India and the ways in which the material expressions of identity at the level of the individual state units of the federation are visibly different from each other.

Each year the states choose to represent themselves on Rajpath through different thematic displays. Although the vocabulary of representation differs from state to state—with some choosing to display their economic identity while others their historical or geographical heritage—all are concerned with representing their difference or the unique position that they occupy in the national spectrum. The diversity of Indian nationhood and the fact that Indianness is a condensation or a coming together of different regionally defined groups is the assumption on which the states design their floats. And built into the regional definition of identity is a notion of territory and territorial distinctiveness. Although the states are organized according to the principle of linguistic homogeneity,[48] language differences are depicted less than are differences in climate, topography, architecture, and plant and animal life.

The state floats thus conform to the invisible logic of landed or territorialized identity, with culture being depicted only if the culture-bearing group, individual, or artifact can be located in a specific territorial space. Consequently, what is showcased are tribes from a particular area, people born in specific states, temples gracing particular metropolitan landscapes, and even religions that can trace their roots to a specific location (e.g., a *peepul* tree in Bihar in the case of Buddhism). In the official nationalist discourse, whether expressed by the center or by the states, Indian nationhood is called up in terms of difference. Moreover, the vocabulary for expressing this difference, whether focusing on the diversities of "nature" or "culture," is one of identity and territory; more specifically, of identity as fundamentally territorial in its makeup.

The symbolic syntax of the Republic Day parades must be read in terms of the complete set of rituals on January 26; here, the significance both of the military procession and of the cultural pageant must be noted, along with the particular form of sequencing that is involved. As we have seen, the military section of the parade foregrounds the paramount strength of the state and its defense forces. Moreover, while the defense forces are presented in terms of their diverse regional origins, they are simultaneously brought together in the service of the entire nation. The military parade thus is a signifier of national unity—a unity that is wrought by, and quite literally realized in, the institutions of the state. Once this statement of unity has been proclaimed, the parade proceeds symbolically to capture the cultural diversity of the Indian nation through the displays of the pageantry procession. Here the floats representing the states gesture toward the different regional identities that comprise nationhood in postindependence India, and thus parcel up the nation's territory into culturally discrete packages. Territory also figured in the first half of the parade, but it did so in terms of an undifferentiated mass or an all-India expanse of land and borders that the military was deployed to defend.

The second half of the parade, with its emphasis on regional, cultural territory, invests the undifferentiated territorial concept with meaning—that is, it specifies the contours of territory for different groups, and in so doing shows that the state and its military protects Naga dances, Keralite cash crops, the subway system in West Bengal, the Ladakhi marriage ceremony in Jammu and Kashmir, and the "harmonious architecture" in Goa. Indian national identity is produced in the spectacle of Republic Day as that which permeates the intimate spaces of the home and the hearth. Instead of asking subjects to step out and merge with Indian nationhood, the official nationalist discourse quite literally brings national identity home and localizes its meaning in the nonabstracted terms of land. The state demands loyalty and sacrifice from its citizens in order to safeguard national identity, which is then produced as an aggregation of particularities, such that being Naga (or Kashmiri or Bengali or Punjabi) is the same as being Indian.

This fragmented vision of culture has been displayed on Rajpath every year, even during periods in which the political and military might of the center was actively engaged in combating the threat of cultural distinctiveness, as various states in the federation have raised demands for further autonomy and even secession. In the freeze-frame of January 26 every year, Punjab, Kashmir, and the northeastern states of Assam, Mizoram, Nagaland, and Manipur—spaces otherwise configured in the national imagination as areas of danger and sedition filled with terrorists and militants—are on display as desirable zones of carefree cultural expression. The defining attribute of culture in this vision is its atemporality and its disconnection from social and political processes of change and contestation. The displays on Rajpath present culture as a stable and permanent resource that underwrites the nation's continuous quest of moving forward and of growing and developing.

As Tom Nairn and Homi Bhabha have observed, the discourse and practices of nationalism are marked by a dual orientation toward time. The "pedagogical imperative" of nationalism produces the nation as unchanging constancy, as that which has existed forever, while the "performative imperative" reinvents the nation as a radical new possibility, gesturing toward not the mists of antiquity but the expansive horizon of the future.[49] The representations of culture on Republic Day reflect this duality. Thus, even as the varied people of India are seen to move toward the future with the protective and enabling guidance of the developmentalist state—the visions of the great national march forward in the floats depicting social and economic progress and in the impressive display of sophisticated weaponry owned by the armed forces—the customs, costumes, songs and dances of the people remain timeless and unchanged as the ever-dependable cultural resources that individuals, groups, and the state can draw upon in the ongoing project of nation building. Even as images of the Kashmir valley in flames, the impenetrable forests of the northeast, and the killing fields of the Punjab entrench themselves in the public imagination, so too do the styrofoam and plywood vistas of lakes, mountains, and Kashmiri *chinar* trees, the vibrant colors of the Naga costumes, and the joyous harvest songs of the bhangra-dancing Sikhs atop the Punjab float.

And if Kashmir has moved from being the favorite destination of honeymooners and the location of song-and-dance sequences in just about every Hindi film to the backdrop against which grim-faced newscasters in flak jackets report the body counts of the day, this shift is not registered on Rajpath. There, Kashmir is forever a stationary *shikara* (boat) floating on the papier-mâché waters of the Dal Lake, driven past the cheering crowds on a remodeled Tata truck on January 26 each year.

The unchanging cultural essence of the nation is also represented by the "unity in diversity" composition of the Republic Day pageant. In the display of national culture as so many colorful bits and pieces, the nation materializes as a kaleidoscope that can be rearranged to produce new patterns that nevertheless convey the same general impression of colorful concatenation. Not all states are represented in each annual parade. A state may be present one year and absent the next, either because the relevant state-level bureaucracy has failed to meet the deadline for submitting details about the proposed float to the organizing committee in New Delhi, or because a pointed message of contestation is being sent to the nation's capital.[50] This happened during the period of the national emergency between 1975 and 1977, when the parade had only two state floats.[51] In addition, sometimes state floats fail to appear because the states themselves disappear, or else are reconfigured as new entities with new names and new boundaries as the composition of Indian federalism is reworked. In the years since the original constitution of India as a federated union, there have been many such shifts in the internal boundaries of the nation and the size and shape of its constituent units. The erstwhile princely states have been merged into the provinces of British India, and the provinces themselves have been enlarged, fragmented, and renamed. And so The Punjab and East Patiala States Union (PEPSU) dissolves into Punjab, Haryana, and Himachal Pradesh; Jharkhand emerges from Bihar; and Sikkim, Goa, and Pondicherry cease being foreign soil.

While histories of protracted and often violent struggle have shaped each of these transformations, the birth of new states is invariably staged as a pristine fait accompli in the Republic Day parade. The freshly minted states take their place in the mosaic of cultural diversity, sharing equal billing with those against whom their demands for sovereignty and autonomy were raised. Neither the significance of interstate tensions—the protracted contest between the states of Punjab and Haryana over the status of Chandigarh, or the ongoing disputes over the sharing of river water between the states of Tamil Nadu and Karnataka—nor the substantive disparities in size, economic wealth, and political power between heartland states such as Uttar Pradesh and peripheral states such as Meghalaya disrupts the equalizing logic of the cultural pageant on January 26.

In terms of commemoration, all of the units are configured as equal contributors toward the production of the aggregate national mosaic, which as noted earlier can be based each year on different arrangements and combinations but the overall impression of a diversity display remains the same. In this regard, the tiered or nested configuration of diversity is significant, expressed at the level of the nation with the individual states coming together to display their cultural identities, as well as at the level of the state as a collection of smaller regional cultures. Like the *matrioshka* (nested) doll effect of Soviet nationality policy,[52] the display of how each level of identity contains within it other levels of identity anticipates future scenarios in which the subgroup can have a state of its own. Thus, when one year the Bombay state float presents *ras garba* dancers alongside performers dressed as the famous Maratha chieftain-king Shivaji and his army, and the next year the new state float from Gujarat presents *ras garba* as its distinctive culture, the effect is one of cultural rearrangement—*ras garba* has simply been reassigned to another state.[53] Thus, future reorganizations of the federal framework are prefigured through this split-level staging of diversity, so that the

Republic Day, 2003 (Pioneer, January 27, 2003).

demand for the recognition of new autonomous identities through the creation of new states is never a regime-destabilizing moment but is staged instead within the accepted parameters of official nationalism.

The diffusion of these official nationalist presumptions is, however, not a task that is undertaken by the centralized state alone, in the form of actions and commands issued from the nerve center of the nation in New Delhi. The significance of Republic Day and the continued reproduction of the officially approved meaning of republican rituals are also upheld and underscored through the actions and interventions of various nonstate and even antistate groups. For instance, as noted above the corporate capital has long seized on the day of the republic as an occasion to sell all kinds of commodities, from shoes to insurance.[54] These campaigns that endeavor to constitute consumption as the ultimate act of patriotism also serve to disseminate the authoritative understandings of Indianness, so that hum sab ek hain ("we are all one") lives on not as a ponderous official slogan, but also in the copy of an advertisement for beedis (handrolled cigarettes): "The synthesis of different beliefs and traditions constitutes Indianness," the bold typeface announces in the morning papers of January 26, 1985, "The makers of Thirty Brand Beedis greet the people of India. JAI HIND!"[55]

The many gestures of opposition and challenge seen on Republic Day each year also play an important part in the dissemination of the official nationalist vision. Protests, walkouts, boycotts of official Republic Day festivities in different parts of the nation, and the convening of "black-flag" public demonstrations are an integral part of the experience of January 26.[56] Each year, the attention is divided between the pleasures of the "main action" onstage in Rajpath, and the dangers unfolding in the wings. However, the contestation is for the most part directed at the state qua political party—a challenge to the particular government in power in Delhi at the time—rather than at the state qua institution. It is a directed and selective challenge of the authority of the people in power rather than of the configuration of power itself. Moreover, the ritualization and routinization of contestation—the fact that such activities are repeated every year—consolidates, through negation, the importance of the day of the republic. Through the choice of January 26 as the day of protest its symbolic significance is underscored, with the master narrative of India as unity in diversity—the naturalness of cultural diversity juxtaposed against the representative unity provided by the state—paradoxically upheld through efforts of negation and disavowal.

The More Things Change? Continuity and Disjuncture on India's Fiftieth Republic Day

New Delhi, January 26, 2000. I had watched the Republic Day parades in 1997 and 1998, and I am back again on Rajpath this year, curious about what might be in store for the first parade of the twenty-first century, which is also the fiftieth anniversary of the Indian republic. In my own narrative of the Republic Day experience the day holds additional significance, and its symbolism of newness is overdetermined. In academic and media circles, the contemporary moment is almost invariably described in terms of political, economic, social, and cultural disjuncture. Cited in discussions of the many differences between India's present and its past are factors such as the emergence of Hindu nationalism as an influential political and cultural discourse in the public arena and its supplanting of Nehruvian secularism, the liberalization of the planned and protected quasi-socialist economy, the growing prominence of the "vernacular public" (those whose social and educational status has historically been a barrier to their entry into the privileged circles of the Westernized elites), and the formation of the new status group of the "new middle classes." To this long list of transformations must be added the substantially reconfigured international identity for the nation-state, as marked by the nuclear tests of 1998 that ended an almost half-century-long commitment to nuclear disarmament, and the progressive hardening of relations between India and Pakistan that culminated in the

Kargil war of 1999, the first protracted military engagement with Pakistan since the war of 1971.

And so I am also here to witness the ritual practices of the new India, to see whether a different display of the nation will be paraded on Rajpath this year—one that rearticulates presumptive understandings of nationhood and introduces new practices of cultural authorization. If, as Benedict Anderson has observed, nations are distinguished by the idiom or the style of the way they are imagined, then perhaps a new national style is emergent today; a style reflecting the many changes that have taken place over the past few years, especially since 1998 when the Hindu nationalist BJP government came to power.

Time at least doesn't move differently this year: the parade begins, with military precision, at 9 AM. Like other years, elaborate security arrangements ensure that audience members (who must purchase tickets in advance) are in their respective enclosures by 8:30 AM, after having passed through a series of extensive security checks.[57] Those who are willing to spend five hundred rupees are seated in comfortable chairs next to the VIP enclosure, while others huddle together on hard green benches at the far end of Rajpath. As I negotiate my final security checkpoint, and sheepishly surrender a ballpoint pen forgotten in my pocket, an explanatory commentary prepared by the Ministry of Defence is being broadcast over the public address system installed along Rajpath; as it alternates between its English and Hindi versions the disembodied voices are muffled and mostly indecipherable. In an illustration of how collective belonging is frequently experienced as a shared stance of cynicism and ironic distance toward the ineptitude of the state,[58] a common sense of exasperation soon leads to increasingly friendly interchanges among audience members. The call and response of *Ab kya bola?* (What did he say now?) is heard all along Rajpath.

Even though we are all here to see the parade, the broadcast commentary is an integral part of the experience; the commentator is at once usher, *sutradhar* or narrator, Greek chorus, and theater critic. The voice settles us down, announces, explains, describes, expounds, prophesies, and reviews. Much of the commentary goes unheard by the immediate object of its address—the audience at the parade ground—either because of the crackling of the loudspeakers or because most people are carrying on their own commentaries. Instead the spoken word survives in writing. Each year, the Ministry of Defence prepares a printed script that is distributed to the press. The newspaper accounts of the parade the next day often reproduce the script verbatim, and the state thus speaks into being the archive of the Republic Day experience.

The commentary begins by explaining the significance of Republic Day, and the words of the twenty-first-century script are identical to those from years past: "The day herald[s] justice, liberty, equality, and fraternity assuring the dignity of the individual and unity of the nation."[59] Indeed, it is a statement that reproduces, almost to the last word, the preamble of the Indian constitution. In this opening announcement no mention is made of the nationalist movement for independence, or of the process by which "our country became a republic." Indian nationhood is not presented as something that needed to be fought for, to be sacrificed for, and to eventually be won after a protracted struggle, but as that which merely needed the quiet, rational, and methodical workings of a "written constitution" to bring it into being.

After settling the issues of meaning, the showing through the means of telling begins. The words (and the voice reading them out) describe the immediate environs of the parade ground, pointing out the architectural landmarks of Rashtrapati Bhavan (the residence of the Indian president), the south and north blocks of the Secretariat (where several ministries are located), India Gate, and the Amar Jawan Jyoti (Eternal Flame of the Soldier). These are sites that gesture simultaneously toward India's imperial past and its republican present, distinctions of time dissolving in the unity of space. The Amar Jawan Jyoti in front of the India Gate burns for soldiers who died serving the British Empire and also those who have died for the sovereign Indian state. Rashtrapati Bhavan once housed the *pati* (head) of a different kind of *rashtra* (state): the viceroy of the Indian empire. Then, as now, bureaucrats walked the red sandstone corridors of the Secretariat. Wild monkeys have made their annual winter appearance on the rooftop of the south block, right above the entrance that leads to the offices of Ministry of Defence, for as long as anyone can remember. Then, as now, they could not be scared away.

The voice introduces the chief guest at the parade, President Obasanjo of Nigeria, and tells us why he has thus been honored, speaking of the many ties of friendship and trade between Nigeria and India. The exercise of annual reckoning now begins and the commentary summarizes the key events that took place in India over the past year. These events usually testify to India's scientific, technological, and economic glories, and this year is no exception. What unfolds is a narrative of progress and development, of marching onward relentlessly, though stumbles and setbacks along the way are dutifully reported as well. Thus, we are told in jubilant terms about the Indian military success during the war in Kargil, but we are also given the sobering news that the annual economic growth rate was lower than expected. It is as if the republic must produce a balance sheet of its assets and liabilities to merit the celebrations on Republic Day, with the deeds of the state rather than of the people/nation showcased as those deserving recognition and applause. What Indians are thus urged to celebrate on January 26 is the state rather than the nation; politics and economics rather than culture; and the organized, structured workings of government rather than the inchoate longings of the national masses.

The parade itself commences with the laying of a wreath at the Amar Jawan Jyoti by the prime minister, and the observation of a two-minute period of silence after certain standard military rituals ("present arms," "reverse arms," "last post") have been enacted. This sets the tone for the constant references to the presence and prowess of the armed forces that mark most of the events of the parade. If the purpose of the parade is to visually depict the Indian republic, then the vision that emerges is one of a territorial entity that is shielded by a protective military framework—an iron cage that exists in particular to guard the frontiers of the national territory. We are constantly reminded that the nation requires security, protection, and watchful eyes along its borders in order to exist. As the commentary points out: "Today we salute the gallant soldiers, sailors and airmen of our forces who are guarding the nation's frontiers and are deployed in high altitude and difficult areas of the country, caring little for their comforts. It is reassuring to know that India's modern and formidable military machine is ready to meet any contingency during war or peace."

The commentary that accompanies the procession points out the function, the composition, the history, and the unique contribution of each troop in serving the nation. For instance: "The President's Bodyguards is one of the oldest regiments of the Indian Army. It was raised in September, 1773, at Banaras by the then Governor General . . . The regiment has a glorious and proud history in combat . . . Among the innumerable campaigns in which it has successfully participated have been in France during the First World War and the 1965 operations. More recently detachments of the Bodyguards served in Sri Lanka with distinction." The temporal break of independence in 1947, or the accompanying transformation from an imperial army to an army of a sovereign nation-state, finds no mention in this seamless narrative of military history that in the space of a short paragraph sweeps from the eighteenth-century world of colonial governor-generals to the twentieth-century world of Tamil Tigers and ethnic conflict in Sri Lanka. The armed forces are imbued instead with an aura of timelessness. They are presented as ever ready, ever reliable, and unchanging; as willing and able to serve the state at all times. Moreover, the emphasis on military continuity across time also consolidates an understanding of the state in similar terms of permanence and constancy, as the institutional authority that has always commanded the allegiance and service of the army, regardless of which political party is in power, and of whether imperialism or national sovereignty is the defining attribute of the state. In the additive logic of militarism, each new war is simply collated with the existing record of valor on the battlefield. This year, the Kargil war updates the military record, serving as the latest manifestation of the Indian army's bravery and will to sacrifice for the sake of the nation.

Seated at the parade ground, it is virtually impossible to ignore the salience of the theme of sacrifice. Winners of the highest military honors ("gallantry awards") such as the Param Vir Chakra, the Ashoka Chakra, and the Victoria Cross—again an honor roll that elides temporality and the transition from colonialism to postcolonialism—feature prominently in the parade, testifying to the honor and glory that is showered on those who value the nation-state above their own individual lives. This year, the decorated heroes returning from Kargil are singled out for special attention, and the commentary draws attention to the individuals, contingents, aircraft, and weapons that were actually deployed during the recent war effort: the troops that have recently returned from Kargil, and the 150mm howitzer guns with their superior firing range (twenty kilometers), against which "the Pakistani 130 mm guns were no match."[60]

Then, as if to underscore the intrinsic value of the sacrificial act, what immediately follows the procession of glory-bedecked award winners is a display of the latest weapons and technology of the Indian armed forces. The floats with the medium-range Prithvi missile and the intermediate-range Agni-II missile occupy prominent positions in the display of military hardware, and the superior weapons-delivery capabilities of Prithvi and Agni-II are repeatedly pointed out to the gathered spectators. Although no direct references are made to the specific target or the theater of operations within which Prithvi and Agni (earth and fire) might be deployed, their placement in the parade directly after the numerous Kargil-related military displays—including the giant statue of a soldier with his hand pointing west against a mountainous backdrop—leaves the gathered audience in no doubt as to who might be the chief interlocutor of this formidable display of Indian strength:

our gaze is diverted westward to Pakistan, across the mountains surrounding Kargil.

Indians are not being asked to lay down their lives in vain—along with Prithvi and Agni, their nation is also the proud possessor of "T-72 tanks, Multi Barrel Rocket Launchers, STRELA 10 M Air Defence Missiles, PMS Bridging Equipments, Emergency Communications Terminals, Jaguar Aircraft with Sea Eagle Missiles, INDRA-1 Radars, and Pilotless Target Aircraft." The acronyms and the capitalization of names only enhance the effect of weightiness and impressiveness: this is surely a nation worth dying for. Then, as the troops file past, the roll call of sacrifice and glory continues, and the commentator enumerates the medals won by each contingent. "A good citizen is a good soldier" is the implicit message of the day—the ideal national subject is one who sacrifices for the sake of the nation. This theme is repeated at the very end of the parade as well, as the nation is treated to the sight of "future soldiers"—schoolchildren who have won awards for bravery and self-sacrifice—seated on elephants.[61]

Although the procession of the military is formally separate from, and precedes, the cultural section of the parade, as the troops move down Rajpath they bring into view numerous signs and markers of cultural difference. The various army contingents, for example, represent different areas of the country—the Bombay Sappers, the Maratha Light Infantry, the Rajput Regiment, the Sikh Light Infantry, the Kumaon Regiment, the Assam Regiment, the Jammu and Kashmir Light Infantry, and the Garhwar Rifles, among others.[62] Each group has a distinct uniform and look, and although this does not necessarily correspond to the traditional costume of the region in question—the Kumaon Regiment, for instance, does not dress in Kumaoni ethnic garb—audience recognition and engagement with the marchers is predicated in many instances on the articulation of regional identity: Look, there are the Gurkhas! Aren't the Sikhs tall? The display of the military's commitment to diversity takes gender into account as well, and a "lady officer" marches in front of each regiment. The all-women contingent of the paramilitary Central Reserve Police Forces draws almost as much applause and exclamations as do the members of the Camel Mounted Band, who, the voice explains to us, are forever immortalized in the pages of the Guinness Book of World Records for their remarkable feat of being able to play musical instruments while riding camels.

Thus far, the parade has been a spectacular but familiar sight. Visible signs of newness and disjuncture continue to elude me. While the images and references to Kargil are unique to this year's parade, as is the mention of the nuclear weapons capability of the Indian state, these all seem to fit neatly and logically into the existing framework of militarism and national security as the characteristic features of Indianness—a framework that, as we have already seen, has materialized on Rajpath since the early 1960s. The otherwise substantial reconfiguration of the Indian state from an ardent advocate of nuclear disarmament to a proud and avid possessor of nuclear capability is, in the logic of the Republic Day parade, rendered in terms of serial or linear progression rather than break or disjuncture, fitting into rather than unsettling established conventions of displaying nationhood in terms of military prowess and the state's quest for national security. Indeed, even though it is precisely to the arena of defense policy that arguments about the "new India" turn for confirming evidence, the ritual idioms and visual practices of defense are themselves unaltered. This manifestation of continuity suggests that the nuclear muscle-flexing and the heightened anti-Pakistani rhetoric of the present Hindu nationalist government may have been prefigured in the national imaginary of the past, through the long-standing practice of placing the state and its security requirements at the heart of normative nationhood.

The cultural section of the parade holds no obvious surprises either. This year, too, the floats constitute a "moving pageant of India's rich diversity" and elaborate the vision of Indian identity that first took shape under the personal supervision of Nehru fifty years ago, in the context of the first Republic Day parade. Each state displays whatever it considers to be the distinctive features of its identity, and what we see this year, like in other years, is a montage that defies any overarching theme or logic, except that of showcasing regional identity as difference. Thus Assam materializes as a tea plantation; Delhi and Jammu and Kashmir both depict the martyrs of Kargil; and Andhra Pradesh creates "Vision 2020" in celebration of the efforts of the present chief minister, Chandrababu Naidu, to harness technology to the task of economic development in a display of farmers gazing at computer screens.[63] For Uttar Pradesh, a historical turn is the order of the day as a tableau commemorating the six-hundredth birth anniversary of the syncretic poet-saint Kabir represents the state on Rajpath. As each successive float appears in view, a friendly guessing game begins among the audience members—Is that Gujarat? Or are those turbans Rajasthani? The usual mix of culture, economic development, and natural resources—thus tea plantations as the identity of Assam—along with the showcasing of visible differences in subnational identity through performers in colorful "ethnic" costumes enacting "traditional" rituals unique to each state, produces an effect of familiarity and uninterrupted continuity.

Even though the BJP-led coalition government at the center has effected significant changes in the arena of official cultural policy, such as the commissioning of new sets of state-approved school textbooks that present a Hindu-nationalist inflected understanding of Indian history in terms of the eternal battles between the Muslim invaders and the indigenous Indian Hindus, the rituals of official nationalism and the diversity vision of Indian culture have not been subjected to equivalent alterations. Thus in this year's parade, the unity of the nation continues to be visualized not through representations of a homogenous cultural essence of Indianness as Hindu identity, but instead through highlighting the labor of unification undertaken by the state. The expression of this unity is seen in floats representing different ministries such as the Indian Railways and the Public Works Department or in the specially commissioned golden jubilee "signature float" entitled "We the People of India," which "symbolizes the entire country and its people" through a gigantic replica of the Indian constitution, propped up on three pillars labeled "Democracy," "Legislature," and "Judiciary."

In a similar vein of "stating the nation," it is with the images of the state in action that the parade concludes. The maximum applause of the audience is reserved for the final demonstration of the state's extraordinary abilities: the spectacular sight of three Sukhoi SU-30 fighter jets turning somersaults in the air while another airborne squadron paints the sky with cloud trails of saffron, white, and green. The traces of the tricolor hover ghostlike, high above the parade ground, as the national anthem plays, the president and his entourage make their exit, and the crowd begins to disperse. We leave our day of national commemoration with the sights and sounds of the state.

The evening news provides a fresh set of reminders of why the national day is the day of the state—it is the day on which protests against the state assume maximum visibility, and thus it is also the day on which the repressive arm of the state reveals itself most clearly. This year, two rockets have been fired at a stadium in Jammu while the parade was taking place. Eight tribal separatist groups in five northeast states called an eighteen-hour strike to "protest Indian rule." A bomb went off in Imphal, the capital city of Manipur. In each of these instances, viewers are told, the agencies of the state were able to restore security and order. The nation is safe because of the timely actions and interventions of its representative institution. There are 65,000 troops stationed in Delhi tonight, guarding the nation's capital to ensure that citizens are free to continue celebrating the day unburdened by undue anxiety.

As we leave Rajpath, so does the parade. The soldiers, floats, and schoolchildren move past the now-empty viewing platform, and march on toward their final destination: the ramparts of the Red Fort, the seat of the Mughal empire. An observer given to flights of fancy may imagine she sees the tents of the imperial assemblage swaying gently in their wake.

Conclusion

Republic Day celebrations in India have ever since their inception been both a means of ideological-symbolic reproduction and a site or an arena for the performance, expression, and practice of nationhood. But what exactly is being reproduced and performed on January 26 every year? Answering this question calls for a move beyond the generic or modular observation of a nationalizing ritual to an engagement with the specificities of the particular national project at hand: in this case, the project of creating and sustaining a new and distinctive form of a nation-statist identity. In bearing out this book's main argument of how a new and distinctive expression of a "stated nationalism" has dominated the political and cultural field in postcolonial India, the commemorative rituals of Republic Day are shown to have enabled the performance and reproduction not so much of "horizontal bonds" of communal solidarity but rather "vertical bonds" of authority, hierarchy, and power between state and nation. What takes center stage on January 26 every year is not the sovereignty of the nation but the indispensable role of the state in enabling, representing, and safeguarding national sovereignty.

That Republic Day celebrations in India have accorded such importance and visibility to the presence and actions of the state is not surprising. After all, republican commemorations as a subset of rituals that explicitly memorialize institutional or constitutional founding moments are primed as state-centric occasions in many other countries as well. What is distinctive, then, is not the fact of a "stated nationalism" per se but instead the particular form and expression that it has taken: the idioms, images, and practices that have centered the state in the national imagination. I refer here to the representation of subnational cultural diversity that has been a staple of Republic Day celebrations for more than fifty years, and the fact that the "strong state" and the "diverse nation" are encountered as paired, complementary formations on January 26 every year. Instead of representing national culture as a homogenous, seamless whole, the Republic Day rituals highlighted the fragmented composition of Indianness, and the "indispensable" role of state institutions and practices in unifying, enriching, and protecting the natural cultural diversity of India.

As this chapter has shown, the Republic Day encounter with the state was selective or partial. Although the commemoration was organized to mark the advent of republican democracy in India, it was the armed forces that represented the state at the Republic Day parade. In a reflection both of the colonial lineages of postcolonial rituals, and of the gradual but unmistakable ascendancy of a national security state culture in the years since independence, Republic Day pageantry showcased one specific "face" of state power—namely that of military might and prowess. This was primarily a product of deliberate design and intent on the part of state actors—the Ministry of Defense was one of the main organizers of the parade. But as the examples of the media commentaries and corporate advertising discussed in this chapter suggest, nonstate actors and institutions also played a role in creating and sustaining this militarist "state effect" on January 26 every year.

The encounter with cultural diversity was selective or partial as well. The displays on Rajpath presented culture as a territorially discrete, politically eviscerated, and temporally static "resource" that can be mined by citizens, communities, and the state. In the tableaux of the Republic Day parades, moreover, culture was always a variable endowment: it belonged to the "folk" rather than the city-dweller, the artisan rather than the factory worker, the dancer rather than the militant.

In their representations of the nation's diversity through a series of identically configured ethnic cameos of territorially discrete cultural communities, the Republic Day floats confirmed the logic of Indian ethnofederalism, whereby territorially discrete ethnic-cultural communities could bargain for political autonomy and claim rights that could not be claimed by groups forged around class, caste, gender, or religion-based axes of solidarity. In a similar vein, the serial and streamlined representation of ethnocultural communities during the Republic Day parade reproduced the lumping effect of legislative and policy vocabularies on issues that seemed otherwise quite distant from the pageantry of Rajpath, such as interventions on the "Kashmir question" that glossed over the considerable internal differentiation of the region, and the efforts of central state agencies to quell militancy in the even more monothically understood northeast of India. In sum, the selective vision of India's diversity was not confined to the exceptional, ritual spaces of the parade ground on January 26. Instead, like the other components of the Republic Day imaginary, it reflected and reinforced a wider set of normative presumptions that have structured the arena of politics and public culture in postcolonial India.

Chapters 1 and 2 have examined the encounter with the Nehruvian nation-state through visual and ritual practices, respectively. Together they document how the nation-state was seen and performed in the most literal sense; how the attempt to transform "subjects into citizens" following the end of colonial rule was about producing citizens as spectators of their nation, their state, and their ideal selves. But images and passive spectatorship do not exhaust the postcolonial project. In the next chapter I investigate another kind of encounter with the nation-state: the policy discourses and practices of "nation-building" that called for the active participation of citizens as "builders" of the new India.

CHAPTER 3

Indian Darkness

Science, Development, and

the Needs Discourse of the

Nation-State

:::

> Mr. Nehru, usually shy of statistics, could tell precisely how many problems India was facing today. He was asked this when he visited Europe recently and he had unhesitatingly replied: "350 million." "Every single individual in India," he said, "is a problem."
> —Times of India, July 8, 1953

> Adversity is part of this independence package. The government needs courageous citizens. We have to lift burdens like strong real men. Colonization meant that we weren't burdened, this was part of being enslaved. We can no longer sit back on a bed of flowers. We need to run on thorns.
> —Minister of Education Maulana Azad, August 15, 1948

In the first few decades after independence, the vocabulary of "nation building" dominated both policy debates and political discourse in India. Receiving special emphasis was the ongoing and necessarily incomplete character of Indian nationhood, along with the connotations of nation building as arduous and perilous work. In marked contrast to the celebratory, even triumphal, registers of nationalist discourse that dominate twenty-first-century India—the ascendant imagination of "India Shining" or the proclamation of India as a significant economic and geopolitical global power[1]—the vocabulary of nation building from the initial years after independence conjured up an "Indian darkness" and defined the nation-state as a collection of persistent and unfulfilled problems, failures, and needs. Moreover, and as the epigraphs above indicate, these charges about the continuing problems, unmet needs, ongoing difficulties, and present failures of the nation-state were leveled not by critics but by the agents of the postcolonial state. Equally, the disdain for politics, construed as the machinations of power-hungry politicians, was endorsed and furthered by the state elites themselves in the foundational years of the postcolonial polity. If political practices are, according to Rogers Brubaker, "crucially famed, mediated, indeed constituted by institutionalized definitions of nationhood and nationality," then the "practical category" of nation building framed postindependence Indian politics in a way that alternative conceptions of nationhood as triumph, ease, or plenitude would not have done, with the vocabularies of consent as well as those of critique confirming the role of the state as the chief protagonist of the nation.[2]

To examine how, when, why, and with what effects this particular understanding of postcolonial nationhood emerged is my aim in this chapter. What kinds of institutional practices and political rationalities were associated with such an imagination of the lacking and needy nation? Why was nation building presented as an arduous, uncertain, and incomplete process? Finally, what are the convergences and divergences between the current emphasis of a shining and modern India and the earlier constitution of a modernizing India, between, respectively, the discourses and practices of fulfilled promises and unmet needs?

In the first section I discuss the origins of the postcolonial imagination of India as a "needy nation." I trace its emergence to processes that were unique to the Indian experience of colonialism, nationalism, and decolonization, and to the ideologies and institutional structures of development that dominated the postwar conjuncture. In the next section I turn to the "need for science"—the most common expression of postcolonial needs discourse in Nehruvian India—and the ways in which it enabled the project of nation-state formation.[3] The discourse of scientific needs was not a seamless formation. The two variants of the "need for scientific expertise" and the "need for scientific temper" often contradicted each other and gave rise to competing understandings of the relation between state, nation, and science. In highlighting these contradictions, I draw attention here to the fissured constitution of the Nehruvian nation-state and its dual commitment to state sovereignty and national sovereignty—the investment of sovereign authority in the state as well as in the people/nation. As I will demonstrate, it is through the interplay of these contending projects that the link between nation and state was elaborated and consolidated, and India was defined in terms of its constitutive problems, unmet needs, and inherent deficiencies.

Locating Needs Discourse: Colonialism, Nationalism, and Development

Like other aspects of the postcolonial nation-state project, the needs discourse of the Nehruvian state had extranational and colonial origins. The conception of India in terms of its essential lack, and the broader ideology of development that shaped this conception, were not new inventions of the postcolonial state. At one level, this transposed within the domestic arena the discourses, practices, and ideas about national development that were globally hegemonic at the particular historical conjuncture of the mid-twentieth century, the moment of Indian independence. India was but one of the many newly sovereign nation-states that had committed themselves actively to a developmental model of rapid economic growth through state intervention, receiving both material and normative support from the new ensemble of international institutions that had emerged in the aftermath of World War II.[4] This endorsement of state-led development also entailed the acceptance of a global teleology, or the idea that all nation-states can be lined up along a continuum of more or less evolved in terms of economy, society, politics, and culture, and that it is possible to move from one rung in the ladder of development to the next through the judicious application of an appropriate mix of policies.

The postwar emergence of new international institutions and norms[5]—linked to transformations in the interstate system, the growing prominence of Keynesian economic ideas, and the global reorganization of capital[6]—is undoubtedly important in explaining this phenomenon of "development hegemony" on a global scale.[7] However, to view development as an idea that emerged "fully formed from the forehead of Truman"[8]—the commonly held view that the idea of development originated with the Marshall Plan for the postwar reconstruction of Europe—is to overlook the considerable historical valence of this concept and its intimate relationship to colonial power. As Dipesh Chakrabarty, David Ludden, and Partha Chatterjee among others have pointed out, the discourse of development in postcolonial India drew upon colonial registers of historicist thought and their attendant dichotomies of civilization and backwardness.[9] Through the operations of the "rule of colonial difference,"[10] and its elaboration of a hierarchical distance between the civilized colonial self and the primitive, to-be-civilized colonial other, colonial historicist reasoning had, from the nineteenth century onward (and possibly earlier as well),[11] placed India and Indians in a "waiting room" outside the progressive march of history.

At times, the historicist injunction took the form of a definitive "not ever" or "never," thereby denying the very existence of India as a substantive national community.[12] As the colonial administrator John Strachey famously observed at the turn of the twentieth century: "This is the first and most essential thing to learn about India, that there is not, and never was an India, or even any country of India, possessing, according to European ideas, any sort of unity, physical, political, social, and religious, no people of India, of which we hear so much."[13] On other occasions, however, the absolute denial of the "never" was tempered by the civilizing imperatives of colonial rule and by the quest to improve and reform the lot of Indians through a flurry of legal, economic, political, and administrative interventions. Thus it was not ever, but some day; which also meant not now, "not yet," and not without the guidance and protection of the colonial state.[14]

The colonial commitment to change was not absolute. Failure was a preordained outcome of all civilizing projects. In upholding the principle of state certitude, or the impossibility of wrong outcomes stemming from the actions of the state, these self-fulfilling failures were linked to deficiencies in Indian character rather than to the constitutive flaws of the colonial reform project itself. Other features of the colonial development regime were the separation that it effected between society and economy so that the economy was produced as an objectlike realm for progressive state intervention,[15] along with the use of statistics and the "logic of number" to classify, enumerate, quantify, and otherwise configure India as a mappable "empirical terrain."[16] The deployment of techniques and policy instruments associated with the "new apparatus of [empiricist] cognition"[17] shored up the authority of centralized state power and constituted the state as the ultimate and sole agent of progress.

Nationalist efforts played their own part in advancing the "transition narrative" and the statist logic of the colonial development regime even as they mounted a critique of colonial policy.[18] For the most part, anticolonial nationalism was premised on a demand for a different kind of state that would be able to fulfill the promise of progress rather than on a rejection of state-led developmentalism or of the notion of development itself.[19] For Indian nationalists, Dipesh Chakrabarty notes, "British rule [was seen as] a necessary period of tutelage that Indians had to undergo in order to prepare precisely for what the British denied but extolled as the end of all history: citizenship and the nation state."[20]

The necessity of a state was upheld in both political and economic arenas. In the political domain the Indian National Congress, the Muslim League, and other organizations strove to establish the capacity of Indians for self-government. The economic program developed by the Indian National Congress from the 1920s onward "promised that its state would do everything that the British were doing, but do it better and do it more."[21] By the end of the 1930s the Indian National Congress' proposal for a system of economic planning after Indian independence gave formal structure and coherence to the idea of state-led economic development. For the National Planning Committee convened by the Congress, a representative and indigenous national state would replace a nonrepresentative and foreign colonial state as the harbinger of development and change. The idea of planning that the National Planning Committee settled upon in the course of its deliberations between 1938 and 1940 was that of planning as an "exercise in state policy" to be undertaken by a state-constituted body of "neutral" or disinterested experts. Even before independence the project of planning, according to Partha Chatterjee, "had emerged as a crucial institutional modality by which the state would determine the material allocation of productive resources within the nation: a modality of power constituted outside the immediate political process itself."[22]

As the possibility of independence drew nearer, and in marked contrast to the earlier nationalist discourses about the sanctity of the "inner domain" of national culture and the need for its insulation from state intervention,[23] the progressive agency of a national state was authorized not just in the context of economic development but in the arena of cultural reform as well. A year before the official transfer of power, the National Cultural Trust would chart a cultural policy for the "new India" in which the state's role in reforming, preserving, and promoting an appropriate national culture would be as salient as its role as the "engine" of capitalist growth and economic development.

The discourses of development and progress in postcolonial India thus echoed earlier colonial and nationalist themes, both in regard to the authorization of the state as the agent of transformation and the accompanying characterization of the Indian people/nation in terms of lack or inadequacies, backwardness, and needs. But there was at least one significant difference in postcolonial discourses of development that reflected the unique conjuncture of decolonization, or the fact that developmentalism and historicist reasoning after 1947 were conjoined with discourses and practices of national sovereignty and democracy. What resulted after independence may best be described as a practice of self-placement in history's waiting room;

the saying of "not yet" to ourselves. In postcolonial India, it was neither the colonial construction of the Indian people as the source of backwardness nor the opposing nationalist contention that backwardness instead stemmed from the colonial state that prevailed. Instead, the needs discourse of this period offered a joint indictment of both state as well as people for the present failures of India, and following from this, a joint authorization of both as the agents of progress and development.

Toward this end, visions of the arduous, incomplete, and perilous project of nation-building were elaborated in the five-year plans produced by the Planning Commission after independence, the apex authority entrusted with the responsibility of formulating and overseeing the project of planned development; in the policy discourses of state agencies engaged in furthering different aspects of the developmental project, from science and youth policies to policies on culture and social welfare; and in the innumerable public addresses delivered by a wide variety of state representatives on exemplary occasions such as days of national commemoration or inaugural ceremonies for laboratories, dams, townships, and factories. The main emphasis of the developmental projects was on the unmet needs and present inadequacies of India and Indians. Poverty, illiteracy, technological stagnation, undisciplined youth, chaotic cities, superstitious villagers, self-interested politicians—all of these were upheld as various signs of Indian deficiencies that required the tutelary interventions of the developmental state.

In this manner, postcolonial development discourse remapped the civilization-backwardness dichotomy of colonial historicism within national space. The "cross of 'inadequacy' " was now born by different fragments of the nation.[24] Thus while "every single Indian is a problem," as Nehru observed to his European audience, certain kinds of Indians were especially problematic: "superstitious" peasants; "indisciplined" youth, and even "unscientific" scientists who were unable to apply their professional training in the conduct of their daily lives.[25]

But the themes of national backwardness and lack and the corresponding authorization of state intervention did not exhaust the developmentalist imagination. The theme of popular participation was of equal importance, or the fact that the legitimization of state-led development in the context of political democracy entailed an emphasis on the consensual, voluntary, and enthusiastic participation of "the people." This in turn led to a very different representation of the state, not simply as a problem solver, but as a subject of needs itself.

Although this has been overlooked in much of the available literature on the developmentalist discourses and practices of the Nehruvian state, the state's "need of assistance" and the call for people to "help the state" were among its most persistent themes, as integral to the representational repertoires of nation-building as was the figure of the backward and needy people/nation. In marked contrast to the premises of state certitude that characterized the colonial development regime, postcolonial developmentalism elaborated visions of state failure and state inadequacy, and presented the task of nation building as perilous, uncertain, and above all incomplete without the willing partnership and active participation of the people.

In sum, what was distinctive about the representational practices and needs discourses of postcolonial development and nation building was not so much their negative constitution of the nation in terms of its deficiencies or the paradox of securing the nation through an insistence on its nonexistence. Such a "performative" expression of nationalism, wherein national becoming rather than national being receives emphasis, is a constitutive feature of nationalist thought and practice across the world.[26] Instead, the mark of distinction was the attribution of lack to the state as well: the fact that the charge of state failure was a state-produced discourse.

Locating Needs Discourse: The Dilemmas of Decolonization

The production of both the state and the people/nation as figures of need, and the related paradox of state-generated discourses of state failure, reflect the specific historical and political conjuncture of postcolonial nation-state formation and its often-contradictory dilemmas and imperatives. Some of these were not unique to India but reflected instead the broader dynamics of decolonization that a wide range of polities across Asia and Africa grappled with in different ways during the period of imperial retreat that followed in the wake of World War II.[27]

In addition to these general dilemmas of decolonization, the project of nation-state formation in India was structured by a unique set of exigencies that reflected the particular historical experiences of colonialism and nationalism in the South Asian subcontinent, as well as the specific mode of transition from colonial rule that India had experienced. First was the particular conjuncture of the "revolution-restoration" or the "passive revolutionary" nature of India's postcolonial transition. According to the political theorist Sudipta Kaviraj, the mobilizations of anticolonial nationalism and the establishment of a sovereign nation-state in India followed the trajectory of a Gramscian "passive revolution," with competing class claims welded together in an unwieldy and often unstable alliance between agrarian, industrial, and bureaucratic sections of the bourgeoisie.[28] In this context, the transformative impulses of development and modernization were inevitably tempered. In some instances, proposals for change were abandoned altogether, as in the case of the ultimate failure to undertake substantive land reform legislations.[29] In other instances they were rolled back, as in the case of the effort to reform Hindu personal law. In the face of concerted opposition by Hindu conservatives both within and outside the legislature, the omnibus legislation was eventually passed in a piecemeal fashion minus several of its original clauses that had called for radical changes.[30]

The representational practices of development and modernization in India—the ways in which the state elites explained, described, and justified these processes to national audiences—were also modulated by a similar tempering effect. As described later in this chapter, the imaginary of development would be simultaneously confident and diffident. Reflecting the unique conjuncture of India's passive revolution, state representations of developmentalist projects would emphasize their sweeping ambition and unstoppable logic and also their partial, gradual, and tentative nature.

Further, the "cartographic anxiety"[31] and "territorial ambiguity"[32] that stemmed from the peculiarities of the partition of British India made the consolidation of sovereign state authority an especially protracted process. The unsettled status of the external borders of the Indian nation-state militated against an unambiguous pronouncement of the state's territorial reach. Within the geopolitical confines of India as well, sovereignty was constituted through a series of negotiations, as the central state had to settle the question of accession with each of the many princely states that had enjoyed (nominal) sovereignty during the colonial period.[33] State sovereignty in this context required not just establishing institutional control over a given territory but also establishing the givenness and the meaning of territory itself. This led to a heightened preoccupation with territoriality, as manifested in the anxiety about the vulnerability of India's borders that has repeatedly surfaced in political discourse over the past fifty years. At the same time, however, there also emerged a parallel strategy of disregarding the territorial predicament altogether. India was reimagined as a space constituted not by land and borders but by the abstract grid of national development.

Finally, the question of national identity posed a substantial dilemma. What was the basis on which Indian unity could be proclaimed, given the profusion of mobilized cultural, linguistic, religious, and ethnic groups in India and the absence of a common colonial enemy against which a

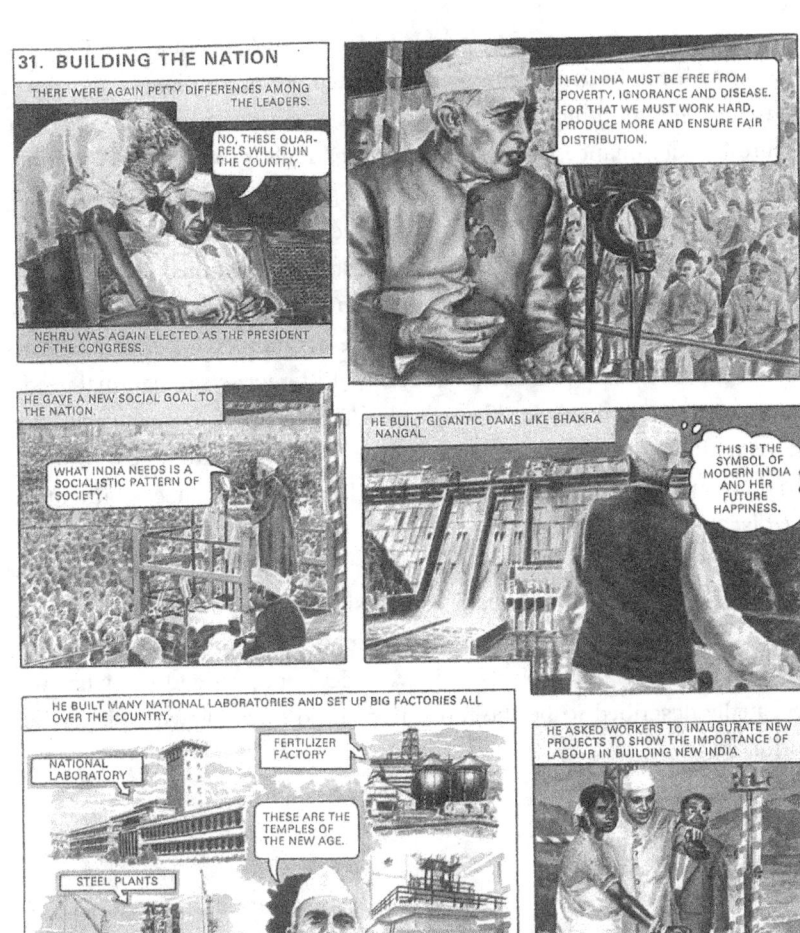

Building the Nation, 1971. From *Chacha Nehru*, a comic book produced by the Publications Division, Government of India.

common front of opposition could be forged? What could serve as the common glue of Indian identity, when every choice of a national language or national religion could be construed in partisan terms as an attempt to secure the dominance of a particular subnational group? Such questions drew attention to the difficulties of imagining the national community along familiar axes of ethnicity, religion, language, race, or even territory, and to the fact that the unity of India and the substance of national identity would have to be proclaimed in and through other registers of belonging. The distinctive forms of a "stated nation," where nationhood is defined in terms of how the state fulfills—and fails to fulfill—different sets of national needs, would play a central role in this endeavor. The homogeneous configuration of the nation-state as a space peopled by identical, substitutable individuals would be enabled in the Indian context by the discourse of needs rather than the discourse of rights or of cultural commonalities.

What exactly did this imagination of the "needy nation" entail? To answer this question, I turn to a specific expression of needs discourse in postcolonial India—namely, the "need for science" and the complex of policies, institutions, and projects that were developed to address what was repeatedly described to be the most acute need of the newly independent nation-state.

Needing Science

The Nehruvian state's enthusiastic embrace of science dominated the postcolonial political and cultural field.[34] The identity of the new India was defined in terms of the privileged place that it accorded to science and technology in all arenas of life. For instance, techno-scientific artifacts such as dams, steel plants, and atomic reactors were hailed as the icons of the new nation-state. Policy debates on the many problems and needs that India faced in economic, educational, social, and cultural arenas emphasized their solution through the application of the objective methodologies and neutral rationalities of science. The years after independence also saw a flurry of initiatives for the development of scientific and technological education. The encouragement of science education in schools and universities, the establishment of research institutes dedicated to specific areas of scientific and technological research, and the creation of state-funded elite institutions of scientific and technological education such as the Indian Institutes of Technology were important and much-publicized priorities for the central state. In all of these cases, the lack of science was defined as the primary national problem, and the "need for science" the most urgent and most palpable national need.

Like the colonial provenances of the "development regime"[35] discussed in the preceding section, the postcolonial state's conception of the national need for science can also be traced to the ideologies, practices, and institutional innovations undertaken by colonial state elites. In addition, nationalist and nonstate actors also had a significant role to play in ensuring the domination of science.[36] The distinctive aspect of the colonial state-scientific field related to the kind of state power that it constituted and authorized. As Gyan Prakash has observed in his discussion of colonial science in India, the "democratic deficit" obtaining under colonialism required the state-scientific episteme to expose rather than conceal the coercive abilities of state power.[37] In other words, the colonial state's scientific vision was linked to coercive rather than hegemonic techniques and rationalities of rule.

The postcolonial state's vision of science took a somewhat different form, although there were significant continuities in scientific institutions, personnel, and policy formations before and after 1947. The institutions, practices, and knowledge formations of official science after independence reflected the different imperatives of national rather than colonial forms and strategies of rule. Now the grammars of state science were inflected by new idioms of democratic legitimization and national representation. Instead of solely enabling the exhibition of the state's ability to know and command its subject population, science was now also the site and means for staging unified national consent to, and willing acceptance of, the state's decisions and actions. Thus, while the link between the development and application of science and the welfare of the "native population" had been established in the scientific discourses of the colonial state,[38] the postcolonial description of this link emphasized its dialogic and consensual nature. The official science policy declarations presented the scientific enterprises of the postcolonial state not as unsolicited initiatives derived from the state's superior knowledge of its population, but instead as "responses" to national needs and as evidence of the new state's commitment to "its own" population.[39]

But what did it mean to need science? Who was the subject of this need, and how was it expressed? By whom, and how, could this need be fulfilled? At one level to define India and Indians in terms of a need for science was to insert India within world historical time and to claim world historical agency for the state as the fulfiller of scientific needs. In this rendition, the specificity of Indian needs received less attention than did the universal nature of the "problems" that India faced. In the rhetoric of Nehruvian India, science was described as a need that manifested itself with equal urgency in new and old, Western and non-Western, and developed and underdeveloped nations. The discourse of scientific needs was harnessed to a wider project of claiming international recognition and commensurability for the nation-state that can be termed, pace Dipesh Chakrabarty, the project of "universalizing India."[40]

For instance, in the context of the legislative discussions on the Atomic Energy Bill in 1948, Nehru's argument for why the state should invest considerable resources in atomic energy research and development activities drew upon civilizational rather than national registers. For Nehru, the development of atomic energy in India was an unavoidable necessity. He argued that it was impossible for India to ignore the call of science, conceptualized here as a universal *geist* that affected all of humankind in the same way and at the same time. Thus while some delegates elaborated visions of an "Indian science" by turning to Hindu religious texts for a prefiguration of the atom, Itty Abraham points out that "the discursive register . . . shifted, in Nehru, to a displacement of the subject 'India' to an abstract humanist understanding of world history . . . India [was] mapped on a world scale."[41] In sum, in this version of the official scientific imagination, the state's commitment to science was presented in world historical terms. The subject of the needs that the Indian state was fulfilling through its development of atomic energy was not circumscribed by bloodlines, history, or territory, but instead was grandly described to be all of humankind itself.

At another level however, the need for science was mapped onto specifically national subjects. Although science was seen to be a universal need, the need for science was described to be especially acute in India. As Nehru noted, "Ours is an urgent way, how we can deal with urgent problems in so far as they affect hundreds of millions of our people. It is they who count and nobody else counts in the ultimate analysis."[42] The imagination of India as a nation defined by its needs and deficiencies was extensive and all-inclusive. In Nehru's words, there were "three hundred and fifty million problems"—a proclamation that explicitly erased any distinctions on grounds of religion, ethnicity, language, or class. Within this undifferentiated vision of the uniformly needy nation, some problems and needs stood out as exemplary, namely, those experienced by "rural India": "The real problems of India are not in cities but in villages. Every politician, every industrialist, who does not have in his eyes the picture of the village has not understood India. Every person in India, who seeks real education, must have this picture of the Indian village before him."[43]

In the Nehruvian national imagination the Indian village had two kinds of problems, both described in abstract and placeless terms: the lack of "basic essentials of life" and the persistence of "narrow mindedness" or "resistance to change."[44] Like the very notion of village India itself, these problems were conceptualized in abstract and general terms, emptied of human agency and disconnected from specific places and times. Needs discourse translated all expressions of popular discontent and incidents of social and individual unrest into one or the other of these two overarching problems, which were constituted as first-order needs, or those from which all others derived. Invoked repeatedly on a wide variety of occasions, ranging from the inauguration of industrial research laboratories and parliamentary discussions on the Scientific Policy Resolution to commencement addresses at institutes for technical education and meetings of science societies, the primary and urgent nature of these needs formed the ground on which official science and technology policy sought legitimization.

While science was prescribed as the solution to India's problems and needs, there were varied understandings of what the scientific solution entailed. Under the sign of science, the new nation-state committed itself to two distinct projects: the development of "scientific expertise" and the development of "scientific temper." As I demonstrate below, each of these drew upon and reproduced a different normative ideal of science and authorized a different set of relations between science, the state, and the nation. Thus the call for scientific experts was premised on a vision of the state as the authoritative problem solver of the needy nation. The call for scientific temper advanced a different understanding—that of how the people/nation could help the limited and inadequate state. The coexistence of these contending perspectives draws attention to the fissured constitution of the official national imagination and the ways in which narratives of failure as well as those of success—celebrations as well as denunciations of state agency and scientific rationality—enable the formation and consolidation of the nation-state.[45]

A Few Good Men: The Need for Scientific Expertise

In order for science to be instrumentalized in the service of national needs and problems, the development of the instrument itself was seen to be a priority. To this end, a series of specialized institutes for scientific research and training were established shortly after independence with the express purpose of developing India's "scientific expertise" and "scientific manpower." The scientific expertise projects addressed the need for "world class" scientists who would undertake pioneering research and advise the state on its developmental projects. The scientific manpower projects addressed the equally pressing requirement of producing a large number of technically trained and qualified individuals who would actually implement development plans by providing their crucial labor power as doctors, nurses, laboratory technicians, or engineers.

The institutional solutions devised to meet these needs included organizations devoted to the pursuit of postgraduate scientific and technological research such as the Indian Institute of Science (IIS) in Bangalore; centers for applied research such as the chain of industrial research laboratories established by the Centre for Scientific and Industrial Research; and degree and diploma-granting educational institutes that imparted techno-scientific training such as the Indian Institutes of Technology or the Indian Institutes of Management. Although expressed in different forms, a common goal of securing the uniqueness of science and technology and asserting the singularity of the scientific expert informed all of these initiatives.

For instance, the theme that dominated the deliberations of the committee convened by the Ministry of Education in 1948 to review the work of the Indian Institute of Science and chart its future course was that of the epistemological or disciplinary-methodological distinctiveness of science—that is, science as a particular object and method of study with rules, conventions, and expectations that differed substantially from those governing other fields of academic inquiry, such as the humanities. In this rendition, science was constituted as a singular episteme, and the successful production of scientific expertise was contingent on maintaining this epistemological and methodological distinctiveness and ensuring that the specificity of science was not "diluted" by adding departments of humanities to the IIS. For the IIS committee, the ideal scientist was exclusively defined by his commitment to the specialized pursuit of techno-scientific knowledge alone: while "an interest in literary, historical and art subjects . . . [could] develop the breadth of view and the general culture of students," it was felt that "a full study of the subject [was] not however, in conformity with the character of the Institute."[46]

In the review committee report, the singularity of science was translated into the singularity of scientists, whose difference from the rest of the population had to be secured. For the IIS review committee, the urgency of India's need for scientific manpower was of note. But it was essential that efforts to increase the quantity of scientists and technologists in India did not lose sight of considerations of their quality. By repeatedly defining scientific expertise in terms of the work carried out by a "few men of high calibre,"[47] the IIS review committee emphasized the constitutive link between the excellence or the "calibre" of work and the selectivity of the scientific community. In their view, the success of the IIS rested on its ability to create and maintain scientific experts as a breed apart. This required the judicious investment of resources in "the development of fewer establishments for advanced training and research," since a more expansive approach would mean that "the general level of technical education and research would be lowered."[48]

Given that the IIS review committee was composed entirely of professional scientists, its emphasis on maintaining the exclusivity of the scientific community was not surprising. But this viewpoint was not restricted to the community of scientists alone. For instance, the quandary of how to juggle the contradictory requirements of increasing scientific manpower and also scientific expertise were expressed by Nehru more than a decade after the IIS review was concluded: "There can be no doubt that science and the scientist will grow in India, grow in numbers, I hope grow in quality. Numbers certainly; already, I have no idea how many people there are in India who can be termed as scientists. The figure must be fairly large . . . They will go on growing. Now, how are you to maintain real quality? . . . I am all for democracy, but democracy normally means mediocrity too. It is a well-known thing you put up with it in a democracy because, well, it is better to have democracy than having something worse. But the fact is that numbers lead to mediocrity specially in the matter of science etc."[49]

The institution-building efforts that were undertaken solely with the manpower mandate in mind—the objective of expanding rather than restricting access to techno-scientific research and education—also emphasized the exclusivity of the scientist and of science. Despite the dissenting opinions of scientists such as Saha who argued for a closer alignment between scientific and technological research and education and the existing network of national universities,[50] these institutes were established outside the university system as separate entities, and as such the pursuit of science and technology was in this way quite literally set apart from other educational endeavors. The institutional infrastructure of higher education in techno-scientific fields such as engineering was developed as a parallel formation with separate budgetary allocations, entrance examinations, fee structures, and curricular frameworks.[51]

Apart from the provision of a separate institutional space, and the careful delimitation of the techno-scientific community through the establishment of stringent entrance requirements that culled excellence from mediocrity, the production of scientific expertise was seen to require the insulation of science from the encroachments of politics, commerce, and bureaucracy. The separation of science from politics was not simply a discursive move but one that took concrete institutional form. The formulation of scientific and technological policy was monopolized by a small group of handpicked scientific advisors who worked closely with Nehru. The aura of scientific expertise meant that extensive parliamentary debates on scientific and technological policy were relatively rare occurrences. As Nirmal Haritash and B. M. Gupta have shown in their survey of parliamentary debates over the past five decades, the number of times that parliamentary representatives have asked questions and have sought additional information and clarification on science and technology policies is extremely low, although there have been vigorous discussions and debates on other issues during the same period.[52]

If the hesitation of lay representatives to enter the abstruse domain of scientific discussions was one way in which science and technology were insulated from the political arena, the conjunction of science and security in arenas such as atomic energy and space research was another. In the name of national security, nuclear science was enshrouded in a cloak of "official secrecy" and kept at far remove from the scrutiny of elected representatives.[53]

The institutional separation of science and politics was transposed to the individual level as well. The ideal scientist, like the ideal planner and others associated with the development regime, was envisioned as someone disconnected from the rough and tumble of the political process.[54] Real scientists did not engage in politics, a category that encompassed a wide range of practices. Criticisms of state policy by scientists, the formation of trade unions within industrial research laboratories, and student agitations in scientific and technological institutes of higher education were variously cited as examples of inappropriately political behavior on the part of scientists. When members of the Association of Scientific Workers—a consortium formed by the employees of state scientific organizations—issued a memorandum criticizing the Planning Commission for its failure to consult with scientists in the course of developing the third five-year plan, their identity as scientists was called into question: "Mr. Nehru chided the Association for its 'contradictory approaches' in some of its draft resolutions and said, 'I am not tremendously impressed by them. In fact, I am distressed by some of them. It seems to me that you are forgetting your science.' . . . Mr. Nehru commented that the resolutions did not show any scientific approach. On the contrary, 'It is an expression of your various contradictory approaches, an angry approach. At any rate, it is not a scientific approach, that is what I am trying to point out.'"[55]

At a certain level, the very existence of an association of scientific workers was a source of concern. Two years prior to expressing his overt disapproval of its "contradictory approaches," Nehru had cautioned the association of the need to ensure that their organizing activities did not take place "at the cost of others."[56] The association was asked to bear in mind the essential difference between science and industry, and to consequently resist from organizing scientific workers along trade union lines. The argument was that they would be better placed if they devoted their energies to the pursuit of science, since "thus only they can advance themselves. When scientific expansion takes place in India, there will be more opportunities for work and more jobs."[57] Similar concerns were voiced when the employees of the industrial research laboratories of the Council of Scientific and Industrial Research began to act more like workers and less like scientists by forming a trade union, thereby undermining the vision of the industrial research laboratory as a distinctive third space that enabled connections to be forged between science and industry even as the separation between these two domains was preserved.[58]

If the purpose of science was to fulfill the unmet needs of the nation, then the ideal scientist as the embodied agent of science had to rise above all considerations of individual gain and focus on the bigger task of serving national needs instead of on petty concerns about career prospects and conditions of employment. In a turn of phrase that illuminated the considerable hierarchies of power inscribed by the call to move beyond selfish individualism, the ideal scientist was described as one who devoted himself to what, in Nehru's words, "we in India consider the Brahminic spirit of service."[59] In the terms of official nationalist discourse, what India needed was not "young men who want[ed] jobs," but those who would "serve India."[60]

The metaphor of the scientist as Brahmin was multivalent. It conveyed both the ability of an elite caste to disengage from the quotidian and material concerns that preoccupied those less privileged, and the unique qualities of creative thought that emanated from the "head" of the social body.[61] The insulation of the scientist from politics and commerce had enabled the first form of transcendence from the everyday. The second move of creative transcendence required another kind of insulation—one that would place the scientist at considerable remove from the deadening effects of bureaucracy.

Despite the close relationship between the political elite and the prominent scientists that actually obtained in the Nehruvian period, the autonomy and separation of scientists from the government was central to the normative vision of scientific expertise. The creative faculties of scientific experts were repeatedly contrasted with the "unimaginative" labors of bureaucracy, and scientists were urged to maintain a distance from institutions of governance. Moreover, in what amounts to a paradox these criticisms of government and bureaucracy were generated by the state itself; the irrelevance of paperwork documented in copious paper trails.

For instance, in presiding over the foundation stone laying ceremony for the Electrical Communication and Engineering Department at the Indian Institute of Science in 1948 in his capacity as the head of government, Nehru noted that "[I am] not sorry that scientists did not reach ministerial office because ministerial office has a mentally corrupting influence. It slightly coarsened the mind. It prevented a person from doing any kind of creative work. In the democratic structure of society, one had to spread oneself out so much and please so many kinds of people that one could not do any solid thinking or any kind of work. This was a problem democracy had to resolve. I am entirely opposed to any serious minded person coming and working in Delhi."[62]

The description of the capital city as a stultifying, "coarsening" environment that impeded the "creative work" of science and the related indictment of administrative labors as meaningless and superfluous were echoed by Nehru in other contexts as well: "I find that here in this city of New Delhi, one could do with a good deal of more imaginative approach but it is a man who sits in an office who becomes static and a dead-weight. And that is why, if I may make a personal confession, I want to run away from New Delhi from time to time, rushing about from place to place. I want to get out of this deadly static atmosphere of this place which cannot think, which forgets that there are people, that there are human beings in India, which thinks in terms of paper and files and ink and all that, which thinks even in terms of figures, but figures are not human beings; figures are only hints or some suggestions as to what human beings are."[63] Reflecting this call to separate science from the static world of "paper and files and ink" that dominated life in the capital city, scientific institutions and artifacts were spread out across national territory. Located in unknown and unfamiliar "elsewheres" they enabled the reimagination of national space along new lines and provided scientific expertise with yet another mark of distinction: a cartography of its own. Each new institute and techno-scientific "fetish"[64] that was built by the Nehruvian state introduced a new name into the existing litany of national geography. Jeolagoda, Sindri, Bhakra Nangal, and Bhilai were sites whose symbolic significance derived not from historical, religious, or cultural registers, but from the abstract grid of the developmentalist imagination.

Like the scientific expert who would inhabit these spaces, the new nation-statist "heterotopias" were presented as spaces unmarked by particularist identities and interests.[65] With this, the establishment of a fuel research institute in Dhanbad could be announced as the fulfillment of the needs of people located several hundred miles away, or the laying of the foundation stone of the new food research institute in Mysore could be a "response" to the drought experienced by residents of Bihar. In this way, the discourses and practices of scientific expertise lent themselves to the central tasks of the nation-state formation project, namely, the constitution of a new subject whose "true" needs and interests were formed and expressed at a national level, and the production of an undifferentiated, state-centered, imagination of India.

Limits of Expertise: The Need for Scientific Temper

In the previous section I explored how the national need for science was addressed through the development of scientific expertise. The expectation was that the scientific expert—the exemplary new Indian man—would solve the pressing national problem of the "lack of basic essentials" by devoting his energies to the development of new technologies. The understanding of science that informed these projects was a fetishized one of science as a visible and distinctive artifact—whether a research institute, a dam, an atomic reactor, a variety of high-yielding grain, or a "made-in-India" tractor. The success of the scientific experts was seen to rest on the insulation of science from politics, commerce, bureaucracy, and local-parochial concerns.

But this still left another problem unaccounted for—namely, the "narrow mindedness" or the "resistance to change" on the part of the Indian masses. The development of a "scientific temper" was proposed as a solution. Nehru's emphasis on the need for scientific temper predated independence. Writing in *Discovery of India* (1946) on the relationship between religion, philosophy, and science, he defined scientific temper as "the search for truth and new knowledge, the refusal to accept anything without testing and trial, the capacity to change previous conclusions in the face of new evidence, the reliance on observed fact and not on pre-conceived theory, the hard discipline of the mind . . . necessary not merely for the application of science but for life itself and the solution of its many problems . . . The scientific approach and temper are, or should be, a way of life, a process of thinking, a method of acting and associating with our fellow-men."[66] If the application of science was the chief concern of scientific experts, with the field of expertise constituted around the notion of science as an instrument, then the project of scientific temper called for the recognition of the limits of such an understanding of science. Science qua temper was characterized by several distinct attributes, all of which were seen to be conspicuously absent from the circumscribed institutional world of experts and their preoccupations with scientific research and application. Discussions of scientific temper were invariably framed in oppositional terms, as an extension, supplement, or otherwise a corrective to the deficiencies of expertise.

First, as the term itself indicates, the temper of science referred to a mentality or an outlook rather than an artifact or a specialized body of knowledge. It was "not the devoted study of a particular subject, but the devoted search for truth."[67] This was described as a broad-based, ecumenical search—the temper of science addressed itself to universalist concerns about "values of life," rather than to narrow and specialized questions of scientific research and application. The pursuit of scientific temper could reconcile the mutually exclusive domains of "spirituality" and science: the advancement of science qua temper would enable the advancement of "the higher things of life."[68] As Nehru stated in 1959 on the occasion of the golden jubilee celebrations of the Indian Institute of Science:

> There is something in life, let us say, like goodness, like truth, something like beauty . . . which presumably are very important in life. And when we put it in this way, how far can science be allied, without destroying its basis, to certain fundamental values in life? If it is not concerned with life as such—if it is independent of these values—then it may make the greatest advance there divorced from those values, but presumably the ultimate result will not be good.
>
> On the other hand, we cannot merely talk of these values in life without science coming into the picture. These are difficult problems and certainly a little beyond my depth. But I do not myself see any essential incompatibility between the temper of science, the spirit of science, the approach of science, and these higher values—provided that even in the search for these higher values the temper of science is maintained.[69]

The second distinctive feature related to the intended scope or reach of scientific temper. Unlike the rarefied and insulated domain of scientific expertise, the project of scientific temper was a call for the diffusion of "science mindedness" throughout the population. The growth of scientific temper was thus measured not by an increase in the number of research institutes and in the levels of scientific manpower within the nation (the number of trained scientists and technical workers), but by the extent to which ordinary people were "apply[ing] the methods of science to all of life's problems"—by their demonstrated ability to take a "dispassionate" and "objective" stand on individual and social problems;[70] by their patience and their refusal to indulge in unconstructive acts of criticism or what Nehru dismissively described as the propensity to "froth and foam";[71] and above all else, by their active commitment to agendas of change and to a vision of a future unburdened by the dead weight of custom and superstition.

Defined by these ideal attributes, scientific temper was seen to elude scientists and nonscientists alike. In Nehru's opinion, the fact that scientists excelled in research skills and developed utilitarian techno-scientific applications had no bearing on their ability to apply the scientific method in their daily lives. The theme of the "unscientific scientist" repeatedly surfaced in his addresses to scientific audiences, illustrated through examples of how scientific experts continued to lead private lives marked by superstition, prejudice, and atavistic customs.

The contradictions between the ideals of scientific expertise and scientific temper were also expressed during ceremonial occasions such as the inauguration of industrial research laboratories. If foundation-stone laying and ribbon-cutting ceremonies for techno-scientific projects were the definitive rituals of Nehruvian India, both in terms of their frequency of occurrence and the widespread media coverage that they received as events of national importance, then the contending ideals of science that were reproduced at each of these ceremonial moments was integral to the ritual repertoire. In the following section I examine in closer detail the contradictory constitution of postcolonial scientific rites and the ways in which the state-centered understanding of nationhood was reproduced through performances of the "clash of sciences," or the contest between the normative goals of scientific expertise and scientific temper.

Ceremonial Contradictions: Expertise, Temper, and the Rituals of Scientific Inaugurations

Under the terms of a scheme developed by the Council of Scientific and Industrial Research (CSIR) and its director S. S. Bhatnagar,[72] in the first two decades after independence several research laboratories were set up in

Jawaharlal Nehru at the foundation-stone laying ceremony of the Kosi barrage in Hanumanagar, April 30, 1959 (Courtesy of the Nehru Memorial Museum and Library, New Delhi)

locations across the nation, each specializing in a different field of industrial research. Together, the laboratories constituted a "chain" that remapped national space along techno-scientific and developmental lines. Among those heralded as the new centers of national devotion, or the sacred pilgrimage sites of the postcolony, were the National Chemical Laboratory in Pune, the National Physical Laboratory in Delhi, the Central Fuel Research Institute in Dhanbad, the Central Glass and Ceramics Research Institute in Calcutta, the Central Food Technological Research Institute in Mysore, the Central Electrochemical Research Institute in Karaikudi, and the Central Building Research Institute in Roorkee.[73]

Given their national-symbolic significance, is not surprising that the inauguration of each new laboratory was a carefully choreographed event, graced by political dignitaries and scientists of national and international renown. The laying of the foundation stone of the National Physical Laboratory in New Delhi in June 1947 was witnessed by Patrick Blackett and other eminent scientists who were in the city to attend the meeting of the Indian Science Congress.[74] In January 1950, Desmond Bernal, Irene Curie-Joliot, and Robert Robinson, the president of the Royal Society (the premier international scientific association) were among those present at the formal opening of the National Chemical Laboratory in the western Indian city of Poona.[75]

Other laboratories were visited by a different array of "chief guests" at each of their two founding moments: the initial stage of laying a foundation

The opening ceremony of the National Physical Laboratory, New Delhi, 1950. (Courtesy of the Nehru Memorial Museum and Library, New Delhi)

stone for the new building and the final stage of the formal inauguration after all the construction work had been completed and the premises were ready for occupancy. The status and rank of these guests varied according to the national-symbolic importance of the particular scientific venture. Thus, the opening of the two pioneer industrial research laboratories, the National Physical Laboratory and the National Chemical Laboratory, attracted more prominent visitors than did the inauguration of the Central Institute of Medicinal and Aromatic Plants in the city of Lucknow in northern India a decade later. Despite these differences, the audiences at each of these inaugural events were comprised of a common mix of national and regional politicians, scientists, students, bureaucrats, reporters, and, finally, representatives of "ordinary Indians": the masons, electricians, and daily wage laborers who had actually constructed the new buildings.[76]

There were significant similarities as well in the practices and procedures that were followed during the inaugural ceremonies. Speakers discussed the national and scientific significance of the particular project being inaugurated and offered more wide-ranging observations about the meaning and future of science and development in India.[77] In some instances, the intimate bond between science and nationhood was represented through visual means, such as the unfurling of the national flag on the roof of the new laboratory;[78] in others, the spoken word constituted this link, as in the case of the address delivered by S. S. Bhatnagar during the inauguration of the National Physical Laboratory. Citing a letter that had been written to him by Gandhi, Bhatnagar likened the work of science and scientists to the "rod and staff" that holds a national flag aloft. While Gandhi had "succeeded in creating a National Flag . . . he had left it to the scientists to create a rod which will hold the flag firmly."[79]

Particular individuals and institutions were then applauded for their role in advancing the nation-building cause. Taking the form of an egalitarian eulogy, these declarations of gratitude and praise traversed a long chain of command all the way from the prime minister to the "bulldozer operators" who had quite literally laid the groundwork for the future of science and technology in India.[80] Finally, the event concluded with the climactic moment of the actual inauguration, when the presiding dignitary would declare the laboratory open.

The inaugurations often took the form of dramatic demonstrations of the magnificent promises of science and technology. For instance, the National Chemical Laboratory was inaugurated "as it should be the case in a chemical laboratory, with a bang."[81] The National Physical Laboratory announced its opening through a similarly impressive technological display. The presiding dignitary, Sardar Vallabhai Patel, a leading figure of the nationalist movement and the home minister of India at the time, was presented with a miniature model of the laboratory. When he cut the ribbon attached to the model, a wireless transmitter was activated and the doors of the laboratory slowly swung open. According to a witness present on the occasion, the spectacular display incarnated the dazzle and wonder of science before the marveling audience; indeed, "Jawaharlal Nehru was so excited that he jumped on to the table to get a better view of the opening doors."[82] Like the prestidigitations of colonial science, postcolonial science drew upon magical registers in the effort to harness popular support and acceptance. Remote-controlled doors and impressive explosions were thus as much a part of the persuasive techniques of official science as were the rational cost-benefit analyses churned out in the dry bureaucratic prose of the five-year plans.

In sum, the inauguration of each laboratory was the site as well as the means for the material representation of the science-state-nation triad that structured social relations in Nehruvian India. The joint presence of state officials and scientists at these events attested to the partnership between science and the state.[83] The acknowledgment of the efforts of elected officials, bureaucrats, and state scientists constituted the state as a multifaceted entity. The figure of the construction worker elaborated a central theme of official nationalism—namely, the active involvement of ordinary people in nation-building projects. If science was staged as a display *for* the nation, it was equally a display *of* popular participation. Both the expert scientist and the nameless worker were authorized as builders of the new scientific nation at these events, although their respective labors were valued in very different ways.

Finally, the inaugural ceremonies were occasions on which the imagination of India as a needy nation was reproduced through texts and performances that showcased both the abilities and the failures of state and science to address the unmet needs of the nation. Thus, on the one hand, inaugurations celebrated the magic of science and the superior abilities of the scientific researchers who would occupy the new laboratory buildings. In speeches, publicity brochures, and newspaper reports, the opening of each new scientific venture was invariably heralded as a sign of national progress toward a modern and prosperous future. The opening of a leather research institute, a ceramics research institute, or an institute for developing more efficient mining technologies were all hailed as significant milestones in the developmental journey of the new nation; that is, as success stories that proved that the state's pursuit of science and technology could indeed reap substantive benefits.

On the other hand, the enormity of India's unmet needs, the uncertainties and hardships of the present, and the exclusion of the masses from the world of scientific expertise were central themes of all inaugurations. Along with the triumphant accounts of scientific successes that were routinely produced on these occasions were the discussions of the limits of institutional science. What was the point of "so many bricks and mortar" in the face of continued ignorance, poverty, and inequality?[84] Didn't the elaborate ambitions of "Big Science" and the penchant for undertaking monumental techno-scientific projects slow down the process of fulfilling national needs?[85] Didn't the call to celebrate the establishment of scientific institutions encourage passive "worship at the altar of science" and transform science into an empty "set of ceremonials and forms . . . a ritual, a religion"?[86] Although hailed as sites where "humanity works for the good of humanity," weren't big dams also places where "thousands and lakhs [a unit of one hundred thousand] of people have worked, have sweated, have shed their blood, have even given their lives?"[87]

What is significant about these interrogations is not so much their content but the fact that the doubts and indictments were offered freely by state elites themselves. In a reflection of the contending political compulsions that structured the postcolonial field—the dual mandate of investing the state as well as the people/nation with sovereign authority that the specific formation of a democratic nation-state required—the discourse of official science deployed vocabularies of praise as well as doubt, questioning the worth of scientific institution building at its very moment of triumph. Moreover, this was not just a stray occurrence but a systematic, even structural feature of the inaugural ceremony. The interrogation of official science was as much a part of the ceremonial status quo as the applause that greeted the cutting of ribbons; the shining visions of national futures was as intrinsic to the inaugural imaginary as the dark images of the troubled present.

Conclusion

Is nationalism a "derivative discourse"? Does the formation of a nation always and necessarily entail a modular transfer of eighteenth- and nineteenth-century Euro-American experiences to other places and times? Raising this question in response to Benedict Anderson's thesis on nations as "imagined communities" that are formed through processes of imitative diffusion, Partha Chatterjee developed an equally influential account of the specificity of nationalist ideologies and practices in the non-Western world.[88] Locating his discussion of Indian nationalism in the specific historical conjuncture of colonial relations, he drew attention to the unique set of political compulsions that structured the anticolonial nationalist movement. In his account, the nation-form in India emerged as a distinctive configuration that was driven not by replication and imitation but instead by the endeavor to differentiate the cultural core of nationhood from preexisting modular templates.

Chatterjee's argument situates nationalism within a historicized field of political and social relations. With this analytical move, the emergence of the nation is no longer seen as a derivative by-product of macro-structural transformations, whether the invention of "print capitalism" identified by Anderson or the more broad-ranging transformation from agrarian to industrial society discussed by Ernest Gellner.[89] Instead, the nation is a politically contingent formation that is shaped by the interplay of particular structures, agents, and practices, and that accordingly assumes different forms in different spatial and temporal contexts. While the transformative logics of modernity, capitalism, and industrialization play an enabling role, it is the mediations of these general processes by localized constellations of social and political relations that determines the actual form and content of nationhood.

Extending this argument to the context of postcolonial Indian nationalism, in this chapter I have located the distinctive imagination of India as a "needy nation," and the attendant discourse and practice of "nation building," within the specific historical conjuncture of the 1950s and the political dilemmas and compulsions of the decolonization project, or the attempt to produce a sovereign nation-state. While efforts to produce and consolidate state and national sovereignty in a host of new nations in the aftermath of World War II drew upon similar sets of developmental ideologies and practices, there were substantive differences as well in the "style and idiom"[90] of the national imagination, and the normative categories of state, nation, and citizen that were produced in each polity. Among the factors that played a role in the production of the particular state-centered national imagination are India's particular historical legacy of British colonialism; the dilemmas of territorial ambiguity that stemmed from the coincidence of independence and partition; the availability of diverse nation-state templates that spanned the political and economic spectrum, from the liberal capitalist democracy of the United States to the democratic socialism of the USSR; and the ideational checks and balances exerted by the moral legacy of Gandhianism on the Nehruvian vision of industrial modernity and planned development.

As noted above, the state-centered national imagination had three distinctive features. First, it fostered a vision of "Indian darkness." The ideologies and institutional practices of nation building insistently drew attention to the perils, problems, and uncertainties that were encountered by the nation-state. Second, it entailed the "defamation of the present."[91] The teleological visions of state-led modernization and development that dominated the political and cultural arenas in postcolonial India, from the moment of independence in 1947 until the late 1980s, deferred the fulfillment of national needs to an ever-receding future horizon, and constituted the present in terms of negativity, difficulty, and lack: a "bed of thorns," to use Azad's words cited at the opening of this chapter, or a unity of "350 million problems," as Nehru would have it.

Finally, it was a contradictory formation that both celebrated and called into question the scientific-developmental endeavors of the state. However, as the example of the contest between scientific temper and scientific expertise has illustrated, the interrogation of the state in the name of national-popular sovereignty did not dismantle the statist coordinates of the national imagination but instead authorized new and different forms of state intervention.[92] In the end, both sets of projects constituted the ideal citizen in suprapolitical terms: the neutral expert scientist insulated from the messiness of the political process; the peasant as a passive beneficiary of scientific and developmental policies, and whose mode of political participation was restricted to "cooperating" and "rendering assistance" to state agencies.

The disavowal of politics is also the central theme of the next chapter, in which I examine the building of the postcolonial nation-state in the most literal sense: the construction of planned townships as the exemplary spaces of the new and modern India. Like the representations of cultural diversity, science, and development explored thus far, the effort to build new urban space would also further, and reflect, normative visions of a national identity beyond politics.

CHAPTER 4

Cities of Hope

Steel Townships and

the Spatial Practices of

the Nation-State

: : :

> A tremendous amount of building is taking place in India and an attempt should be made to give it a right direction . . . so that new types may come out, new designs, . . . new ideas, and out of that amalgam something new and good will emerge.
> —Jawaharlal Nehru, 1949

> Durgapur Steel Township today presents a notable example of lapse.
> —Town and Country Planning Organization, 1971

In 1957 the Indian state announced its second five-year plan. Explicitly borrowing from both the form and the content of Soviet-style economic planning, a program of economic development was proclaimed that committed significant financial, political, and human resources to rapid state-sponsored industrial growth and the creation of large-scale projects such as hydroelectric stations, steel plants, shipyards, and locomotive, cement, and fertilizer factories.[1] The mandate of the second plan (and the third plan, with its continued emphasis on heavy industrialization) also included the building of several industrial townships in areas adjacent to the plan projects. The rationale for township development was expressed in terms that went far beyond practical or utilitarian considerations of providing housing for workers. Instead, the townships were described as entirely new kinds of places inhabited by new kinds of people who would directly participate in the grand project of building the nation—that is, nation builders in both the narrowest sense of physically enabling the manufacture of new industrial products and infrastructure and in the broadest sense of becoming the ideal "producer-patriots" of the new nation. In the words of a brochure issued by the Steel Authority of India (SAIL) to commemorate three decades of the Indian steel industry: "Nehru wanted the steel plants [and the associated steel townships] to be special places, inhabited by special people."[2]

If the postcolonial nation took the abstract form of, in Salman Rushdie's words, a "dream we all agreed to dream,"[3] then industrial townships like Durgapur, Bokaro, Bhilai, and Rourkela were its grounded and inhabited "dreamworlds"[4]—namely, locations in which a dramatic and substantial reworking of existing spaces, times, and subjectivities could take place. As the state's Town and Country Planning Organization noted in a report on Durgapur steel township in West Bengal, an industrial township built to house the workers of the steel plant in the area, the expectation was that Durgapur would be a "grown-up city," with its adulthood or coming-of-age marked by its "well planned nature" and by the fact that the state would, through the provision of superior civic amenities, enable the existence of a "better civic life."[5] Moreover, unlike the vexed task of planning and developing already existing and inhabited cities, the activity of planning and developing these industrial townships or "steel towns" offered the nation-state an opportunity to realize its vision from scratch. Located in underdeveloped areas of the country, far from the large metropolitan centers of colonial India, the steel towns would enable the postcolonial state to break new ground.

The idealization of an "elsewhere" that informed the project of building steel towns was echoed in other contexts as well. In the years after independence, the urban spaces most celebrated by the discourses and practices of official nationalism had neither a significant geographic-material presence nor a historical one. They were instead unknown sites with unfamiliar and in many cases invented names, populated by relatively small numbers of people. Like the steel towns, these were all new urban spaces built by the postcolonial state, ranging from regional capital cities such as Chandigarh (Punjab) and Bhubaneswar (Orissa) to refugee "model towns" such as Faridabad, Nilokheri, Kalyani, and Ulhasnagar that were built to house the displaced refugees who had recently arrived from Pakistan.[6] While the spatial practices of colonialism were informed by strategies of centering—the building of capital cities with newly demarcated "city centers" containing imperial buildings, central promenades or avenues, parks, fountains, and monuments—postcolonial spatial practices were shaped by the imperative of decentering. Neither the capital city nor the national borders were the primary objects of the official nationalist gaze. Instead, it was to the "elsewheres" that lay between the center and the limits of the nation, to the new urban places filling in the abstract space of the national map, that official nationalism drew attention. They were upheld as the exemplary national spaces of the new India—spaces that would enable the birth of new citizens and bring forth the future of national time; spaces in which the state could foreground activities undertaken on behalf of the nation and thereby render visible its representative nature; spaces in which the dream of "national integration" or the harmonious coexistence of diverse ethnic and religious groups would be realized.

Within a span of fifteen years, the symbolic significance of the steel town was substantially revised. By the early 1970s, specific examples of crime, corruption, communal riots, residential segregation, labor unrest, and the inadequate supply and distribution of essential municipal services in steel towns were cited as material evidence for the multiple failures of the nation-building project and as proof of what happens when the pace of development is too rapid or when plans are carelessly implemented. According to the government's report on Durgapur, the brave new citizen had become a "victim of haphazard and unplanned growth and uncongenial environment" and the new city a place of "low and uneconomical densities, wastage of space and inability to optimally utilize existing infrastructure, ill-distributed facilities, loose planning, [and] monotonous housing."[7] The dreamworld of the steel town was thus renamed as catastrophe, now cited as a "notable example of lapse" rather than a manifestation of the Nehruvian promise to realize "something new and something good."

The journey of the steel town from exemplary promise to exemplary problem is the subject of this chapter. I am interested here not so much in the reasons for this downfall but instead in the political stakes of the narrative of the steel town as failed promise. How was the steel town produced as a dreamworld—that is, what kinds of desires and expectations were invested in it and what were the practices undertaken to realize the dream? What were the grounds on which its failure was proclaimed, and what were the solutions offered? In addressing these questions, this chapter examines the spatial practices—both the locations and the dislocations—and the temporal visions—the utopian as well as dystopian imaginations—that consolidated the distinctive formation of the Nehruvian nation-state.

By tracing this journey, I draw attention to three specific aspects of the nation-state formation project and the encounter with the nation-state that is the main subject of this book. First, I examine how the production of the steel town as an exemplary national space entailed symbolic and institutional strategies of separation or differentiation—notably the status of the steel town as a national ideal deriving from its radical difference from the "rest of the nation" and its insulation from the surrounding local environment of "backwardness." In a departure from the prevailing accounts of nation building as a project of generating an undifferentiated, seamless, and homogenous sense of national space and community,[8] the projects of nationalization and state-centrism in postcolonial India are shown here to be localizing or fragmenting in their impulse and effect.[9] Unlike the spectacular commemorative practices of Republic Day that located the nation within the delimited time-space of the center of the capital city, or the cinematic imagination of the Films Division that privileged a similar central node of national articulation, namely the Bombay headquarters where production and distribution decisions were made, the nation-building projects discussed in this chapter unfolded in scattered and dispersed locations. In this regard, the chapter serves as a reminder that the nation-state could be, and was, encountered far from the delimited coordinates of capital city culture. If the widespread recognition of the state and its authoritative idioms of nationhood explain the endurance of the Indian nation-state, then it is in the unmindful, ordinary, and everyday practices of life and work in the steel towns of India as much as in the self-consciously "nationalist" audiences who gather to witness spectacular displays of state power on the streets of New Delhi that such acts of recognition may be documented.

Second, the chapter examines the inherent tensions of nation-state formation and the array of competing projects that were in play during the initial decades after Indian independence. As I establish in the next section, the building of the steel town was informed by multiple and contradictory imperatives—for example, the effort to represent the state as both the authoritative benefactor and the accountable "servant" of the nation; the normative idealization of the citizen as a docile worker as well as an autonomous agent; and the dual emphasis on the diversity and the unity of Indian nationhood. In this context, the "lapse" of the steel town, or the revision of its exemplary status from dreamworld to catastrophe, was not surprising since the achievement of any one set of nation-state goals would *necessarily* mean the failure of others. Thus, as I demonstrate below, when the steel town lived up to the expectation of being a meticulously planned and ordered space that reflected the reign of state reason, it meant that the goal of bringing forth an engaged, autonomous, and "free-willed" citizenry had not been realized. Similarly, to the extent that the ideal resident of the steel town was a good worker, he was found to be a bad citizen, with his disciplined obedience running counter to the requirements of vibrant, engaged, participatory action demanded by the ideal of democracy. By highlighting these tensions and contradictions, this chapter amplifies a theme that has run through this book, namely, the reconceptualization of the nation-state project as a fissured arena or field of political discourse and practice, where the trope of failure is as much a part of the official national imagination as are triumphalist pronouncements of achievement and success.[10]

Finally, by documenting the transformation in the steel town's symbolic significance, I highlight the flexible logics of nation building and the sedimented or multilayered and dynamic character of nation-state discourse and practice. Thus far in this book I have examined how the imagination of institutions and the naturalization of diversity were articulated, elaborated, and consolidated through different kinds of encounters with the nation-state in Nehruvian India. In this chapter I explore how in the mid 1960s a new idiom of nationhood supplemented existing formulations, and India and Indianness increasingly came to be described in terms of the unfortunate "persistence of communalism."[11] The steel town was a critical site for this reformulation, with the thesis of communalism advanced by actors from the state, media, and civil society in the wake of the mass violence that took place in the steel township of Rourkela in 1964. In modifying the colonial state's primordializing rhetoric about the inevitable and enduring "clash of civilizations" between Hindus and Muslims in India, the political rhetoric in late Nehruvian India advanced an instrumentalist explanation for religious violence. For the most part, the official commissions of inquiry and parliamentary discussions on the Rourkela riots as well as independent investigations carried out by civic action groups and journalists converged on a common explanation of the violence as an exceptional event that had been brought about by cunning political entrepreneurs and their ability to manipulate gullible populations. Not surprisingly, the solution was seen to lie in the disavowal of politics, the reinvigoration of unifying structures of governance, and the recuperation of the "true" ethos of tolerance and diversity in India.

New Amalgams: The Promise of the Steel Town

The origins of steel towns and industrial townships in India can be traced to the process of capital accumulation in the colonial period. Jamshedpur in eastern India was the first such planned settlement, built in the first decade of the twentieth century to house the workers of a steel plant located nearby. Subsequently, townships were also set up in the princely state of Mysore and in Asansol in conjunction with the development of steel industries in those areas. All of these townships, like the industrial projects with which they were associated, were developed primarily through nonstate or private capital: Jamshedpur was built by the firm of J. R. D. Tata, a prominent member of the indigenous-colonial bourgeoisie; the Mysore complex reflected the capitalist aspirations of a princely state; and Asansol resulted from the entrepreneurial activities of the private British firm Burn and Company.[12]

In contrast, the steel towns built during the postcolonial period were all direct and exclusive creations of the national state.[13] They emerged within the framework of a state-led program of national development, not simply to house workers of steel plants but rather workers of *nationalized* steel plants. Moreover, the manufacture of steel itself was invested with considerable national symbolic importance. Like other building blocks of the Nehruvian "architecture of energy,"[14] steel was much more than mere industrial substance: as stated in a government publication, "the production of steel is the foundation for the industrial superstructure, for the prosperity of modern man."[15] The making of steel thus was an intrinsic part of the glorious task of "serving the nation," to quote a newspaper advertisement on the occasion of India's tenth Republic Day in 1953.[16] Postcolonial steel towns were sites in which the transition from the dependent colonial economy to the sovereign and planned national economy, and from the unfree subject to the productive citizen proudly serving her nation, could be enacted in and through everyday practices—sites that, through owing their existence to the decisions and actions of the national state, proclaimed the birth of the sovereign nation.

The decision to build a series of steel townships was first announced in the context of the second five-year plan, and subsequent efforts at township planning and development were undertaken by the Hindustan Steel Company, a public-sector corporation created by the national ministry of steel and mines to oversee the production of steel. The steel town was thus a state artifact in the most literal sense. It was built and supervised by the state, with every aspect of its existence—from its location to its street lighting, from local governance structures to the quality of fruits and vegetables being sold in its marketplaces—determined by agencies of the national state.[17] Moreover, being the creature of the state was also the chief identity of the steel town. Through an insistence on the steel town's artificiality or the planned and deliberated nature of its origins; its strangeness or disconnection from the surrounding environment; and its newness or the fact that before it came into being there was nothing there, the steel town was built to bear witness to the agency of its creator. Like the other institutional and cultural-ideological innovations introduced in the early post-independence period, the building of steel towns was shaped by the imperative of "state visibility," or the effort to establish the difference of postcolonial India through making visible the representative activities undertaken by the newly sovereign state.

The first steel plant was built in Rourkela in the state of Orissa. Bhilai in Madhya Pradesh, Durgapur in West Bengal, and Bokaro in Bihar soon followed.[18] The preconstruction locations of these industrial complexes (plants along with residential townships) were largely understood to be empty. For instance, accounts of the sites in which the townships were developed describe how the advantages and disadvantages of the natural topography influenced the layout and design of the plan: that is, the ways in which planners could take advantage of the natural incline of Bokaro to develop storm water drainage systems, and how the existence of "beautiful and high hills" around the area of the proposed township of Rourkela would serve as an "excellent buffer to maintain the quiet character of the town from the noise of the steel plant, the state highway, and the main Calcutta-Bombay railway line."[19] In these accounts, the encounter between the planned township and its natural environment is staged in terms of the present—a present that is expected to bring forth a new and different future, and a present that bears no traces of any being, thing, or place that came before.

But from these descriptions of the blank natural slate on which the steel township realized itself—the story of the encounter between the urban plan and nature—fleeting glimpses of other presences emerged. Thus, the land acquired for the development of Bokaro township was described to be "partly under intensive cultivation of paddy."[20] In another instance, the story of the development of the industrial township of Chittaranjan in West Bengal, built in 1951 in association with the locomotive manufacturing factory established there by the railway ministry, mentions in passing that people from the eight villages of Sundarpahari, Amaladahi, Fatehpur, Durgandi, Beramuri, Simjuri, Namkoshia, and Uparkeshia were displaced in the process of acquiring land for construction. Subsequently, three of the residential sectors of Chittaranjan township were named after these villages.[21] Is there a Sundarpahari, an Amaladahi, or a Fatehpur elsewhere? Did the villagers who left their names behind as they were relocated outside the urban area come up with new naming practices? These questions went unanswered in the official narratives, where the birth of the new urban was invariably described as an act of location rather than dislocation.

However, literal and metaphoric acts of dislocation and insulation were critical to the establishment of the steel town and to its symbolic significance as an exemplary national space. With all of the steel townships and steel plants built in areas where there was a high concentration of *adivasi* (indigenous-tribal) populations, the displacement of these groups and the rejection of their customary and collective claims to land were an integral part of the urban development process. Now placed outside the steel town and the steel plant, the indigenous population could in the areas in which it had previously lived only enter as temporary "unskilled labor" in the plant and as domestic servants in the township. For instance, the Bauri community members living in the areas outside the Bokaro township worked as maids, rickshaw pullers, and truck loaders. Within the steel plant, they were primarily employed in temporary positions, or in "Grade IV" services, as orderlies and sweepers.[22] There were thus significant numbers of people for whom the encounter with the nation-state was experienced in and as force, dispossession, "destitution," and insecurity.[23] The fact that these experiences unfolded at a historical moment otherwise characterized by the widespread support and legitimacy of the Nehruvian project is a reminder that the character and effect of state power is more mixed and variable than uniform, and that the "recognition of the state" is produced in multiple ways, harnessing registers of consent and affirmation as well as those of coercion and fear.

After being emptied in this manner, the spaces of the steel town were subsequently filled with the presence and the future promise of steel. The repletion took place in several ways. First, urban planning decisions about how much land to acquire and how many houses to build were shaped by a single calculation: How many workers does it take to produce one million tons of steel ingots, the initial production target assigned to each plant? Thus, the Town and Country Planning Organization estimated that 7,500 workers would be employed in the pursuit of the one million ton goal, and an "additional 2,500 persons will be required as secondary workers to cater to the various needs of 7,500 primary workers." Taking as the benchmark an average family size of five, planners set about the task of developing houses, shopping centers, schools, hospitals, police stations, parks, and entertainment centers for a community of 50,000 people.[24] Projections of the future growth of the towns were similarly shaped by calculations about increases in steel production.

Second, the question of proximity to or distance from the steel informed the determinations of the city limits and also the design of roads and transportation systems: How could these enable the ease and efficiency of journeys to and from the steel plant? For instance, the "circulation plan" for Rourkela—the layout of roads within the township—placed a "ring road" along its "main spine" that would connect the township to the steel plant, the railway station, and the highways beyond. All other roads within the town wound their way to this central avenue, with the chief imperative being that each worker's house should be no more than a short walk away from any arterial road, and consequently from the public transport vehicles of the steel plant.[25] At the same time, too much proximity was deemed undesirable. A critical distance from the "noise of the steel plant" also needed to be maintained, whether through the utilization of features of the natural landscape as buffers (such as the hills around Rourkela township) or through placing the township on another side of the railroad tracks or the highway. Both sets of considerations entailed understanding Rourkela in relation to the steel.

Third, hierarchies of work were directly mapped onto the landscape of inhabitation. The development of different types of housing and their allotment among the residents were determined by the salary structures of the steel plant. As Niranjan Benegal observes in the case of Bokaro township, "The size and location of a living quarter is directly proportional to the salary of the occupant. The cost of the house is recovered over a period of time by a 10% monthly deduction of salary."[26] In some townships, the spatial layout of the entire town reflected the relative earning power of its residents, as houses belonging to different socioeconomic categories were segregated into separate and "self-sufficient" residential sectors. In other townships, a conscious effort was made to ensure a form of (gradual) mixing—thus the first three tiers of the socioeconomic scale would be clustered together in one residential block, and the next three tiers of the scale in another.

Taken together, these three features of the steel town—its location, its roads, and its houses—defined its identity as a town of and for steel, and consequently as a paradigmatically national space, given the central significance of steel in the imaginary of developmentalist nationalism. The spaces of Rourkela, Bhilai, Bokaro, and Durgapur were also the sites for the realization of other and related aspects of postcolonial national desires, such as the Nehruvian insistence on newness and change as the defining characteristics of the sovereign nation-state, or that which set it apart from the colonial and precolonial past of "static conditions." To quote Nehru: "Even before the British came, we had become static. In fact, the British came because we are static. A society which ceases to change ceases to go ahead, [and] necessarily becomes weak."²⁷ In contrast, India after 1947 would be marked by change and the relentless drive to move forward—impulses that would necessarily strengthen the nation.

The newness of India was also proclaimed in relation to an international canvas—the idea that the experiments underway in India would be different from those existing in the rest of the world. Thus, although the dominant imperative of the postcolonial moment, according to Sankaran Krishna, was to "catch-up" to "what has supposedly already happened elsewhere," the process of catching up—the actual journey of development charted by the Indian nation—would take India beyond existing models and trajectories.²⁸ In the logic of Nehruvian nation building there was no contradiction between practices of borrowing from modular templates and the proclamation of national uniqueness and distinctiveness. Through adaptation and "creative synthesis," copies that were substantively distinct from and far better than the originals were expected to emerge. The formation of a "mixed economy" that combined principles of socialist and laissez-faire economics; the articulation of a "third way" foreign policy of nonalignment with the cold war superpowers; the commitment to a "unitary federalism" that drew upon features of the centralized state structure of Britain as well as the federal design of the United States; and the enshrining of group rights as well as individual rights in the constitution were all examples of this effort to produce something new by combining features from disparate external exemplars.

The urban plans for the steel towns were also marked by this logic of newness as bricolage, or, to use Nehru's words quoted at the beginning of this chapter, a belief that "out of this amalgam something new and good will emerge." Planners selected concepts and designs from a wide range of often-contradictory urban planning paradigms. For instance, while the idea of self-contained residential neighborhoods was derived from the "garden city" plan, other principles of the garden city, such as the requirement of preserving an expanse of agricultural land outside the city or the concentric-circle spatial layout, were rejected.²⁹ The urban planners' efforts to form the steel towns as spaces of modernity came from a view of the modern as multifaceted with multiple imperatives and requirements. As modern, the new urban space was to be marked by independent living and self-sufficiency; hence the development of contained residential sectors, each with their own shops, schools, parks, and entertainment centers. At the same time, the new urban also had to respond to the modern imperative of legibility or transparency—that is, to be unlike the inscrutable and inward spaces of the "old" city—which meant that the residential sectors could not be completely closed off into themselves. Thus, Durgapur came about as both garden city and "band town," with its self-contained residential clusters strung along a single arterial road instead of being laid out in concentric circles.[30] And it was precisely through its synthetic combination of these different features that Durgapur's newness was proclaimed: in its "planned hybridity" it was set apart both from Indian cities and from past and present urban spaces in the rest of the world.[31]

Apart from the innovations in urban design, the steel town's claim to novelty also rested upon the distinctive subjectivities, practices, and social relations that it would bring forth—that is, the fact that life within the steel town would be unlike anything experienced anywhere else. Thus, community life and opportunities for political participation were structured very differently within the steel town, with the presence and involvement of the state serving once again as the grounds for differentiation. All Indian towns and cities had structures of local government. Decentralized mechanisms of self-government were also being realized in villages at the time, with the directive principles of the Indian constitution committing the state to the active development of village *panchayats* or councils. However, in contrast to other rural and urban spaces, the steel town had no representative or participatory structures and mechanisms in place. All decisions were taken and all policies enacted by the officials of Hindustan Steel. The general manager of the steel plant (appointed by the Ministry of Steel and Mines) was the de facto mayor of the township, and his wife was the ex-officio chair of the cultural clubs and organizations run by the "ladies" of the town.[32] The state thus took upon itself the task of expressing and meeting the present needs of steel town residents as well as anticipating their future desires. Liberated from the demands of political participation in this manner, residents of the steel town could occupy themselves with cultural, educational, and recreational activities such as the development of community gardens, the encouragement of "wrestling, freehand exercises, gymnastics and other [forms] of physical culture,"[33] and the organization of religious festivals. The resulting apolitical subjectivity of the citizen-resident—what we might even term "antipolitical" in that it actively denies the presence and possibility of political action—and the seamless or unmediated connection forged between state and citizen within the steel town, set it off from the messy and sordid world of politics outside.

Finally, the steel town was different because its spaces showcased both the diversity as well as the unity of the nation. While all Indian cities were marked by considerable cultural, linguistic, and religious diversity, and heterogeneity is in fact taken to be the defining feature of the urban condition the world over, the steel towns of India were to be distinct in their ability to bring together these differences in a harmonious way. Along with the absence of politics, life in the steel town was to be marked by the absence of conflict and social antagonisms. With people from all parts of India living together in the joint pursuit of steel production, Durgapur, Bhilai, Bokaro, and Rourkela were going to realize the official nationalist mantras of "unity in diversity" and *hum sab ek hain* ("we are all one").[34]

As Durgapur, Bhilai, Bokaro, and Rourkela were transformed from imagined spaces into inhabited places, their symbolic significance changed. Increasingly, they were described as examples of national problems and failures—as "notable examples of lapse," to paraphrase the government's 1971 report—rather than as exemplary national "dreamworlds" or ideals. And just as the utopian imagination of the steel town was a many splendored thing, the chronicle of its catastrophe was similarly multifaceted. The list of its problems was as detailed as that of its promises: steel towns were economically polarized; they were sites for violent communal riots between Hindus and Muslims; life within the steel town was boring and colorless; the spaces were overcrowded, public services were in scarce supply, and nothing seemed to work properly. In addition, the dividing line between the inside and the outside of the steel town was easily muddied: residents went outside for their daily shopping, outsiders lived in unsightly and illegal dwellings within. Finally, not only had steel towns failed to be self-sufficient and "generative cities" that brought about regional economic growth by spreading prosperity in the surrounding backward areas—the only acceptable form (and direction) of boundary-crossing activities between the steel town and its local environment according to the terms of the original promise—the "parasitic" steel towns may even have contributed to the further immiseration of the surrounding areas.[35] In the following sections I discuss some of these indictments in further detail, along with the ways in which the revised imagination of the steel town as "catastrophe," like the earlier utopian construction, enabled the consolidation of the postcolonial nation-state.

Catastrophic Encounters: The Steel Town as Problem

The steel town's identity as an exemplary national space was linked to its distinctiveness—to the fact that the times, spaces, subjectivities, and practices associated with it would be manifestly different. As the utopian steel town was transformed into a lived reality, its distinctiveness did manifest itself, although in unintended and unforeseen ways. Take, for instance, the imperative of state visibility, which was indeed realized within the steel town. However, given the multilayered understanding of the representative principle that structured the postcolonial political field—whereby centralized institutional interventions of planned development that represented the people by "acting for" them as well as democratic political structures that represented the people by "standing as" them were jointly authorized—to see the state was actually to behold multiple visions.[36] Some of the multiple faces of the state that were encountered in the steel town include the state as the "model employer" of the citizen-workers who inhabited the steel town; the state as the "developmentalist agent" that was laboring to realize the "fruits of advancement" for the nation as a whole; the "pastoralist state" concerned with the minutiae of individual lives within the township, from the grocery shopping decisions made by housewives to the daily travel time of commuters; and the "totalizing state" engaged in the task of integrating the national population.[37] The significant role played by international institutions, ideologies, and interests in the creation of the postcolonial steel projects also contributed to this effect—it was not simply the facilitating labors of an "Indian state" that were sighted in the spaces of the steel town but the sights and signs of German, Soviet, and British state authority as well. Outside the city limits of Rourkela the lettering on the highway signpost—"Wilhelmshaven: 10,000 km"—served as a permanent reminder of the steel town's transnational constitution.[38]

As the steel town became a reality, so too did its contradictions and aporias. Over time, the incompatibility between the different components of the nation-statist project became increasingly apparent. In the most general sense, the goals of "making workers" and "making citizens" led to conflicting outcomes, and the difference between the "industrial" and the "township" components of the industrial township, or the efforts of capital and civic development respectively, proved to be difficult to reconcile. For instance, the decision to allocate housing on the basis of workplace hierarchies entrenched class-based divisions within the township and acted as a barrier to the development of neighborhood solidarities and related forms of social capital and civic belonging. One of the most persistent complaints about the steel town was its economic polarization and the manifest lack of cross-class interaction. Approximately a decade after the townships were built, a series of reports on the "present condition" of the steel town by the urban planning agencies of the state as well as by nonstate national and international organizations, such as the Ford Foundation and UNESCO, concluded that the act of tying housing to salary had led to a reinscription of workplace inequalities and hierarchies within the urban area. Moreover, since the residential sectors of the townships were largely homogenous with regard to housing type, this meant that for the most part the poorer people lived together and in isolation from those more prosperous. The self-sufficient design of the residential sectors served as an additional deterrent to interactions between different economic groups, since other than going to work there was no reason for anyone to venture beyond the confines of his or her sector, which was a similarly polarized space. In townships with "mixed housing" sectors the situation was no better. In fact the specter of relative deprivation and envy that hovered over all attempts to get the haves and the have-nots to share space possibly made matters even worse.

Economic polarization and segregation were considered to be especially problematic because of the ways in which the economic disparities between different categories of workers mapped onto colonial inequalities of caste, religion, and region. As the steel plant responded to the "full employment" mandate of the Indian state, it registered a steady rise in the numbers on its payroll without a corresponding increase in the amount of money available for distribution among its employees. Since the plant's managerial and other white-collar staff was considered to be nationally competitive, their salaries were held relatively constant. Consequently, the practice of "overemployment" had a disproportionately adverse effect on nontechnical, semiskilled and "unskilled" labor—categories comprised of people who had been denied educational opportunities in the past. In short, instead of undoing old hierarchies, the new urban spaces of the steel town reproduced them.[39]

Pursuing the goal of rapid industrial growth also had other kinds of unintended consequences on life in the township. As the industrial capacities and outputs of the steel plant increased, so too did the size of the informal labor sector.[40] With this came the proliferation of camps, slums, and other forms of makeshift housing settlements on the outskirts of, and also within, the planned environment of the towns. There was also an acute shortage of housing for formal employees of the steel plants. Indeed, the Town and Country Planning Organization's 1971 data on employee housing at the Durgapur steel plant revealed that 47 percent of steel plant employees lived in shared housing, 27 percent in "labor camps," and 11 percent in *bustees* or slum dwellings. In other words, only 15 percent of the employees lived in their own houses within the township—the place that had been built to meet the housing needs of the steel plant.[41] However, the fortunate few who had a house of their own within the steel town had their own share of problems to contend with: overcrowded schools, poorly equipped hospitals, and a "semi-developed market disguised as a Central Business District."[42] In order to satisfy their basic needs, residents often had to venture outside the township, where vegetables were cheaper, schools were better, and even health care, though more expensive, was more reliable. As a result, the boundary between the inside and the outside of the steel town proved difficult to maintain, and the town's identity as a self-sufficient space was called into question.

Steel towns were also sites in which the constitutive contradictions of the "mosaic nationalism" project and its simultaneous emphasis on the fragmented and on the totalized character of Indian nationhood became apparent. Thus on the one hand, and in keeping with the multiculturalist logics of India's unity-in-diversity formula of nationhood, the existence of distinct ethno-religious communities in steel towns was critical to the town's identity as a nationally representative space. On the other hand, these displays of subnational distinctiveness could very easily become expressions of insular parochialism, with intra-ethnic solidarities strengthened at the expense of inter-ethnic connections. Steel town residents were commonly described as being trapped within the narrow prison houses of regional identity; instead of relating to each other as fellow "producer-patriots" they were seen to reproduce ethnic, linguistic, and caste barriers within the township. According to Bagaram Tulpule, who served as the general manager of the Durgapur steel plant between 1971 and 1974, the frequent incidents of labor unrest during his tenure had a lot to do with the fact that the Bengali employees of the steel plant were unable to get beyond their cultural milieu of bhadralok (genteel bourgeois) identity and to reconcile themselves to their status as "physical labour." In the account of this state official, the problem of "labor indiscipline" was linked to the persistence of parochial identity and the failure of the steel town to realize new, "national" attitudes and practices. Instead, the Bengalis continued to be Bengalis: "Discipline in the conventional sense of unquestioning obedience to or suppliance before their officers is naturally irksome to them."[43] Tulpule's account of labor unrest as ethnically derived behavior can be called into question. Of significance, however, is not his explanation of the steel town's problems but the problematization itself—the fact that the very ethnoregional identity that the steel town was expected to protect, display, and foster was seen as a destabilizing threat to be kept at bay. The steel town was thus a site in which the inconsistent embrace of diversity in postcolonial India—the understanding that subnational diversity is something valuable as well as dangerous—found expression.

In a final example of the contradictions of the steel town project, while the meticulously planned nature of the steel town may have been a "success" as far as the goals of order and rationality were concerned, it had a negative effect on the quality and experience of life within the township. As one observer noted: "With dusk comes a lull over the town. Human activity almost comes to an apparent stop. There is very little communication between people. Everyone, as it were, recoils into his domestic cell. The life, activity, colour and gaiety of an urban area is strikingly absent."[44] The urban planning agency of the state concurred with this perspective, describing Durgapur in terms of the "monotony of the city environment" and how its lack of a "skyline and visual urban effects" had "taken away the much desired element of human living."[45] In the state's own assessment, steel towns did not look or feel "urban" and their inhabitants did not behave like engaged citizens.[46]

Perhaps the most unexpected outcome of the steel town project was the fact that it contributed to the proliferation and intensification rather than the erasure or transcendence of antagonisms and conflict. Reports about crime and "law and order" problems in the steel towns and in the surrounding areas increased over the years. Contrary to the expectation that the steel town and the steel plants would "transcend" politics, there were significant interunion rivalries, and frequent incidents of "industrial unrest." The promise of shedding "atavisms" of identity was likewise belied. As Jonathan Parry's rich ethnography of workers in the Bhilai steel plant establishes, the policy of the caste-based reservation of jobs for state workers meant that, for many, caste identity and the possession of a "caste certificate" was the means for entering the "caste-free" utopia of the world of steel.[47] Steel towns also proved unable to either transform or keep at bay one of the most pernicious atavisms of the old India: the problem of communalism or interreligious violence. Thus in March 1964 the town of Rourkela witnessed "indiscriminate killing, loot and arson."[48] In an event in which the police and the local administration proved to be either unable or unwilling to take any precautionary measures, approximately thirty-four Muslims were killed over a twenty-day period and more than five thousand left their homes. Researchers visiting Rourkela in the aftermath of the violence were struck by the high level of "communal mistrust among various sections of the people."⁴⁹ Once again, the "new amalgam" of the steel town had broken the original mold.

Programs of Reform

By the 1970s attention turned to the question of whether salvage or recovery was possible; of how, if at all, the problem of the steel town could be fixed. The failure of the steel town was attributed to three specific causes: "unrealistic plans," "inadequate implementation," and "hasty development." Accordingly, solutions considered how urban plans that met the needs of the people could be designed, how these user-friendly plans could be better implemented, and how the pace of growth and development could be slowed. While the specific policy recommendations were diverse and wide ranging, they all drew upon and reproduced a common set of assumptions. First, all efforts at problem solving distinguished urban space from urban practice—the idea that built structure and inhabitants are two separable parts of a city, and that it is possible to design structure to fit inhabitants and to change inhabitants by redesigning structure. According to the terms of this logic, the steel town was seen to have failed because the needs of its inhabitants had not been adequately known and anticipated. Therefore, carefully designed surveys and better demographic projections of population growth would make a difference. Alternatively, the problem was seen to stem from the passivity and inwardness of the inhabitants. Thus, the logic went, the development of more playgrounds and community halls were in order.⁵⁰ What was called into question (and what in turn presented itself for solution) was not the idea of nationally produced urban planning but rather the specific flaws within the existing urban plan. As Michel Foucault notes in his discussion of the history of prison reform projects in Europe: "Prison 'reform' is virtually contemporary with the prison itself: it constitutes, as it were, its programme." The proliferation of reform discourses and practices around the "failure" of urban planning in the steel towns had a similar constitutive or productive effect—the critique of existing plans was simultaneously an authorization of the planning enterprise and the rationalities, technologies, ideologies, and practices of nation-state building.⁵¹

Second, the solutions to the problem of the steel town continued to reproduce the assumption that the citizen-worker was the ideal national subject. How could residents of the steel town be productive and disciplined in the steel plant and neighborly and active in the township? How could a rich community life emerge from the shadows of a hierarchical workplace? In different ways, these questions attempted to grapple with the constitutive contradiction of the steel town—the fact that to the extent that it fulfilled its goal of being a *steel* town, a place where docile workers lived, it failed to be a steel *town*, a space inhabited by engaged citizens. A radical revision of the conditions of work and the presumptions of citizenship may have been one possible way to mediate this contradiction, but this path remained uncharted.

Third, the solutions offered for the problem of the steel town were, like the promise of the steel town, located and bounded within a specific urban area. Something had gone wrong inside the steel town, and reform efforts would accordingly focus on this inner space. In other words, the problem of Rourkela, Bhilai, Bokaro, and Durgapur was conceptualized as a problem *within* Rourkela, Bhilai, Bokaro, and Durgapur—a conceptualization premised on the assumption that urban and nonurban spaces could be differentiated and that problems and solutions were localized. Within this framework, the problem of economic polarization could be addressed by redesigning the system of housing allocation. Thus if workers' houses were matched to family size rather than salary, then economic disparities would be less visible within the town.[52] This solution did not engage with the question of structural inequalities—of how and why some people earn so much more than others.[53]

However, not all instances of reform were "programmatic" in the sense of reiterating existing, established, and discursive-institutional programs. Attempts to restore, salvage, and fix the lapsed utopia of the steel town also generated new ideologies and practices, as well as new forms of nation-state encounters. The discourse of "communalism" was one such innovation. Arguably the primary "master narrative" in contemporary India, its postcolonial revitalization took place in the steel town. The promise of bringing forth new life had heralded the establishment of steel towns in the late 1950s as exemplary national spaces. Less then a decade later, the violent deaths within the steel town of Rourkela would establish their exemplarity once again, but this time as examples of everything that was wrong about India.

Death and the Nation: The Reinvention of
Communalism in Postcolonial India

On March 21, 1964, the steel town of Rourkela dominated the headlines in national newspapers, thereby fulfilling its original promise of being a place of remarkable and unprecedented occurrences.[54] However, the actual nature of the occurrences did not conform to the celebratory and optimistic pronouncements that had heralded the establishment of the steel town—in fact, it directly contravened their utopian terms. Rourkela's newsworthiness stemmed from the outbreak on March 20 of riots between Hindus and Muslims in the steel town and its neighboring environs, during the course of which at least twenty-eight people were killed and fifty-nine were seriously injured. With the declaration of a curfew in the township, the dispatch of the Indian army, and the flurry of official visitors to investigate the causes and consequences of the riots, the steel town's place in the national imagination acquired a new, and unforeseen, centrality: it was now the site in which the postcolonial nation-state's attempts to combat the "virus of communalism" were on display.

Why did the riots take place? In response to this question, central and state officials (both elected representatives and bureaucratic agents), media commentators, academics, and civil society associations advanced a range of explanations. There were varied accounts as well of the sequence and nature of events and of what exactly constituted the nameable and knowable universe of the "riot."[55] In the national media reports, the riot was given four defining features: violence, suddenness, locatedness (isolable to a discrete time and place), and impersonality or namelessness.

The riots that became a "national news story" on March 21, 1964, followed the death and injury of several people; the imposition of a curfew in the steel township of Rourkela and the neighboring towns of Jharsuguda and Brajarajnagar; the dispatching of the national army to the area; and the official nomination of the event as a riot in public statements issued by Orissa government officials. It was thus comprehended as a spatially and temporally discrete or contained event that could be mapped onto a specified set of violent actions (the killing and wounding of people) and institutional responses (the declaration of a curfew; the authorization of armed intervention to restore law and order). Further confirming this reading of the riot as an isolable "event" or a bounded occurrence that took visible, tangible forms of violence rather than an ongoing, diffuse, and elusive process, the "suddenness" of the riot was repeatedly singled out for comment. Moreover, although exhaustive details were provided on the aftermath of the riot, there was no information available on the preceding period. This narrative choice consolidated the impression of the riot as a radically disjunctive event: an "eruption" for the *Times of India*; a "spontaneous" occurrence for the *Hindustan Times*.[56]

If the riot stood out as a discrete set of violent actions and the institutional responses elicited by them, then the anonymity, or the lack of specific, named agents of violence, was equally distinctive. The generalized vocabularies of "mobs," "crowds," "people," and "anti-social elements" were used to describe the perpetrators as well as the victims of violence. The details of death and destruction were provided in general, even vague terms: a "riotous mob" had gathered in the "Jalda area" of the Rourkela township on March 20; there were "stray incidents of arson"; "the death and injuries were caused mostly by stabbing"; and, finally, the terse pronouncement that "the situation in the two towns [Brajarajnagar and Rajgangpur] in the vicinity of the steel town] was officially reported to be tense."[57]

The first time that the violence in Rourkela was reported in a news article, there were no qualifying adjectives used to name (and therefore explain) the nature of the violence. On March 21, readers were informed about an "orgy of violence" and of unspecified "clashes" that had taken place in Rourkela on the preceding day. By the second day of the news coverage, the riots had acquired an additional description, and now entered the media landscape as examples of "*communal frenzy*." From a strictly semantic perspective, the redescription of the riot as "communal" did not add any new information, since the conflict had already been described as one between communities. However, to an Indian-reading public, the reference, as indeed its vagueness, was clear. In the intricate guessing game that the reading publics in postcolonial India perform on a daily basis, where a range of journalistic neologisms and euphemisms have been developed to circumvent the customary restrictions on the direct naming of religious communities in press articles about inter-religious hostility,[58] the "communal frenzy" was implicitly mapped onto the relations between two particular communities: Hindus and Muslims.

For the most part, India's free press and the Indian state initially described the riot in similar terms. In parliamentary discussions in New Delhi and in public statements by the chief minister and governor of Orissa, the home state of Rourkela township, the riot was similarly produced as an event and attributed with a violent, sudden, located, nameless, and "communal" character.[59] State and media texts also provided convergent explanations for the riots and identified similar sets of proximate and root causes. At one level, the spontaneity of the riot was its defining characteristic: the "outbreak" of violence that "spread" from one locality to another without any apparent organizational structure or motivated leadership. From this perspective the riot was effectively inexplicable, located in the mysterious stirrings of crowd psychology, and unknowable and therefore unpreventable.

While this was the prevailing explanation in the immediate aftermath of the riot, other sets of more specific causes emerged in later days, and the question of agency became central to the understanding of the riots. Now, the spontaneity of the crowds was seen as a symptomatic effect of other, "real" causes, namely the instrumental manipulation of gullible populations by "anti-social elements."

The official narratives soon dispensed with the generalized vocabulary of "anti-social elements" and explicitly named "Pakistani agents" as the chief instigators. According to Biju Patnaik, the former chief minister of Orissa, the riots were a part of "a concocted game for the purpose of advancing Pakistan's case in the Security Council [concerning the dispute with India over Kashmir]." Patnaik's explanation was unambiguous: "Pak agents engineered the whole riot with the political stunt that the army and police of India would be busy in the places of disturbances and there will be good opportunity for Pakistan to invade India."[60] The role of Pakistan was also discussed in parliamentary debates on the Rourkela riots. Some members of parliament provided specific coordinates for Pakistani agency and called for the closure of the Pakistani High Commissioner's office in Calcutta, since "certain persons ... were indulging in undesirable activities."[61]

The connection between the Rourkela riots and Pakistan was also made in another, more indirect, way. Within a week of the riots, they were no longer seen to be exclusively local in origin or significance but were linked instead to events and processes that occurred far from the immediate confines of the steel town. The events in Rourkela were now seen to be part of a larger, contemporaneous, wave of Hindu-Muslim violence that was affecting other areas of India, and whose origins could in fact be traced to locations and events occurring outside India. Two weeks before the events in Rourkela there were riots in the city of Calcutta, 225 km away; a month before, there was extended violence in the city of Jessore in East Pakistan. As trains carrying "Hindu refugees" from Jessore (via Calcutta) to the resettlement colony of Dandakaranya in the central Indian state of Madhya Pradesh stopped at Rourkela station, rumors about the events in Calcutta and Jessore reached the steel town and "the virus spread far and wide."[62] Rourkela's riots had now acquired an international cause and were connected with the treatment of Hindus in East Pakistan. And with the metaphor of the virus, their significance was generalized as well. Although the riots had taken place in Rourkela, the entire body politic was susceptible to the infection of communalism.

What kinds of solutions were in order? The immediate task at hand was the restoration of civil order in Rourkela, a task that was entrusted to the military and law enforcement agencies of the central and regional governments. The provision of relief and rehabilitation for displaced Muslims was another issue requiring urgent attention. The more long-term question of preventing future riots also dominated state and media discussions. How could the virus of communalism be controlled and possibly even eliminated? There were some concrete proposals offered in response to this broad dilemma, such as the flurry of debates in the Indian parliament about the need to develop a "firmer" foreign policy toward Pakistan; to register a formal complaint with the United Nations; and even to curtail diplomatic ties with the neighboring state. For the most part, however, the solution was conceptualized in terms as broad as the problem itself: "political elements" must be kept at bay. The restrictions on "politics" took multiple forms, from the call to curb union activities at the steel plant to the disallowing of questions, motions, amendments, and legislative discussions in response to the home minister's statement on the "recent incidents of violence" before the Lok Sabha (House of the People) on March 23, 1964. Ruling against a proposal for a parliamentary discussion on the central government's management of the conflict, the speaker of the house noted: "Raising questions at this time is not good for our nation. Please accept this."[63]

Although there were no further incidents of serious rioting in Rourkela after March 1964, riots took place with increasing frequency in other parts of the country in the years that followed. As in the case of the Rourkela riots, the dominant official and media narratives that were applied to each of these cases was that of the spread of communalism. The narrative of communalism reinvigorated some of the key terms of political discourse in postcolonial India, such as the "fear of politics" and the call for a social order without any conflict, antagonisms, or dissent. It shored up as well the "need for a state" that was a central pillar of the Nehruvian imagination. Neither the official narratives nor the media accounts of the Rourkela riots engaged with the significance of the riot's location in a steel town. Was there a relationship between state policies of national development and the violent events of March 1964? Why did *adivasis* participate in the violence against Muslims, thereby departing from the historical accommodation between these two communities in this area? Were there other, "nonreligious" explanations for the steel town riots? The master narrative of communalism disallowed such questions.[64] When riots were explained in terms of the exogenizing logic of the communal virus, the possibility that state policies might have played a role was ruled out. In fact, the diagnosis of a virus renewed the call for an expert state to heal the diseased national body.

Finally, the discourse of communalism contributed to the naturalization of diversity in postcolonial India. In colonial India, the master narrative of communalism had endowed religious identity with primordialist and unchangeable attributes—"communal riots" were expressions of the natural enmities between religious communities in an essentially religious society. The postcolonial state's reinvention of communalism rejected this primordializing framework: riots had political-artificial rather than cultural-natural roots; communalism was a "virus" and not a natural endowment. And in its place a different kind of essentialism emerged: the natural tolerance of Indian diversity; the "peaceful coexistence" that "really" characterized India; the synthetic cultures of unspoiled communities; and the deep structures of composite nationhood that "evil doers," "anti-social elements," "fissiparous tendencies," "foreign hands," and "corrupt politicians" could temporarily obscure but never vanquish. The reviled other of the nation-state, the specter of communalism, appears in fact to have enabled its consolidation.

Conclusion

In tracing the transformation of the steel town from a celebrated national dreamworld to a disavowed national catastophe, this chapter has drawn attention to the constitutive role of spatial strategies of differentiation in the project of nation-state formation. The creation of a national community is commonly understood to entail an emphasis on cultural sameness or homogeneity, with nation-building described as a project of enabling the emergence of "one" out of "many." However, in this chapter, as in the rest of this book, I have argued that this generation of homogenous cultural community is only one aspect of the project of nation-state formation. In contrast to the creation of the nation, the production of the nation-state draws upon and fosters different sets of practices, which are directed toward the constitution of cultural identity as well as the consolidation of institutional sovereignty and authority.

In this chapter I have elaborated on this difference in one specific context, namely the spatial practices of nation-state formation. As the preceding discussion has shown, the nationalization of the steel town entailed its production as an exemplary space that was manifestly out of step with and disconnected from the "rest of the nation." To borrow from a useful distinction developed by Donald Handelman in a discussion of the symbolic strategies of nationalism, the steel towns of India served as "models for" rather than "models of" the nation,[65] built to visibly showcase the promises of the as-yet-unrealized future rather than the realities of the national present or the memories of the national past. The future that the steel town was expected to bring forth was that of a "stated nation," one that manifested the innate and indissoluble bond between state, nation, and citizen. Indeed, the chief identity of the steel town was that of a state-made space. Its exemplarity was linked not to its timelessness, naturalness, or other sets of organic-fatalist attributes but instead to its characteristics of novelty and artifice, its made rather than found existence.

As a model for the desired Indian future, the steel town was thus invested with the multiple desires of the nation-statist project. Consequently, by examining the formation of the steel town dreamworld we can gain a better understanding of the coordinates of this project and of the specific content of the nation-statist imagination in Nehruvian India. Its many contradictions and impossibilities also come to light, along with the noncohesive, multilayered, and inherently messy constitution of nation-statist ideologies and practices. Thus, as this chapter has shown, the steel town was a site that saw the valorization of the free-willed citizen as well as the industrious, docile worker as the ideal subjects of the nation-state; that is, the representation of the state as both a munificent employer and a constrained "servant" of the people and the celebration of India's "essential" diversity alongside dire warnings about the dangerous and destabilizing effects of diversity "gone wrong."

Within a decade of its existence, the status of the steel town underwent a radical transformation that was then hailed as an example of national failure. However, like the steel town dreamworld, the steel town as catastrophe also played a central and productive role in the consolidation of the nation-state. Thus the failure of the steel town led to a flurry of reform programs that further secured the dominant idea of India as a "stated nation." From the ruins of the steel town a new specter of communalism would emerge—one that would soon become one of the structuring principles of the postcolonial political field, invoked by a wide range of state and social actors. The call to "combat communalism" by reviving the natural tolerance of Indian society, integrating the diverse nation, and "rising above" politics did not undermine but instead shored up the three key pillars of the nation-statist imagination: the natural diversity of the nation; the unifying agency of the state; and the disavowal of politics.

CONCLUSION

After Midnight

:::

In this book I have explored the cultural politics of nation-state formation in India—the range of symbolic, discursive, and material practices through which the postcolonial Indian nation-state came to exist as an authoritative entity that structured political and social life. In the latter half of the nineteenth century, discourses about Indian national identity began to proliferate in colonial India's public cultural and political arenas.[1] As the rich historiography of this period has established, this "anticolonial nationalism" was neither a singular nor a cohesive formation. Rather, several distinct and contending visions of nationhood competed for authorization at any given point in time. For instance, the definition of India as the *punyabhumi* and *pitrubhumi* (holy land and fatherland) of Hindus was advanced by the Hindu nationalist ideologue Vinayak Sarvarkar at the same time that the Indian National Congress endorsed a secular-pluralist understanding of nationhood.[2] Despite variations in motivation, form, and content, the diverse national imaginations that were produced in the colonial period shared a family resemblance. They all found expression in and as oppositional discourses, produced in the course of efforts to modify, resist, and eventually reject the authority of the colonial state and its agents.

With the formal proclamation of Indian independence in 1947 came the dissipation of this oppositional charge—or what might be termed the "insurgent consciousness" of nationalism.[3] In the discourses and practices of Indian nationalism "after midnight," national community and state authority, once pitted against each other, were now reimagined as aligned, even twinned, formations: people as well as institution, nation as well as state, now jointly called up in the name of India and Indianness. Instead of being directed against state power, idioms of nationhood in the postcolonial period would energize and legitimize the project of state empowerment.

What exactly did this transformation entail? How was a social movement imaginary of anticolonial nationalism transformed into an institutionalist discourse and practice of postcolonial nation-statism? What were the means by which nationalists were to be turned into nationals, colonial state into sovereign national state, and subjects into citizens—shifts that entailed, among other things, a radically different orientation toward state authority? Such questions press for a sequel to the familiar account of "freedom at midnight," in which discussions of Indian nationalism end with the suitably dramatic and symbolically overdetermined moment of national independence. In the preceding chapters I have addressed this task: taking this nationalist "moment of arrival" as the starting point for my investigation, I have examined the cultural interventions and symbolic-representational practices that materialized new ideas of India after 1947.[4] I have argued that Indian nationalism in the decades after independence was overwhelmingly nation-statist, and that this statist form simultaneously emphasized the natural diversity of its populace even as it presented itself as the unifying agency that coalesced this diversity into a unity, and that all this was underlain by a claim to a transcendent space of the supra- or anti-political occupied by the state. Here I revisit my argument by considering the broader theoretical implications and the future research agendas that are suggested by it. I also address the question of whether and how the nation-statist imagination is being transformed in twenty-first-century India.

Nation into Nation-State

In the first few decades after Indian independence, visual representations, ritual practices of commemoration, discourses on science and technology, and urban planning schemes were among the primary sites and means for the transformation of nation into nation-state. Taken together, they illuminate three key aspects of the nation-state project. First, that it was an active project—a historically layered, contradictory, dynamic, and open-ended process of making that cannot be encapsulated within a discrete and seamless "postcolonial" framework. For instance, the lineages of visual, ritual, discursive, and spatial practices in Nehruvian India can all be traced to colonial institutions and policies. Republic Day parades emulated the pageantry of colonial durbars. The Films Division of India replicated many of the institutional structures of colonial propaganda organizations such as Indian News Parade and Information Films of India. The discourses and policies of techno-scientific modernization and development, indeed the broader formation of state-led development itself, reworked the colonial presumptions and techniques of governance. Finally, even the establishment of steel townships as the exemplary spaces of the new India was not a novel innovation of the Nehruvian state—planned industrial settlements had existed since the early years of the twentieth century.

In a similar vein the reimagination of India as a nation-state did not result from the singular actions of an omnipresent and monolithic state. Instead, the state-centrism of the postcolonial national imagination, and in fact the very myth of the powerful and transcendent state itself, were "coproduced" by the interactions, negotiations, and interventions of different sets of social actors. Those who played a role in producing and reproducing the postcolonial nation-statist imagination include the corporate advertising agencies that urged consumer-citizens to participate in republican commemorations on January 26 every year; the filmmakers who fiercely guarded their sense of artistic autonomy but were nevertheless eager to negotiate production contracts with the Films Division; the scientists who confirmed the vision of India as a nation in urgent need of techno-scientific modernization; and the journalists and civil society activists who, concerned by the rapid spread of the communal "virus" in the hitherto antiseptic spaces of the steel township, renewed the call to disavow politics.

These were elite actors for the most part, and the political field mapped in this book is in this sense a decidedly "nonsubaltern" formation. However, the varied social and political locations and affiliations of these actors make this formation more heterogeneous and internally diverse than accounts of dominant ideologies of state-centric nationalism would lead us to believe. The difference between the radical left political imaginary of filmmaker K. A. Abbas, who played a role in advancing the cinematic imagination of the Films Division (discussed in chapter 1), and the centrist political views of the scientist S. S. Bhatnagar, who played a key role in elaborating the scientific needs discourse of Nehruvian India (discussed in chapter 3), are but a few examples of the divergent logics that motivated the participation of individual agents in the project of reimagining India as a nation-state.[5]

The second aspect of the postcolonial nation-state project highlighted in this book is its distinctive mode of reproduction; that is, the fact that the nation-statist imagination was disseminated in and through "encounters" that took place in different contexts and locations, and involved individuals from diverse social-cultural backgrounds. As noted in chapter 3, for instance, both metropolitan scientists and rural stone masons encountered the needs discourse of the Nehruvian state at the various foundation-stone laying ceremonies for new scientific and technological projects.[6] Moreover, as the ponderous, didactic, bureaucratized, and even boring address of the postcolonial nation-state made manifest, the project of nation-state formation drew upon affective registers of "disenchantment" that were distinct from those that enabled nationalist mobilization in the colonial period and the movement politics of nationalism in general. Its success had less to do with the psychological processes of internalization and acceptance (the existence of people who buy into dominant nationalist ideologies) than with recognition and repeated exposure (the existence of spectators who "see" and "know" the state). The iterated deployment of nation-statist idioms and practices by diverse social actors rather than their internalized belief or affective resonance is the key to understanding the mechanisms of reproducing the new ideas of India in the years following independence.

The concept of encountering rather than believing in the nation-state allows for an important analytical delimitation. The point here is simply about the ways in which, as a result of repetition and ubiquity as well as institutional endorsement, certain understandings about nation, state, and citizen acquired presumptive status in the political arena of postcolonial India. As Rogers Brubaker and Frederick Cooper have observed in a related context, "[this] implies nothing about the *depth, resonance,* or *power* of such categories in the lived experience of the persons so categorized." Instead, the argument is about how encounters with the nation-state "make certain categories readily and legitimately available for the representation of social reality, the framing of political claims, and the organization of political action. . . . The extent to which official categorizations shape self-understandings . . . are open questions that can only be addressed empirically.[7]

The third aspect concerns the distinctive impulses of the nation-statist project and the common themes that are woven through the various visual, ritual, discursive, and spatial encounters considered in this book. Prominent among these was the imagination of institutions or the central importance accorded to a particular kind of authoritative institutional form—the sovereign and representative national state. The statist imagination took several different forms, of which scholarly attention has been largely devoted to the "command economy" and the "command polity" variants—the constitutional, legal, as well as ideational commitments to a statist model of planned economic development and centralized state authority that characterized the Indian regime for the first four decades after independence. But as the preceding chapters have noted, the imagination of institutions also structured the understandings of culture, nationhood, and citizenship, with India and Indianness defined around the enabling presence and agency of the sovereign national state. This statist configuration of Indian national identity, whereby nationhood and citizenship were asserted to be artifacts that were state produced (or at the very least, state facilitated), was arguably the most distinctive feature of the postcolonial national imagination, especially when considered against the contrastive backdrop of the social movement imaginary of anticolonial nationalism that had energized nationalist actors in the years prior to national independence.[8]

The natural diversity rather than the homogeneity of the nation was another emphasis—and one that was consistent. As I argue in chapters 1 and 2, the centralized state and the fragmented nation were tightly linked and co-constitutive pillars of the nation-statist imagination in Nehruvian India, and would in fact go on to structure the national cultural and political field well beyond the death of Nehru in 1964. The postcolonial embrace of diversity or the concerted institutional-ideological efforts to protect, foster, and otherwise recognize subnational regional cultures—whether through educational, language, and cultural policies or through the very framework of ethno-federalism itself—was neither a reflection of nor a response to a natural or preexisting order. Instead, it entailed the active production of an "arboreal pluralism," or the selective inclusion and transformation of group identities into a particular state-supporting matrix of cultural diversity in which only certain kinds of identities—namely, those based on regional cultural differences—were recognized as constitutive of diversity. This arboreal pluralist logic was most clearly (and most visibly) revealed in the cultural floats of the Republic Day parades and in the films on Indian culture produced by the Films Division that invariably represented Indian identity as a montage of diverse ethno-regional cultures.[9]

Finally, encounters with the nation-state were sites and occasions for articulating a disavowal and condemnation of politics, a broad category that encompassed a wide range of mobilizational, electoral, and organizational practices and actions that contradicted, subverted, or escaped institutional channels and governmental purview. The political field of postcolonial India was structured around the call to reject or transcend politics, as the naturally diverse nation, the transcendent state, and the ideal citizen were all constituted in supra-political, even anti-political, terms.[10] In a peculiar paradox, even as the postcolonial nation-state celebrated the distinctions and achievements of its democratic constitution, the mechanisms and manifestations of democratic practice, such as elections, organized protest, popular mobilization, or general forms and expressions of social and collective conflict, were singled out for sustained criticism—whether as objects of distaste, contempt, fear, or general disapproval—in the public cultural discourse of Nehruvian India.

Why did the postcolonial national project take this particular form? Answering this question calls for a reconsideration of Nehruvian India and postcolonial modernity as historically contingent social-political formations. From this perspective, state-centrism, the emphasis on the natural diversity of the nation, and the disavowal of politics are not the products of choices made by unconstrained national elites. Instead, they are shaped by the distinct exigencies and logics of mid-twentieth-century efforts to establish a nation-state following the formal end of colonial rule. For instance, the state-centrism of the Nehruvian national imagination reflects the general imperative of simultaneity that structured the process of decolonization—the fact that in contrast to the sequenced trajectories of nation and state formation in Europe and Africa, the task at hand in India and other former colonies was the *simultaneous* formation of nation and state.

A state-centric, diversity-embracing national imagination did not, however, emerge in all of these cases. The significant variations among contemporaneous nationalisms[11]—in India, Pakistan, Indonesia, Algeria, Vietnam, Ghana, Malaysia, and Algeria, to name just a few of the "new nations" that were established in former European colonies between the 1940s and the 1960s—suggests that contextually specific sets of factors played an important role. For instance, the conjunction of a strong state as well as diversity recognition, and the complementary interplay of region and nation, ethnic and civic, modes of belonging built upon and furthered the accommodative logics of colonial rule and the concatenated mobilizations of anticolonial nationalism that were specific to India. These and other examples stress the importance of a situated rather than an invariant engagement with the project of nation-state formation, one that highlights the historical contingencies and uncertainties rather than the predetermined outcomes of a modular postcoloniality. A situated understanding of nation-state formation must also engage with questions of transformation: whether, how, and why new ideas of India emerge outside the particular historical moment of the Nehruvian project to enable and constrain the field of politics in different ways.

Transforming India: "India Shining" and the Neoliberal Imaginary

There have been significant institutional reconfigurations of state and social structures and changes in the distribution of political authority over the past sixty years. In contrast to the one-party dominant political system that characterized the Nehruvian period, political authority in contemporary India is considerably more diffuse and layered. There are multiple, and new, contenders for political power, such as regional political parties, new sets of class and caste actors, nongovernmental organizations, and multinational corporations.[12] There has been a similar pluralization in the sites of public culture. With the dismantling of the long-standing media monopoly of the state in the late 1980s, there has been a proliferation of public cultural arenas and actors, and television and Internet media have come to play an increasingly important role in setting the cultural agenda.

Substantial shifts in economic policy have also taken place. Starting in the 1990s, the shift from state socialism to free market models displaced the "humble peasant" and the "hungry masses" from their iconic roles in the developmentalist national imagination. Today, the normative subject of economically liberalized India belongs instead to the "new middle classes." Triumphant declarations of fulfilled promises and achieved modernity have taken over from the diffident uncertainties of nation-building discourses; enticing visions of the easy pleasures of consumption have replaced from an earlier moment the ascetic exhortations of Maulana Azad to "lift burdens like strong real men."

An apt illustration of these changes is the "India Shining" campaign undertaken in 2004 as an initiative of state and nonstate actors. In November 2003, the Indian state hired the multinational advertising agency Gray Worldwide to devise an advertising campaign that would project a new image for India. What began as the airing on television networks in December and January of a sixty-second video that highlighted the economic achievements of the existing Hindu nationalist Bharatiya Janata Party–led coalition government soon grew into a multimedia extravaganza with full-page advertisements in newspapers and magazines and giant billboard displays throughout the country, at a cost to the government of at least 650 million rupees ($140 million).

The brand concept for the campaign was "India Shining"; the tag line of which appeared in all advertisements and was accompanied by pictures of smiling Indians. In one image, a classroom of schoolchildren eagerly raise their hands to answer a question; in another, an old man in a Muslim prayer cap holds a lotus in his hand; and in a third, a housewife plays cricket. The explanatory text that accompanied each photograph listed the many reasons for celebration. These included the accelerating economic growth rate, the abundance of foreign exchange reserves, the successful provision of basic education, the multibillion dollar information technology industry that had made India a leading global player, the availability of new career opportunities for men and women, the ease with which bank loans for personal and home improvement could now be accessed, and the dramatic improvements in road, health, and telecommunication networks in the country.

The campaign was notable not only for its ubiquity—the fact that between November and February one could not escape the triumphant pronouncements about India's shine—but also for the quick synergies that it established in a wider public cultural domain. Numerous other advertising campaigns appropriated the slogan of India Shining in the ensuing months. It was used to describe events and moments unrelated to economic growth, such as India's victory over Pakistan in an international cricket test series. Reproduced in commercials, special issues of national magazines that surveyed the current state of India, and publicity material developed by the Indian Tourism Board, India Shining materialized in words and images the abstract message of a "resurgent India," a phrase used in recent years to describe the ascendancy of the new middle classes and India's global importance as the "world's largest consumer market," the "info-tech hub of the developing world," the "world leader in business process outsourcing," and hence the "engine of the new global economy."

At one level there is a similarity between the imagination of India Shining and that of the earlier Nehruvian national imagination. While India Shining proclaims the triumphant arrival of India into the world of modernity, in marked contrast to the deferred vision of an ongoing journey that informed the earlier conception of a troubled India, both reproduce a common logic of statism. In the contemporary moment, the accomplishment of a shining India is also presented as the fruit of statist labors: the adoption of farsighted economic policies; the constitutional configuration of India as a democracy; and the stability and durability of the political system that together (and in contrast to "rival" China) create a conducive environment for international investment. Although formulations of national identity now define the nation as an arrived presence instead of a deferred horizon,[13] the link between nation, state, and individual continues to be maintained and reinforced. In the shining light of the twenty-first century, as in the murky light of mid-century, the nation remains "the name for a relationship that links a state (actual or potential) with its subjects."[14]

But the differences between the two national imaginations are also worth contemplation. The political openings and closures that stem from an envisioning of India's troubled darkness are not those constituted by the triumphalist imaginary of the present. To begin with, the temporal fluidity of the "logic of deferral" in the needs discourse of Nehruvian India is missing from the resplendent shine of twenty-first-century India. The needy nation was an expression of faith in the future. The fulfilled nation closes off any horizons beyond the here and now.

Next, the conflation of economic success and nationhood in the glossy advertisements of the India Shining campaign inscribes a rigid division between those who are presently reaping the benefits of the economic miracle, and those who remain outside the circle of light. As noted in chapter 3, the nation-building imagination had placed all Indians in the waiting room of history and put everyone's future on hold. In contrast, India Shining constitutes the nation as a limited membership club.

Finally, the language of needs in Nehruvian India lent itself to an unexpected and unintended set of creative appropriations. Needs discourse provided marginalized groups and individuals with a way to make claims on the state and to hold it accountable for failing to live up to its promises. As Partha Chatterjee has recently argued, slum dwellers in Calcutta, who otherwise remain outside the elite circles of civil society and associational politics, have been able to appropriate governmental categories of welfare and needs to establish their political agency and make claims on the state.[15] Similar observations also hold for the specific case of scientific needs discourse. For instance, the "people's science movement" coordinated by organizations such as the Kerala Sastra Sahitya Parishad (Science Writers' Forum of Kerala), the Delhi Science Forum, and the All India People's Science Network have harnessed the scientific needs discourse of the Nehruvian state to highlight the limits and failures of existing science and development policies. Whether the liberal discourse of rights and the neoliberal discourse of individual initiative ushered in by the India Shining imagination will open up spaces of political agency and hope in equivalent ways remains an open question. These differential political possibilities are ultimately what separate the tarnish and the shine of India, the uncertainties of modernization from the certitudes of modernity.

Transforming India: "Saffronization" and the Hindu Nationalist Imaginary

Perhaps the most dramatic and most discernible change in recent years has to do with the ascendancy in contemporary India of Hindu nationalism as a political and cultural force that reached its apex with the Bharatiya Janata Party forming the government after the general elections of 1999. The fact of state complicity in the mass killing of Muslims in Gujarat in 2002 was the most direct evidence of the steady erosion of the secular-pluralist commitments of the Nehruvian national imagination in recent years. But as pointed out in the considerable scholarship on Hindu nationalism and the transformations of Indian secularism, there are numerous other examples, both less extreme and less visible, of the daily and lived transformation of secular-pluralist national identity by Hindu nationalism. To use Amartya Sen's characterization, there has been a substantive shift from a "large" to a "small" idea of nationhood in contemporary India.[16]

Upon closer look, however, these claims of Hindu nationalist disjuncture may be overstated. Thus on the one hand Hindu nationalist organizations and actors have put forward ethnicized, primordialist understandings of nationhood as a factor of religious identity that are at considerable remove from the civic, pluralist criteria that were endorsed in Nehruvian India. These include the redefinition of India as a Hindu nation, where Muslims and other religious minorities enjoy at best a second-class existence conditional on their acceptance of the superiority and priority of Hindus; the assertion of monolithic and permanent religious communities of Hindus and Muslims that enable such a definition; and the production of elaborate historical narratives about the long-standing persecution of Hindus by "foreign" Muslim rulers.[17]

These ideas and understandings have enjoyed official sanction and have been disseminated by state agencies and institutions. Some of the activities undertaken by the BJP government at the national and state level in recent years included the rewriting of school textbooks and reorganization of university curricula; the development of new commemorative rituals such as the mandated daily morning prayer to the Hindu goddess Saraswati by government officials in the state of Uttar Pradesh; and the elaboration of new national symbologies with an overtly Hindu cast. As a result of these institutional interventions, nation-statist encounters in contemporary India entail practices and experiences of seeing and recognition that are quite different from those mapped in this book. To encounter the nation-state in late-twentieth-century India is to come upon a vision of religious majoritarianism and exclusivity; to recognize a particular, monolithic, masculinist, and upper-caste version of Hindu identity as the enabling ground of national belonging.

On the other hand, themes of state transcendence, natural diversity, and the fear of politics that enabled the conjunction of nation and state in the immediate post-independence period continue to be reproduced in contemporary political and cultural arenas. Thus, the vision of a strong and authoritative state, along with its counterpart of vulnerable citizens and endangered nation continue to be central in Hindu nationalist discourse and practice.

If the preoccupation with national security—understood in terms of the inviolability of the territorial extent and authority of the central state—first emerged in the 1960s in the context of a series of internal and external challenges to centralized state power,[18] it received its fullest expression during the recent reign of the BJP government. The nuclear tests of 1998; the ascendant discourse of anti-terrorism that was backed up by legislative measures such as the Prevention of Terrorism Act passed in 2002; and the proposal to introduce a national identity card that would facilitate the identification, prosecution, and deportation of illegal immigrants from Bangladesh who had "infiltrated" India are but some concrete expressions of the reauthorization of statist command by the BJP government and its allied organizations in the Sangh Parivar (literally, the joint family of cultural, political, and social organizations that advance Hindutva ideology).

Another elective affinity or point of convergence between the Nehruvian and Hindu nationalist imaginations is the disavowal of politics. Like Nehruvian nationalism, Hindu nationalism also locates the ideal citizen, the nation, and the state in a transcendent domain outside electoral mobilizations, political organizations, and popular protests. If for Nehruvian India, communalism reflected the corruptions and dangers of politics, these are mapped onto the formation of secularism—or what proponents of Hindutva refer to as "pseudo secularism"—in Hindu nationalist India. Mirroring each other, Nehruvian and Hindu nationalist discourse have both constituted their ideal citizen as a nonpolitical subject and the nation-state as a suprapolitical entity and arena. Moreover, the discourses and practices of secularist activism that have emerged in contemporary India to withstand and reverse the ascendancy of Hindu nationalism also further this disavowal of politics, as the call to "combat communalism" launched by civil society activists is most frequently phrased in terms of the urgent need to recuperate the essential ethos of a tolerant India by "leaving politics behind."

The Swarna Jayatri Rath Yatra organized by the BJP to commemorate the fiftieth anniversary of Indian independence, 1997. (Courtesy of the Bharatiya Janata Party, New Delhi)

Finally, although its majoritarian aspirations would lead us to expect otherwise, Hindu nationalist organizations nevertheless reproduce the imagination of India's natural diversity. This convergence can be explained by practical-strategic considerations. Given the ethno-linguistic organization of political space in the Indian federation, any political formation with national aspirations can speak for and of the nation only through the additive or aggregated rhetoric and logic of regionalism. Here, the contrast between the two mass-mobilizational campaigns undertaken by the BJP in 1989 and in 1997 is instructive. As scholars of Hindu nationalism have documented, the infamous Ram Janmabhoomi, or Liberation of Lord Rama's Birthplace campaign, undertaken in 1989 marked the inauguration of the BJP's cultural-political campaign to remake India as a Hindu nation. The campaign explicitly and unambiguously advanced Hindutva ideals, as the party and the larger social-cultural formation that energized it defined themselves as representatives of a *Hindu* nation.

Less than a decade later, similar mobilizational tools and symbologies were deployed in a new chariot procession launched by the BJP and allied Sangh Parivar organizations, this time to mark the fiftieth anniversary of Indian independence. In contrast to the homogenous "Hindutva effect" of the Ram Janmabhoomi campaign, the primary symbolical effect that the Swarna Jayanti Rath Yatra (Fiftieth Anniversary Chariot Procession) sought to convey in summer 1997 was that of Hindu nationalism's diverse constitution—the fact that being Hindu, just like being Indian, was about "being something else at the same time."[19] The carefully plotted pan-regional route of the procession; the icons of Hindu nationalist heroes from different regions of India that decorated the sides of the Toyota truck-cum-chariot; and the collection of samples of "sacred earth" from each state in India to be placed in an urn of "national unity" that occupied the procession's pride of place were among the symbolic and ritual practices that enabled Hindu nationalists to perform their allegiance to the sacred mantra of Nehruvian nationalism: unity in diversity.

These and other findings of convergence call into question the understanding of Hindu nationalist disjuncture. Moreover, and to echo Thomas Hansen's trenchant observation, the "ease" with which Hindu nationalism fits into and furthers "authorized discourses" of Indian nationhood invites a consideration of whether the naturalization of Indian diversity by the Nehruvian national project may in fact have *enabled* the discursive and practical maneuver of unifying the nation through Hindu majoritarianism in later years.[20] For instance, the Nehruvian reproduction of an essentialized, unitary, unchanging, and depoliticized understanding of ethno-regional cultures; the representation of subnational diversity "in need" of an overarching unifying agency; and the negative exemplars of the destabilizing, dangerous, and "anti-national" expressions of diversity that constituted the limits of the pluralist imagination, have all lent themselves to Hindutva's quest for national legitimization over the past decade. From this perspective, the distance between the diversity-embracing framework of Nehruvian nationalism and the monocultural aspirations of Hindu nationalism—between history and the present—may be shorter than we would hope.

NOTES

INTRODUCTION

1. According to Paul Brass, the "systematic" manner in which the mass violence against Muslims took place, the "precision" of the killings, and the considerable evidence of the involvement of political organizations distinguish it from the more spontaneous forms of inter-religious "riots" that have taken place in India. Ashutosh Varshney advances a similar observation, and he adds to the definition of a "pogrom" the ideologically motivated nature of the violence and the involvement of the state government in perpetuating and condoning the acts. See Brass, "The Gujarat Pogrom of 2002"; and Varshney, "Explaining Gujarat Violence." For a detailed discussion of the events in Gujarat, see the collection of media reports and analytical essays compiled in Varadarajan, Gujarat.
2. These approximations are based on an investigative report by the Human Rights Watch. There is some amount of variation in the statistics reported by different civil society organizations and human rights groups that investigated the violence. The figures cited by the state were considerably lower. See Human Rights Watch, "We Have No Orders to Save You."
3. The election results surprised political analysts, most of whom had been predicting a victory for the incumbent coalition government. The reasons for the National Democratic Alliance's defeat are complex, and do not necessarily indicate a rejection of Hindu nationalist ideology (or conversely, a vote in favor of secularism and tolerance). Widespread dissatisfaction with the economic policies of the government and the "anti-incumbent factor" are among the alternative explanations that have been advanced. Yogendra Yadav has in fact ruled out broad national-level explanations altogether, and has argued instead that the final outcome was an aggregation of regional and district-level electoral verdicts and social-political changes that were driven by specific, localized factors. See Yadav, "Radical Shift in the Social Basis of Political Power."
4. "Detoxification" was the term used by the state officials themselves to describe the project of replacing BJP appointees in educational agencies such as the National Council for Educational Research and Training (NCERT) and withdrawing the history textbooks that had advanced a Hindu nationalist version of Indian

history. For an assessment of the Hindu nationalist historiographical project and a longer-term perspective on the politics of history writing in India, see Lal, *The History of History*. See also the thoughtful assessment of the limits and possibilities of the "detoxification" project by the Indian historian Shahid Amin in "Educational Reforms."

5 This question about the relationship between the apparent exceptionalism of the Gujarat violence and the normal practices of democratic politics in India also informs a recent volume of essays, *Violence and Democracy in India*, which I coedited with Amrita Basu.

6 The thesis of Gujarat as an exception, and the corollary observation about the resilience of Indian secular institutions and ideologies, has been discussed by Steven Wilkinson, Sunil Khilnani, and Bhikhu Parekh, among others. Although these writers argue that the existing institutional-ideological structures of secularism require considerable strengthening and energizing in order to prevent future Gujarats, they all concur on the *absence* of a total collapse or breakdown of secularism in the present. See Wilkinson, "Putting Gujarat in Perspective"; Khilnani, "Branding India"; and Parekh, "Making Sense of Gujarat."

7 The term "holding together" is used by Alfred Stepan to describe the particular federal structure of India's "multinational democracy." He distinguishes this from the "coming-together" federalism of the United States, where national unity (the decision to form a federation) was the product of a contracted agreement made by state units. According to Stepan, the fact that the Indian federation survives in the absence of such a foundational "voluntary bargain" and, moreover, that it survives as a flourishing democracy (unlike the "coercive effort by a non-democratic centralizing power" that underwrote the "putting-together" federalism of the USSR) is what makes India an exemplary success story. Stepan, "Federalism and Democracy," 22.

8 The movement for Khalistan was a militant effort to establish an autonomous homeland for Sikhs in the state of Punjab in the 1980s. The central government increasingly resorted to armed force and repressive legislation in the effort to counter the violent tactics of the movement. The spiral of rapidly escalating violence culminated in the Indian army's siege of the Golden Temple in 1984. Four months later, Prime Minister Indira Gandhi was assassinated by her Sikh bodyguards in retaliation for the desecration of the Sikh religion's holiest shrine; her death in turn was "avenged" through the mass killing of thousands of ordinary Sikhs in Delhi. See Axel, *The Nation's Tortured Body*; Gupta, *The Context of Ethnicity*; and Mahmood, *Fighting for Faith and Nation*. For an overview of ethno-nationalist movements in postcolonial India, see Brass, *Language, Religion and Politics in North India*; and Kohli, "Can Democracies Accommodate Ethnic Nationalism?"

9 "The holocaust was not an irrational outflow of the not-yet-fully-eradicated residues of pre-modern barbarity . . . [but] a paradigm of modern bureaucratic rationality" (Baumann, *Modernity and the Holocaust*, 149–50).

10 Prakash Upadhyaya makes this argument in the context of a discussion of Indian secularism, and Faisal Devji offers a similar critique through a more general interrogation of postcolonial culture and politics. See Upadhyaya, "The Politics of Indian Secularism"; and Devji, "Hindu/Muslim/Indian."

11 This position is usually linked to a more wide-ranging "critique of modernity" or the critical interrogation of modernist institutions, ideologies, and governmental technologies. The writings of Ashis Nandy are a paradigmatic example. See the collection of essays in Nandy, *The Romance of the State and the Fate of Dissent in the Tropics* for a recent elaboration of this argument. Similar arguments about the limits of state-sponsored multiculturalism and other institutionalist attempts at "diversity-management" have also been raised in discussions of the United States, Canada, and Australia, among others. See Chow, *The Protestant Ethnic and the Spirit of Capitalism*; Hage, *White Nation*; Goldberg, *Multiculturalism*; and Mackey, *The House of Difference*.

12 According to the philosopher of science Imre Lakatos, every research program is grounded in a "negative heuristic" or a "hard core" of unfalsifiable, unquestioned (and unquestionable) assumptions. See Lakatos, "Falsification and the Methodology of Scientific Research Programmes," 135.

13 The geographical landscape traversed by this line of inquiry is vast, moving from the future of postwar Iraq to the increasing use of headscarves worn in French schools. Ongoing discussions about the emergence and viability of a European identity also reflect a similar set of concerns, namely that of how to secure a nested arrangement of differing scales or levels of identity so that it is possible to be simultaneously Italian and European, or Basque and European, or for that matter to have Germany and Estonia share a common identity.

14 For example, see the proposals outlined in Coakley, *The Territorial Management of Ethnic Conflict*; Dasgupta, "India's Federal Design and Multicultural National Construction"; Easterly, "Can Institutions Resolve Ethnic Conflict?"; Lijphart, *Democracy in Plural Societies*; and Lustick, "Stability in Deeply Divided Societies."

15 The variable or dynamic, symbolic, and subjective/situated aspects of ethnic identity—the fact that ethnicity is a meaningful and lived category that is differently experienced (even by the same individual) at different points in time—is overlooked by institutionalist-proceduralist approaches. On the problems of "thin" understandings of ethnic identity, see Hale, "Explaining Ethnicity" (especially 462–63); Horowitz, *Ethnic Groups in Conflict*; and Okamura, "Situational Ethnicity."

16 The instability of postcolonial "new" nation-states was a dominant theme in the political development literature of the 1960s. While the teleologies of modernization that related the difficulties of "national integration" to the absence of the requisite modern "pattern variables" in the societies outside of the West have since been disavowed, the proposal that there is an inverse relationship between the longevity of institutions and ethnic instability continues to be advanced in discussions about postcommunist states—most recently in discussions about post-

war Iraq and Afghanistan. For an early statement of the problems encountered by "new nations," see Binder, *Crises and Sequences in Political Development*; and Geertz, "The Integrative Revolution."

17 The dialectic of remembering and forgetting" that Ernest Renan identifies as one of the core constituents of nationhood (necessarily) takes place over an extended duration of time: the institutional production of amnesia requires the absence of living memory. The exemplary forgetting that Renan pointed to is the case of the St. Bartholemew's Day massacre, an event that took place seven centuries before the time of his writing. Anthony Marx's recent discussion of how the forgetting of past practices of exclusion and violence sustains the myth of national unity in European nation-states is also based on an implicit argument about historical distance, or the need for "enough time" to have lapsed between the violent, illiberal origins of nationalism and the pacific liberal environment in which it presently flourishes. But how much time is long enough? The temporal distance between the present and the past is a constituted effect rather than a quantifiable accumulation of years (itself another construct), and in this sense it is not the passage of time as such but rather the construction of time as passing and/or past that we need to consider. See Renan, "What Is a Nation?" 19; and Marx, *Faith in Nation*, 165–206.

18 The fiftieth anniversary of Indian independence in 1997 saw the emergence of a new body of scholarship on the experiences of partition. See, for instance, Butalia, *The Other Side of Silence*; Menon and Bhasin, *Borders and Boundaries*; and Nandy, "The Invisible Holocaust and the Journey as an Exodus." The main thrust of this project was to undo the silences of the official narratives of Indian history, where partition is discussed only fleetingly, if at all. Moreover, the efforts of scholars such as Butalia to compile oral histories of partition memories marked another departure from the dominant historiographical practices of a state-centered "history from above." Although the project's immense political-ethical value as well as its scholarly value cannot be denied, the contrast between the voices recuperated by the partition-memory project and the silences that otherwise prevailed may be somewhat overstated. For instance, public cultural texts—films, literature, poetry—have been a significant site and means of representing and communicating the meaning of partition as an embodied or lived experience of violence and dislocation. The films of Ritwik Ghatak, Nemai Ghosh and the fiction of Saadat Hasan Manto, Krishna Sobti, Bhisham Sahni, Rajinder Singh Bedi, Narendranath Mitra, and Jyotirmayee Devi have all engaged in the "speaking" of partition. Finally, although the political use and effect is very different, memories of the violence of partition have been kept alive in the *shakhas* or branches of the Rashtriya Swayamsevak Sangh (RSS), the nodal organization of Hindu nationalism.

19 Cited in Linz, Stepan, and Yadav, "Nation State or State Nation?" 20–21.

20 The agencies of nationalization-modernization discussed by Weber include schools, the army, transport and communications (roads), and the church. See Weber, *Peasants into Frenchmen*.

21 See Buck-Morss, *Dreamworld and Catastrophe*; Dobrenko and Naiman, *The Landscape of Stalinism*; and Haynes, *New Soviet Man*.
22 See Mosse, *The Nationalization of the Masses*.
23 For Syria, see Wedeen, *Ambiguities of Domination*; for Iraq, see Makiya, *Republic of Fear*.
24 According to Benedict Anderson, the advent of national consciousness is explained by social-cultural processes such as the standardization of vernacular languages, and by cognitive shifts such as the emergence of new understandings of time (as "simultaneous" and "empty"). Both of these transformations are linked to the innovations of "print capitalism." See Anderson, *Imagined Communities*.
25 According to Michael Billig, the everyday, habitual encounters with visual signs of the nation such as the national flag and other "banal" or routine reassertions of the nation-state's existence enable the consolidation and naturalization of nationalism in the established nation-states of the West. Moreover, it is the "unmindfulness" that attends these experiences and enables their productive effect: "This reminding is so familiar, so continual, that it is not consciously registered as reminding. The metonymic image of banal nationalism is not a flag which is being consciously waved with fervent passion; it is the flag hanging unnoticed on the public building" (Billig, *Banal Nationalism*, 8). For a discussion of the historical transformation in the symbolic repertoire of banal nationalism in the United States, see Zelinsky, *Nation into State*.
26 For a fascinating discussion of the "cult of Ataturk" in Turkey, and its visible, material manifestations in statues, monuments, and iconographies, see Navaro-Yashin, *Faces of the State*, 188–204.
27 Under the terms of the Flag Code of India, civilian displays of the national flag were only permitted on six authorized "national days" every year.
28 See Marx, *Making Race and Nation*. For a polemical statement about the analytical and political-ethical problems of "importing" to other social historical contexts (the study of Brazil, for instance) the concepts and models for the study of race and racial inequality that are based on the specific American experience, see Bourdieu and Wacquant, "On the Cunning of Imperialist Reason," 44–46. As these writers argue, "[the] commonplaces of the great new global vulgate that endless media repetition transforms into universal common sense manage in the end to make one forget that they have their roots in the complex and controversial realities of a particular historical society, now tacitly constituted as model for every other and as yardstick for all things" (42).
29 The "lumping effect" of ethnicity also obscures the significant variations within ethnic categories. For instance, the differential histories, population sizes, and social-economic relations in the states of Uttar Pradesh and Gujarat configure the identities and differences attached to "Hinduness" and "Muslimness" in very different ways. However, discussions of "religious conflict" seldom take this local-regional variation into account, and focus instead on a singular, nationally

aggregated problematic of ethno-religious identity and conflict. For a notable exception, see the attempt to theorize local (in this case, urban) variation in Varshney, *Ethnic Conflict and Civic Life*.

30 Systemic endurance, resilience, or stability is understood here in a minimalist and negative sense as the absence of prolonged periods of social disorder, political upheavals, civil wars, and protracted secessionist movements.

31 Drawing upon Deleuze and Guattari's discussion of epistemological formations, William Connolly develops a contrast between the institutionalist structures and practices of an "arboreal pluralism" where group identities are configured as "limbs branching out from a common trunk fed by a single taproot," and a fluid, decentralized formation of a "rhizomatic pluralization." See Connolly, *The Ethos of Pluralization*, 93.

32 Sankaran Krishna has developed a similar argument about how the "threat" of ethnicity is produced as a necessary supplement of state power by the rhetoric and practice of nation building, international relations, and foreign policy. See Krishna, *Postcolonial Insecurities*, especially 59–100, for an extended discussion of "the unredeemable debt that nation-building owes to ethnicity and vice versa" (60).

33 For discussions of the formation and evolution of epistemologies of identity, along with a critical evaluation of the "identity paradigm," see Brubaker and Cooper, "Beyond Identity"; Gleason, "Identifying Identity"; Hacking, "Making Up People"; Hopf, *Social Construction of International Politics*; Handler, "Is 'Identity' a Useful Cross-Cultural Concept?"; and Weldes and Laffey, "Beyond Belief."

34 Balibar and Wallerstein, *Race, Nation, Class*, 93.

35 See Smith, *The Ethnic Origins of Nations*, for a statement of this "ethnosymbolic" perspective on nation formation.

36 Socio-biologists link the formation of national, ethnic, and other large social groups to the operations of kin selection, inclusive fitness, altruism, and other evolutionary mechanisms. See Van der Berghe, *The Ethnic Phenomenon*; and Johnson, "The Architecture of Ethnic Identity."

37 In Smith's account, it is through the interventions of political agents, and as a result of political, economic, and social structural changes, that an *ethnie* is transformed into a nation. See the overview of Smith's ethnosymbolic approach in Guibernau and Hutchinson, "History and National Destiny."

38 Gellner, *Nations and Nationalism*.

39 Adams, "Culture in Rational-Choice Theories of State Formation," 109. Adams uses this phrase to describe the existing conceptualizations of the family. In an argument that is of considerable relevance to the subject of this book, she argues for a move beyond the mere assertion and imputation of emotion and affect to the family; and for a consideration of the "path (or paths) by which forms of elite masculinity come to be linked to ideologies of rule" (109)—that is, a consideration of the political and social structures, mechanisms, and implications of affect formation.

40 Hroch, "From National Movement to the Fully-Formed Nation."
41 Hechter, *Internal Colonialism*; Nairn, *The Break-Up of Britain*.
42 Although it has all of the shortcomings of ideal-typical classifications, the scholarship on nationalism can be arrayed along a typological spectrum of "primordialist," "constructivist," and "instrumentalist" approaches. The constructivist perspective on nations and nationalism addresses the historical contingency, fluidity, and dynamism of identity as well as its "stickiness" or durability—the fact that while identities may be "made" or artifactual, they are experienced as "found" or natural. For a discussion of the approaches to nationalism, see Eley and Suny, introduction to *Becoming National*. From the moment of social history to the work of cultural reproduction."
43 Anderson, *Imagined Communities*, 21.
44 Unlike Gellner, Anderson does not define industrialization as a prerequisite for the emergence of nationalism. The advent of print capitalism occurs in a *pre-industrial*, mercantile capitalist order.
45 Anderson, *Imagined Communities*, 19.
46 The "ineffability" assumption made by primordialist conceptions of the nation, or the view that the emotive power of national bonds is self-evident, invariant, and sui generis, is the subject of a thoroughgoing critique by Eller and Coughlan in "The Poverty of Primordialism."
47 Although Anderson's argument endorses a version of ineffable reasoning, there are elements of an alternative framework in his book, although he does not take up these himself in any sustained fashion. These relate to the structuring effect rather than the ideological affect of the nation form. For instance, as Jonathan Culler and Pheng Cheah have recently noted, Anderson's discussion of the novel as a nationalizing vehicle is based on its structural role (the form of the novel and how it interpellates the reader as a national subject) rather than its thematic/ideological content. See Culler and Cheah, *Grounds of Comparison*, 8. Culler describes this as the work of the "novel as an analogue to the nation" rather than a "representation of the nation." In his words, the novel is a "structural condition of possibility" for imagining the nation. Instead of providing representations of the nation, it enables the "formal adumbration of the space of a community" (Culler, "Anderson and the Novel," 33, 48, and 50).
48 Herzfeld, *The Social Production of Indifference*, 98.
49 The opening question of Anderson's book is about how to explain or account for the violence and "bloodshed" of conflicts between socialist states. While he goes on to argue that these conflicts drew attention to the power and persistence of the national idea even in regimes that endorsed non-national/inter-national ideologies, the relationship between violence and nationalism, or the ways in which the "imagination" of the nation actually went on to affect and structure the actions, practices, and emotions of subjects, remained unexplored. Thus, while his book documents the emergence of the nation and nationalism, it does not provide an explanation of its emotive significance or its role as an incitement to particular

kinds of (violent) action; that is, the question of what it is that made people kill, or die, for their "imagined community" is not addressed. See Anderson *Imagined Communities*, 1–4.

50 Anderson is hardly alone in this neglect. A similar tendency to psychologize the nation also marks the work of other scholars, with the dominant understanding of nationhood as that of an "*idée-force* which fills man's brain and heart with new thoughts and new sentiments and drives him to translate his consciousness into deeds of organized action" (Kohn, "Western and Eastern Nationalisms," 162).

51 Cited in Billig, *Banal Nationalism*, 19.

52 Kelly and Kaplan, *Represented Communities*, 35.

53 See Anderson, *Imagined Communities*.

54 Ibid., 83–111.

55 Cassirer, in his *The Myth of the State*, notes the signifying practices and symbolic representations that imbue the state with an authoritative presence and a (particular kind of) material reality. Cassirer's notion is reworked by Thomas Blom Hansen in his "Governance and State Mythologies in Mumbai" to include a consideration of policy discourses as well as bureaucratic-institutional technologies (for instance the "commission of inquiry").

56 Wedeen, *Ambiguities of Domination*.

57 This is also a shift from the individualizing premises of the identity and belief model to a consideration of the social determination and intersubjective constitution of identity—the "formal matrix of relations, or networks in which individuals are enmeshed" (Berezin, "Political Belonging," 358).

58 As Brubaker observes, "To understand nationalism, we have to understand the practical uses of the category 'nation,' the ways it can come to structure perception, to inform thought and experience, to organize discourse and political action." This effectively shifts the terrain of enquiry from the ontology of nationhood (the "what is a nation" question) to the political and cultural processes of its institutionalization. See Brubaker, *Nationalism Reframed*, 10, 16.

59 Van der Veer, *Imperial Encounters*, 53.

60 Abrams, "Notes on the Difficulty of Studying the State," 58.

61 The work of Partha Chatterjee is a notable exception, in that his analytical object is nationalist *thought and practice* rather than national emotion or identity. He maps the discursive field that was constituted by political elites and intellectuals writing and acting in the name of the nation, and in so doing he steers clear of imputations of effect and reception. See Chatterjee, *Nationalist Thought and the Colonial World*.

62 Billig, *Banal Nationalism*, 8.

63 Ibid., 11.

64 Mbembe, *On the Postcolony*, 103.

65 The demand for the recognition of language identity is seen as a claim for political and economic power sharing (a demand for greater autonomy for regional state units, and for the reorganization of the existing federal structure through setting

up new state units). The claims-making practices of religious groups are, however, accommodated within a nondistributive register; that is, they are seen as claims for the protection of religious customs and traditions, rather than for political and economic equality. The controversy over the Uniform Civil Code is linked to this logic of cultural recognition/minority protection, whereby "Muslims" are viewed as being naturally attached to "their" religious law, and secularism is interpreted as the preservation and protection of these legal frameworks. This is a position that does not accommodate the demands of Muslim women for a restructuring of gender relations *within* the monolithically understood "Muslim community." See Hasan and Menon, *Unequal Citizens*, for a carefully disaggregated discussion of this issue.

66 In fact one of the key findings of this study is that the charges of state failure, inadequacy, or ineffectiveness were state-produced discourses in Nehruvian India; a common technique of state legitimization has been what we might term the "manufacture of dissent."

67 Mitchell, "Society, Economy, and the State Effect," 81. See also Mitchell, "The Limits of the State," 93–95.

68 This is somewhat different from Billig's discussion of the reproduction/naturalization of nationhood through "forgotten reminders." The logic of the encounter is predicated not on "forgetting" but instead through the continued recognition of forms or the expression of authority and power. See Billig, *Banal Nationalism*.

69 Wedeen, *Ambiguities of Domination*, 33–35.

70 This in turn requires that we take seriously the practices of ideological *production* or the ways in which authoritative discourses and "monopoly claims" are articulated, instead of placing causal importance on the *reception* of ideology. In this regard, I depart from the culturalist arguments about state formation that continue to attribute a determinative role to some form of "political unconscious," such as the notion of state as "fetish" advanced by Michael Taussig or the discussion of the "phantasmatic forces that effect and the psychic work that regenerates the state" in Navaro-Yashin's study of state power in Turkey. See Taussig, "Maleficium"; and Navaro-Yashin, *Faces of the State*, 16. For the concept of the "political unconscious," see Hunt, *The Family Romance of the French Revolution*.

71 Departing from the Foucauldian understanding of the microcapillary, invisible, and internalized workings of disciplinary power, the naturalized appearance of the "cultural arbitrary of the nation-state" discussed in this study is seen to depend upon practices and effects of externalization and visibility. See Mitchell, "The Limits of the State," 93–95.

72 Hansen and Stepputat, *States of Imagination*, 37; emphasis added.

73 As Hansen and Stepputat have observed in their discussion of the cultural practices of state-formation, such practices entail the use of "symbolic languages of authority" (the institutionalization of law and legal discourse as the authoritative language of the state; the materialization of the state in signs and rituals; and the

production of national cultures and national landscapes) and "practical languages of governance" (the assertion of territorial sovereignty; the gathering of knowledge of the population; the development and management of the national economy) (*States of Imagination*, 6–8).

74 As Hansen and Stepputat have noted, "state power is fetishized through displays and spectacles but becomes effective as authority only because it invades, and is appropriated by, everyday epistemologies of power, of the magical, the spiritual, and the extraordinary" (*States of Imagination*, 20). Among the studies that highlight the everyday forms, sites, and agencies of state formation are "Blurred Boundaries," Akhil Gupta's ethnography of how the state is imagined by the residents of a north Indian village; *On the Postcolony*, Achille Mbembe's discussion of the "conviviality" of power or the ways in which "state power and subjects share the same living space"; and *Faces of the State*, Yael Navaro-Yashin's exploration of how the farewell ritual enacted by soldiers and their families in Turkey reinscribes the existence and the authority of the nation-state. See also Joseph and Nugent, *Everyday Forms of State Formation*.

75 VVIP is the acronym for "Very Very Important Person," a bureaucratic-security category for elite office-bearers of the state, such as presidents and prime ministers. For an engaging institutional and political history of "securitization" practices in postcolonial India, see Lal, "Black Cat Commandos, Gunmen, and other Terrors."

76 Enacted in 1987 in the aftermath of Indira Gandhi's assassination by sympathizers of the secessionist Khalistan, TADA circumvented the due process of law and invested discretionary powers in the state to detain suspected terrorists and try them in "special courts." As several human rights groups have since documented, TADA was frequently used against groups and individuals contesting the structures of state power used as an instrument to quell social protest in different parts of the country. Although TADA was eventually withdrawn, the renewed international emergence of anti-terrorism legislations in the aftermath of the World Trade Center attacks led to the passage of a Prevention of Terrorism Ordinance (POTO) in 2002.

77 For a discussion of the "spectacular" and "magical" representations of state power, see Taussig, *The Magic of the State*; and Coronil, *The Magical State*.

78 The "Nehruvian India" of postcolonial India refers to the formative role played by the nation's first prime minister, Jawaharlal Nehru, in laying the institutional and ideological scaffolding of the new nation-state in the 1950s and 1960s. The periodization of Nehruvian India that is used throughout this book corresponds to the years 1947–1969. While Nehru died in 1964, there were no significant transformations in state-society relations and the structures of governance under his immediate successor, Lal Bahadur Shastri (1964–1967), and during the initial years of Indira Gandhi's premiership. The break that I identify—following Frankel, Rudolph and Rudolph, Corbridge and Harriss, and others who have written extensively on this period of postcolonial Indian history—relates to the structural

transformations of the "Congress system" that Gandhi introduced through her split with the original Congress Party in 1969; her decision to discontinue internal elections within the party; and the resulting centralization of the party structure around a personalized and increasingly populist node of leadership. See Frankel, *India's Political Economy, 1947–1977*; Rudolph and Rudolph, *In Pursuit of Lakshmi*; and Corbridge and Harriss, *Reinventing India*.

79 Moreover, like the encounters with the many pleasures of diversity, the dark countervisions of diversity's dangers manifested themselves in a variety of arenas and were replicated by both state and nonstate actors and institutions. The designation of the northeastern state of Manipur as a "disturbed area" rife with militants and the subsequent passage of a special Armed Forces Special Powers Act in 1958, as well as the "peace marches" by social activists in the aftermath of communal riots in the steel township of Rourkela in 1964 (the subject of chapter 4), played different but complementary roles in advancing the logic of the unity-in-diversity worldview: the former by forcefully quelling alternative assertions of group identity and practices of claims making, the latter by echoing the state's familiar call to "leave politics behind."

80 For the most part, the ideal citizen of Nehruvian India was imagined as a masculine subject, iconically represented as a young boy. Contrast this with the feminized imagination of Mother India advanced by sections of the anticolonial nationalist movement, and by the Hindu nationalists in pre- and post-independence periods. For a discussion of the "erotic logics" of nationalisms and the feminization of the nation, see Ramaswamy, "Maps and Mother Goddesses in Modern India."

81 Here I draw upon Thomas Hansen's discussion of the distinctions between the "sublime" sphere of state action and the "profane" domain of ordinary politics that is riven by partisan conflict, self-seeking behavior by political entrepreneurs, and the "petty" concerns of individuals and groups whose discontent with the existing status quo reveals their inability to appreciate the intrinsic worth of statist reason. See Hansen, *The Saffron Wave*, chapter 1.

82 Hansen and Stepputat, *States of Imagination*, 5.

83 Although an investigation is beyond the scope of this particular study, encounters with the nation-state have also varied significantly across governance levels: representations of state, nation, and citizen that emerged at the local level have been quite different from those that structured regional and national political fields. As Joel Migdal has observed, "If states have to be viewed in their social contexts, it is important to study not only the peak organizations of states and key social groups, often located at the center of the polity in the capital city, but also state-society interactions at the periphery" (Migdal, introduction to Migdal, Kohli, and Shue, *State Power and Social Forces*, 3. For an interesting counterpart to the nationalizing effects of the nation-state encounter presented in this book, see the ethnographic discussion of an encounter with the state in a village in West Bengal in Ruud, "Talking Dirty about Politics."

84 This argument about the contradictory, incoherent, even *tentative* (in the sense of reversible or nonpermanent) operations of state power calls into question the liberal view that individual and collective freedom and autonomy require a constrained or minimalist state, as well as the corollary of this view, that "big states" *necessarily* engender unfreedom and social leveling. Each chapter interrogates and sets aside the false dichotomy of such liberal reasoning by showing how an unequivocally state-centric national imagination can equally be one that fosters, elicits, and produces various forms of individual and collective political agency.

85 Wedeen, *Ambiguities of Domination*.

86 Although the "ideas of India" that I work with in this book are similar to those identified by Sunil Khilnani (democracy; secularism; stateness; development), I am more interested in their institutional-material determination and effects, or ideas qua ideologies, rather than their political-philosophical lineages. See Khilnani, *The Idea of India*.

87 "Communities are to be distinguished, not by their falsity/genuineness, but by the style in which they are imagined" (Anderson, *Imagined Communities*, 6).

88 My use of the term "enframing effect" departs from the cognitive-internalized presumptions of "frame theory." In other words, I do not use it in the sense of a mental schemata or "shared meanings, which assumes that individuals "accept" dominant frames and then formulate their thoughts and actions accordingly. Instead, my focus is on how certain discourses are empowered or sanctioned in the public arena while others are not. Thus, the "enframing effect" is produced through the coercive technologies of state power as much as through its consensual aspects, or rather, through a combination of the two. For a recent critical assessment of frame theory that draws attention to the neglect of the social-institutional *processes* and *effects* of framing and its endorsement of a "black box" approach to mental cognition, see Oliver and Johnston, "What a Good Idea."

89 As Rogers Brubaker has argued, variations in the "practical category" of citizenship and nationhood in France and Germany, and in the complex of institutional structures, policy formations, and political practices to which they gave rise (such as the differences in naturalization laws and in the public cultural attitudes toward "foreigners" and "minorities" in each country), can be explained by their divergent geopolitical histories and cultural-ideological legacies. While it may be implausible, and indeed impossible, to trace a direct line of causation between the discrimination faced by Turkish *gastarbeiter* (guest workers) in twenty-first-century Germany to the dilemmas of institutionalization and legitimization that occupied state builders in early-modern Europe, Brubaker has nevertheless made a persuasive case for the embedded and historically sedimented character of cultural-political formations such as nationalist ideologies, and the consequent need to ground discussions of contemporary political discourses and practices in a consideration of social, cultural, and institutional histories. A similar argument is made by Anthony Marx in his comparative analysis of "race and nation" in the

United States, Brazil, and South Africa. Although parts of his argument can be called into question (such as his largely unsupported assertion that it was indeed possible to "bind up the nation" in and through ideologies of racial homogeneity and their counterpart, racial othering), it is notable for its call to locate the contemporary predicament of racialized politics in each country in a historical consideration of the experiences of state formation in each country. See Brubaker, Citizenship and Nationhood in France and Germany; and Marx, Making Race and Nation.

90 Wedeen, Ambiguities of Domination, 156.
91 See Scott, Refashioning Futures.
92 As Scott has argued, the dominant preoccupations and scholarly debates of postcolonial studies often fail to take cognizance of the transformations in the larger political context that have taken place since the initial formulation of postcolonial theory, and the new constellation of issues, questions, and stakes that require address if theory is to maintain its critical edge and compulsion. See Scott, Refashioning Futures, 3–15.
93 Ashcroft, introduction to Ashcroft, Griffin, and Tiffin, The Postcolonial Studies Reader. In a similar vein, the "postcolonial" of Sandra Harding's "postcolonial science studies" is about the "people's sciences" and "subaltern sciences" in non-Western contexts that stand outside, and in opposition to, the dominant paradigms and institutions of "Western science." The many initiatives of "official science" that were undertaken in these polities in the course of the effort to build new nation-states, and the intimate relationship between science and state power in postcolonial polities, find no mention in what amounts to an unqualified celebration of the necessarily progressive character of postcolonial science. See Harding, Is Science Multicultural?
94 As the vocabulary of postcolonial "condition" implies, the relative inattention to issues of social and political context and historical variation can be explained by the formative influence of psychological and psychoanalytic paradigms on postcolonial theory.
95 For an exception, see the following ethnographic studies of postcolonial modernity as a lived, socially historically situated experience: Gupta, Postcolonial Developments; Ferguson, The Anti-Politics Machine; Hansen, Wages of Violence; Chatterjee, The Nation and Its Fragments; Krishna, Postcolonial Insecurities; and the collection of essays in Breckenridge, Consuming Modernity. Differences in disciplinary location can partly explain why this group of scholars configures their object of analysis, "the postcolonial," very differently from those who work with literary studies. For a discussion of the variegated epistemologies of postcolonial studies, see Young, Postcolonialism.
96 Cohn, Colonialism and Its Forms of Knowledge.
97 See Cohn, Colonialism and Its Forms of Knowledge; Jones, "Religious Identity and the Indian Census"; and Chakrabarty, "Modernity and Ethnicity in India." According to Ian Hacking, the "dynamic nominalist" effect of the census and other statistical

projects is about how "numerous kinds of human beings and human acts come into being hand in hand with our invention of the categories labelling them." See Hacking, "Making Up People," 236.

98 The description of precolonial forms of identity as "fuzzy communities" that lacked a dichotomous sense of group boundedness (the notion of an absolute difference between self and other) and accommodated a layered notion of identity is found in Kaviraj, "The Imaginary Institution of India." See also Appadurai, "Number in the Colonial Imagination."

99 For a discussion of the "construction of communalism" by colonial discourse and institutional practice, and its appropriation and revitalization in the postcolonial period through the pervasive tendency of representing socially and politically grounded acts and moments of violence as expressions of an essential "pathology" of communalism, see Brass, *Theft of an Idol*; and Pandey, *The Construction of Communalism in Colonial North India*.

100 See Barua, "Inventing Race," for a discussion of the "martial races" theory that informed the design of military recruitment strategies; Hasan, "The Myth of Unity," for a discussion of the institution of "separate electorates" for Muslims by the Morley-Minto administrative-legislative reforms of 1909; the collection of essays compiled by Jones, *Religious Controversy in British India*, for a discussion of the colonial protection of separate personal law codes for members of different religious communities; and Brown, "Ethnology and Colonial Administration in Nineteenth Century British India, and Yang, *Crime and Criminology in British India*, for a discussion of the ethnicizing and racializing effects of criminal legislation (the designation of certain communities as "criminal tribes").

101 The idea of a separate state for Muslims, although within the overall framework of a united India, was first articulated by Mohammad Iqbal at the annual session of the Muslim League in 1930. The transformation of this demand for increased autonomy to an agitation for a separate Muslim nation-state in 1946 (via the 1940 Lahore Declaration that Muslims were a separate nation) was by no means a preordained outcome, but rather one that was influenced, among other things, by the intransigence of Congress leaders toward the political accommodation of the Muslim League and the demand of its leader, Mohammad Ali Jinnah, for a weaker federation. As Ayesha Jalal has pointed out, the "uncertainties and indeterminacies of politics" in late colonial India must be taken into account in order to understand how the idea of a distinct Muslim *nation* was transformed into a demand for the separate *nation-state* of Pakistan. See Jalal, "Exploding Communalism," 93.

102 "Language politics" gained new momentum in the first decade after independence as different groups mobilized around the demand for linguistically homogenous state units. In 1956, the States Reorganization Commission announced the federal reorganization of the Indian polity along linguistic lines. For a discussion of language politics from the perspective of center-state relations, see King,

Nehru and the Language Politics of India. For a historical discussion of the mobilizational strategies and ideologies of the Tamil linguistic nationalist movement, see Ramaswamy, Passions of the Tongue.

103 The various volumes in the Subaltern Studies series provide rich and compelling evidence of the interplay, and also the tension, between national and local resistance movements during the colonial period.

104 See Jaffrelot, Dr. Ambedkar and Untouchability; Omvedt, Dalits and the Democratic Revolution; and Dirks, Castes of Mind.

105 For instance, the death of Sardar Vallabhai Patel in 1950 removed a potential political opponent for Nehru and unified the Congress around the particular Nehruvian vision of secularism and democratic socialism. A recent issue of the English-language national weekly Outlook was devoted to an exploration of such historical counterfactuals or "what-ifs" that included, among others, speculations about the alternative course of Indian history had Sardar Patel not died in 1950 or had the Congress leaders known that Jinnah was terminally ill during the negotiations over the demand for Pakistan in 1946–1947. See Guha, "What If."

106 For instance, the "bifurcated" legacy of the late-colonial experience in Africa, whereby "citizens" and "subjects" were differentially constituted along racial and ethnic lines, respectively, was absent in the Indian context. See Mamdani, Citizen and Subject.

107 Thus, for instance, Indian decolonization can be explained by the distinctive leadership styles and political-ideological visions of individuals such as Jawaharlal Nehru, Mohandas Gandhi, Mohammad Ali Jinnah, as well as by the transformation of economic and geopolitical relations around the time of World War II that rendered infeasible the project of holding onto the empire. For a recent attempt to combine agent-centric and structural explanations of democratic state formation in India, see Adeney and Wyatt, "Democracy in South Asia."

108 Although it is beyond the scope of this book, the lineages of the Nehruvian nation-state must also be traced to the world-historical conjuncture that prevailed at its founding moment, and the influence of global structures and ideologies on the formulation of national identity and state-society relations within India. For instance, the commitment to represent and protect cultural diversity made by the Indian state mirrored the contemporaneous commitments that were being forged at the international level by the newly established United Nations system. Similarly, the authorization of a statist model of development for India also drew upon and reflected broader sets of international norms and institutional practices. For a discussion that locates the formation of the postwar "new nations" in the broader world-historical conjuncture of the postwar order, see Kelly and Kaplan, Represented Communities, 9–22.

109 "At the stroke of the midnight hour, when the world sleeps, India will awake to life and freedom" is how Jawaharlal Nehru famously described the moment of Indian independence (Nehru, "A Tryst with Destiny").

110 For a discussion of the negotiations with the princely states, see Copland, *The Princes of India in the Endgame of Empire*; and Jenkins, "Turning Princes into Subjects."

111 Maulana Azad, radio broadcast to Indian children, All India Radio, August 15, 1948. Transcribed from the All India Radio archives, New Delhi, March 3, 1997.

112 Among other things, this meant that the delegates were elected on the basis of an extremely limited franchise. For an assessment of whether and to what extent India's constituent assembly was a representative body, see Austin, *The Indian Constitution*; and Jha, "Representation and Its Epiphanies."

113 Until the first general elections were held in 1952, India was governed by representatives who had assumed office (as delegates to the Constituent Assembly) according to the terms of the colonial Government of India Act of 1935. The Indian Independence Act of 1947 entrusted the Constituent Assembly of India with the task of governing the Indian Union during the transitional period. It convened as the Constituent Assembly of India (Legislative) until the adoption of the Constitution in January 1950, and then as the "Provisional Parliament of India" until the newly elected parliament was constituted in 1952. The Constituent Assembly vested executive responsibility in a fourteen-member cabinet headed by Nehru as prime minister and Patel as deputy prime minister. There were five non-Congress members in this cabinet: S. P. Mookerjee of the Hindu nationalist organization; the Hindu Mahasabha, B. R. Ambedkar; the Dalit leader, John Mathai; C. H. Bhabha; and Shanmukham Chetty.

114 The continuities were not just ideational but also structural-institutional. The "nation-state encounter" that forms the subject of this book was first enacted during this transitional period: thus, documentary film productions commenced in 1948, as did the frenzy of scientific institutional building discussed in chapter 3. Moreover, the Films Division of India and the Center for Scientific and Industrial Research were replicas of colonial institutions (the Information Films of India and the Board of Scientific and Industrial Research, respectively)—specifically, institutions that had been set up in response to the colonial emergency of World War II. Differently put, the norm of the postcolonial nation-state's efforts of cultural production is rooted in a moment of colonial exception.

115 This represented a substantial departure from the colonial period, where the establishment of separate electorates had linked political claims making to religious and caste identity rather than to language and regional culture.

116 India's war with China in 1962 also effected another substantial transformation. It was an occasion that saw the emergence of what might be called the "ethnicization of the nation" or the determination of national belonging in primordial terms of blood and race. The declaration of a national emergency was followed by the enactment of a new piece of legislation: the Foreigners Law (Application and Amendment) Ordinance, which applied the Foreigners Act of 1946 in requiring the registration of foreigners, defined as "any person not of Indian origin who was at birth a citizen or subject of any country at war with or

committing external aggression against India." Along with the registration requirement, the rights of such foreigners to move the courts for constitutional protections were suspended. However, of ultimate significance is the footnote that was soon added to the ordinance, which stated that the definition of "person" meant "any person who, or either of whose parents who, or any of whose grandparents was, at any time a citizen or subject of any country at war with, or committing external aggression against India." With that footnote, second-generation Chinese Indians, and arguably even third-generation Chinese Indians (since only "one grandparent" had to be born in China for the grandchild to qualify as a foreigner), were constituted as foreigners. The same definition of "foreign person" was also applied by the Foreigners (Internment) Order of November 1962, whose provisions enabled the arrest and detention, without cause, of any "suspicious person." By February 1963, according to the Indian government's own records, there were about 2,100 detainees in the Deoli internment camp in Rajasthan. While "normal law" and jus soli criteria of citizenship were restored after about two and a half years, other aspects of the "emergency" lingered on, thereby reconfiguring the political and cultural field of democracy and nationhood in imperceptible but significant ways. For a discussion of the racialized-ethnicized discriminations of emergency law during the India-China war of 1962, see Cohen and Leng, "The Sino-Indian Dispute over the Internment and Detention of Chinese in India"; and Oxfeld, *Blood, Sweat, and Mahjong*. A discussion of the military and political circumstances of the 1962 war is available in Maxwell, *India's China War*; and Hoffmann, *India and the China Crisis*.

CHAPTER 1 *Moving Pictures*

Portions of this chapter previously were published as "Moving Pictures: The Postcolonial State and Visual Representations of India," *Contributions to Indian Sociology* 36, nos. 1–2 (2002): 33–63.

1 See Anderson, *Imagined Communities*; Brubaker, *Nationalism Reframed*; Verdery, *National Ideology under Socialism*.
2 According to Anderson, nationalism is an expression of homogenous "fraternity" that dissolves and overlooks any differences between fellow nationals and emphasizes instead the distinctions between those who belong to the nation and those who remain outside its enchanted realms of belonging and desire. A similar description of nationalism as a homogenizing force also emerges in other accounts, with nation formation seen for the most part to entail the establishment of 'horizontal' bonds of solidarity between individuals. See Anderson *Imagined Communities*.
3 Brubaker, *Nationalism Reframed*.
4 *Report of the Committee on Broadcasting and Information Media on Documentary Films and Newsreels*, 1967, Ministry of Information and Broadcasting, New Delhi; hereafter referred to as the Chanda Committee Report 1967.

5 Quoted in Mohan, *Two Decades of the Films Division*, 10.
6 For a discussion of the specific cultural mandate of UNESCO during this period, see Girard, *Cultural Development*; and Sewell, "UNESCO." For a general discussion of the Ford Foundation's ideological practices of development and philanthropy, see Berghahn, "Philanthropy and Diplomacy in the 'American Century.'" The documentary filmmaking effort in India also benefited from the corporate sponsorship of organizations such as Burmah Shell, the petroleum conglomerate in South Asia. Burmah Shell's publicity/filmmaking unit in India was headed by James Beveridge of the National Film Board of Canada and employed several independent documentary filmmakers to make publicity and training films for the organization, but also films of "aesthetic merit" that traveled to international festivals. See Mohan, *Two Decades of the Films Division*, and Woods, "From Shaw to Shantaram."
7 Cited in Barsam, *Nonfiction Film*, 2.
8 For example, *Reception Given to Senior Wrangler, Mr. R. P. Paranjpe* (1902); *Great Bengal Partition Movement and Procession* (1905); *Bal Gangadhar Tilak's Visit to Calcutta and Procession* (1906); *The Terrible Hyderabad Flood* (1908); *Delhi Durbar and Coronation* (1911); and *Cotton Fire at Bombay* (1912).
9 Narwekar, *Films Division and the Indian Documentary*, 12.
10 Ibid., 16.
11 Pathy, "A Document on Indian Documentary."
12 Narwekar, *Films Division and the Indian Documentary*, 15–16.
13 According to Richard Barsam, Rotha's "humanistic" vision of the documentary film and its creator derived inspiration from Percy Bysshe Shelley's vision of the true artist as a "legislator of mankind." See Barsam, *Nonfiction Film*, 10.
14 For a discussion of the war propaganda filmmaking effort, see Woods, "Chappatis by Parachute."
15 Narwekar, *Films Division and the Indian Documentary*, 23. In fact, there was no official film production unit present to record the transfer of power at midnight on August 14–15, 1947. The event was documented by international camera units and, in India, by a two-person team of independent Indian filmmakers. Mohan, *Two Decades of the Films Division*.
16 Krishna, *Postcolonial Insecurities*, 5. For a similar argument, see Abraham, *The Making of the Indian Atomic Bomb*.
17 "Central to nationalisms everywhere is the metaphor of nation as journey, as something that is ever in the making but never quite reached. I call this social and political process by which outlined tasks are repeatedly postponed and defined destinations are never quite reached a logic of deferrence. The logic of deferrence secures the legitimacy of the postcolonial state by centering its historical role in the pursuit of certain desired futures" (Krishna, *Postcolonial Insecurities*, 17).
18 Abraham, "Landscape and Postcolonial Science," 164.
19 For a discussion of the state-documentary partnership in other contexts, see Barnouw, *Documentary*; MacCann, *The People's Films*; Swann, *The British Documentary*

Film Movement, 1926–1946; Roberts, Forward Soviet; and Taylor, "Now That the Party's Over" and Film Propaganda.

20 Sangeet Natak Akademi, Seminar on Film in India, 8.

21 This phenomenon has persisted well beyond the immediate circumstances of its emergence in the initial years of the postcolonial period. Thus, as Tejaswini Ganti has observed in her examination of the social worlds of Hindi commercial cinema in the late 1990s, Indian filmmakers continue to reproduce a "developmentalist discourse" in their discussions of their craft. This may well have stemmed from strategic calculations about gaining legitimacy and recognition from the state. However, the issue at hand is not so much the origins and motivations of such sentiments but rather their constitutive effects—the fact that the understandings of filmmaking as a pedagogical enterprise of nation building, and of the national audience as infantile and (therefore) in need of reform and education, were reproduced outside the narrow circles of official propaganda. See Ganti, Casting Culture.

22 Participants included filmmakers and film critics such as Sohrab Modi, P. K. Atre, Kalidas Nag, Vishram Bedekar, M. K. Siddhanta, and Marie Seton. See Government of India, Symposium on Historical and Biographical Film.

23 Quotes here are from ibid., 9, 18. For a discussion of the production of such "people's films" by the commercial film industry of the 1950s, see Chakravarty, "National Identity and the Realist Aesthetic" and National Identity in Indian Popular Cinema; Prasad, Ideology of the Hindi Film; Kapur, "Cultural Creativity in the First Decade"; Srivastava, "Voice, Gender and Space in Time of Five Year Plans"; and Vasudevan, "Addressing the Spectator of a 'Third World' National Cinema."

24 In addition, a cameraperson affiliated with the Films Division was stationed in each state capital to provide on-the-spot coverage of news events for the production of newsreels. See Mohan, Two Decades of the Films Division.

25 In the first twenty years of its existence, approximately 75 percent of Films Division productions were done "in house," and the rest were produced by individuals who were not formally affiliated with the organization. See Mohan, Two Decades of the Films Division; see also Garga, "Turbulent Years" and "Is Anyone Watching?"

26 For a different but related discussion of how citizenship discourse in capitalist states invariably addresses an "ethically incomplete" subject that "needs" improvement and managerial intervention, see Miller, The Well-Tempered Self.

27 Apart from commissioning work from individual filmmakers, the Films Division also distributed films received from a range of different national and international agencies, including state governments, central government organizations such as the Khadi and Village Industries Association, civil society organizations such as the Independent Documentary Producers' Association, and international sources such as the United Nations Film Board, the United States Information Services, and the World Health Organization. See Mohan, Two Decades of the Films Division, 62–63.

28 A total of 12,000 such films were distributed for free (one print for every 250,000

people), and therefore each print required 12,000 projections in order to cover the entire population. But the life of each print was only 200 projections, as the Chanda committee noted in its 1967 report, thus effectively limiting coverage to only 10 percent of the population. According to the committee, the lack of "motorable roads" in rural areas also limited the viewership of Films Division documentaries.

29 Narwekar, Films Division and the Indian Documentary, 25.

30 "The word 'People' is an expansive word representing the people inhabiting the length and breadth of the country with their languages and economic systems, determined by geography and agro-climatic divisions" (Mohan, Documentary Films and National Awakening, 93). This book was commissioned by the Films Division and provides a discussion of the Films Division and its activities from the perspective of the organization itself. Further, the author of the book, Jag Mohan, was actively associated with the Films Division for many years and produced several films for them.

31 Vadya Vrinda (1956) is a documentary about the All India Radio's "unique experiment" in creating a national orchestra of musical instruments from different regions of the country.

32 The Nehruvian state's tutelary discourse on citizenship both resembled and departed from the "infantile citizenship" ideal in the United States and the "socialist paternalism" of Romania. For the former, see Berlant, "The Theory of Infantile Citizenship"; for the latter, see Verdery, "Whither 'Nation' and 'Nationalism.'"

33 For instance, Democracy in Action (1951) introduced citizens to the procedures of voting and elections in anticipation of the first general election of 1952. In 1956, six five-minute films detailed the mechanisms of different types of ballot boxes, and in 1959, New Way to Vote depicted the use of a new type of ballot sheet.

34 "The Case of Mr. Critic," quoted in Pati, Films Division Catalogue of Films.

35 For instance, in Ideal Citizen (1959) the title was given meaning through depictions of exemplary individuals who "[kept] their surroundings clean," organized schools and dispensaries, paid their taxes, exercised their right and duty to vote, and cooperated with the police.

36 For a discussion of the Gandhian "detour" and the eventual "triumph" of Nehruvian nationalism in the last decade of colonial rule, see Chatterjee, Nationalist Thought and the Colonial World.

37 See Austin, The Indian Constitution; and Seth, "Nationalism, National Identity, and 'History.'"

38 For a discussion of the political-philosophical notion of "Ram Rajya" or the ideal "Kingdom of God" as articulated by Gandhi, see Parekh, Colonialism, Tradition and Reform; and Mukherjee, The Penguin Gandhi Reader.

39 Not only did Gandhian discourse considerably influence postcolonial political rhetoric, but it also shaped several policy initiatives, such as the community development and rural cooperative schemes that were introduced after independence. See Hansen, The Saffron Wave; and Sinha, "Development Counter-Narratives."

40 Mohan, *Documentary Films and National Awakening*, 96.
41 *Rabindranath Tagore* (1961) was directed by the eminent Indian filmmaker Satyajit Ray.
42 For instance, *Magic Moments* (1962) on the visit of Jacqueline Kennedy to India; *Mitrata Ki Yatra* (Journey of Friendship, 1955) on Nehru's visit to the USSR; and *Out of the Blue* (1963), a defense film about helicopters.
43 Pati, *Films Division Catalogue of Films*, 96.
44 Narwekar, *Films Division and the Indian Documentary*.
45 Sundaram, "The Bazaar and the City."
46 Pati, *Films Division Catalogue of Films*, 31.
47 Ibid., 412.
48 We can in fact describe this as the emergence of a new postcolonial narrative of temporality and progress (the saying of "not yet" to *ourselves*, to rephrase Dipesh Chakrabarty), which had ambivalent political effects, empowering as well as marginalizing the agency of ordinary citizens. See Chakrabarty, *Provincializing Europe*. In chapter 3 I develop this point in further detail through a consideration of the "diffident developmentalism" of Nehruvian India.
49 However, despite the divergent constructions of the here and now as certainty and uncertainty respectively, both the representation of spectacular modernity and that of deferred modernity evacuated the present of substantial, lived meaning. Thus, while in *My Land My Dreams* (1968) it was the "struggles" of the past or what was described as the "historical exploitation of farmers" that invested their present freedom with meaning, in *Grow Hybrid Maize* (1967) the significance of the present was as a harbinger of future prosperity.
50 See Scott, *Seeing like a State*. In a similar vein, and despite the difference in their understandings of state autonomy, Marxist theories of the state as well as the scholarship on "bringing the state back in" have failed to disaggregate the state along levels of governance and have overlooked the multiple and contradictory effects of "stateness." "The capitalist state" was theorized as a (mostly) singular formation in the Poulantzas-Miliband debates of the 1970s, and the "statist" scholarship of Skocpol and others took the state to be a unitary actor. See Poulantzas, "The Problem of the Capitalist State"; Miliband, "The Capitalist State"; and Skocpol, "Bringing the State Back In."
51 The leadership of Jean Bhownagary, Ezra Mir, and P. V. Pathy left a distinctive, creative imprint on the Films Division. Further, Sukhdev's *An Indian Day* (1971) is a case in point of a film that through editing techniques uses the familiar visual vocabularies of the Films Division in surprising and even subversive ways. The fact that this film was commissioned by the Films Division, shown to national audiences, went on to win international and national awards, and is today eulogized in the Films Division's narrative of its own history illustrates the ambivalences of the state effect.
52 Although the official catalogue of the Films Division overlooked these films, the annual reports of the Ministry of Information and Broadcasting list several films

on Kashmir and a film on "the Muslims of India" that were produced in 1956. However, no further information is available on this film.

53 Interestingly, there are no films about partition or about India's foreign policy toward Pakistan during this period.

54 Indeed, several films posited continuity between colonial and anticolonial institutions and infrastructure, as they celebrated "one hundred years of the telegraph" and "one hundred years of the railways."

55 See Zelinsky, *Nation into State*; and Spillman, *Nation and Commemoration*.

56 As Susan Buck-Morss among others has shown, the enthusiastic embrace of socialist "dreamworlds" was not restricted to India alone but instead was a wider world-historical formation that had a considerable influence on the projects of postcolonial nation-state formation that were undertaken in the mid-twentieth century. Surprisingly, the influence of this "utopianism" is not among the international factors discussed by Kelly and Kaplan in their otherwise persuasive account of the effect of global norms and institutions on projects of decolonization. Their focus is almost exclusively on the hegemonic effects of the United States and the Bretton Woods system. See Buck-Morss, *Dreamworld and Catastrophe*; and Kelly and Kaplan, *Represented Communities*.

57 As the introductory chapter has noted, the China war saw the emergence of militarist rhetorics of citizenship and nationhood and a more unitary conception of the nation-state. The production list of the Films Division reflected this shift, with a flurry of films produced between 1963 and 1965 that emphasized "national security" as the primary issue at hand.

58 The films that were produced between January and March 1963 under the "national emergency" scheme all related to various aspects of the war effort: official explanations of the causes or reasons for the war; appeals for public support; and foregrounding the prowess, sacrifice, and bravery of the military. See, for instance, *Shifting Line* (explaining India's position on the international border dispute); *Road to Victory* ("people's reaction to China aggression"); *Service before Self* ("supporting the armed forces"); *Letter from the Front* ("what to donate and what type of work to do"); *A Proud Tradition* ("Hero of Chusul: Late Major Shaitan Singh"); *Meet the Challenge* ("role of women in national emergency"); *They Are Not Alone* (role of *panchayats* [village assemblies] in national emergency); *A Privilege* ("officer recruitment"); *Careless Talk* ("security consciousness"); and *An Unavoidable Internment* (Chinese Internees in India). See Government of India, Annual Report, 1962–63.

59 Government of India, Annual Report, 1964–65, 4.

60 The Indian constitution promulgated in 1950 did not provide a definition of secularism, and the term is itself missing from the constitutional text (the existing preambular definition of India as a "sovereign socialist secular democratic republic" was introduced by the 42nd amendment in 1976). Despite this formal constitutional absence, however, secularism understood as "equal respect for all religions" (and thus distinct from both the Anglo-Saxon variant of the "wall of

separation" between church and state and the French *laic* variant of "civil religion"), served as the normative as well as pragmatic touchstone of legislative reform and social and cultural policy making in Nehruvian India. While the secular embrace of India's multireligious composition is at considerable remove from the Hindu nationalist vision of India as a Hindu nation in which non-Hindus are "second-class citizens," the internal distinctions of secularism are not without their own problems. As this brief discussion of visual representations of religious diversity has suggested, Nehruvian secularism had a particular "minoritizing" effect, whereby certain communities were constituted as the object of secular laws and policies (those requiring tolerance) while others were authorized as secular subjects (those invested with the power to tolerate). For an extended discussion of the powered dimensions of discourses and practices of tolerance and diversity, see Hage, *White Nation*.

61 The allotments were 12,000 feet of raw film stock for the eastern region, 13,000 feet in the south, and 400 feet for trailers. See Government of India, *Annual Report*, 1950–51.

62 Placing the positive injunction of the Films Division alongside the censorship prohibitions of the Indian Cinematographic Act of 1952 is instructive in this regard, as all the "shall nots" of the act are transformed into "shall dos" when it comes to Films Division films. For example, the statement that "the sympathy of the audience shall not be thrown on the side of crime, wrong-doing, evil or sin" authorized the production of films that elicited audience sympathies with "the side" of goodness and truth. For a discussion of the policies and effects of cinema censorship in India, see Vasudev, *Liberty and License in the Indian Cinema*; and for a different discussion of the "productive" power of film censorship, see Gopalan, *Cinema of Interruptions*.

63 As Nehru observed during his remarks to the 1955 Film Seminar (the national meeting of representatives from the film industry and state officials in New Delhi that was convened to discuss "the role of film in nation-building"), the government will compete through the production of documentaries "not . . . with the desire to compete, but to some extent the results might be a setting up of standards by a certain measure of competition" Sangeet Natak Akademi, *Seminar on Film in India*, 15.

64 For a discussion of the unique complex of "high and low stateness" that characterized the Indian state, see Rudolph and Rudolph, *In Pursuit of Lakshmi*.

65 Government of India, *Annual Report*, 1950–51, 1.

66 See Hansen, *The Saffron Wave*, 50–51.

67 Chanda Committee Report 1967.

68 According to Foucault, these are the distinctive features of disciplinary power, in contrast to the centralized, exterior, and visible or "spectacular" operations of juridical-sovereign power. See Foucault, *Discipline and Punish*; and Faubion, *Power*, vol. 3.

69 Ann Anagnost discusses the imperative of visibility in her examination of the

formation and legitimization of the party-state in China. See Anagnost, *National Past-Times*, chapter 4. Her account modifies the Foucauldian premise about the invisibility of modern disciplinary power, which was based on an understanding of how the Benthamite panopticon allows an authority figure to observe a prison inmate without being observed himself. As Anagnost continues, "The tower at the center is not entirely a darkened space inhabited by an invisible gaze but an illuminated stage from which the party calls, 'Look at me! I make myself visible to you. Your return gaze completes me and realizes my power' " (116).

70 "The cold words written by the commentary writers turn flesh when the commentators take over. It is they, who with their accents, pauses and exclamation convey to the 'captive audience' the importance and significance of the visuals. Sam Berkeley-Hill, the late Nobby Clarke, Romesh Thapar, Zul Vellani and Partap Sharma have done the salesmanship for the Films Division in the English language." Mohan, *Two Decades of the Films Division*, 50. See also Thapar, *All These Years*, for a vivid autobiographical reminiscence of her husband Romesh Thapar's audio commentaries for the Films Division.

71 As Philip Corrigan and Derek Sayer have observed in their examination of the distinctive cultural repertoires and practices of state formation in England, "States, if the pun be forgiven, *state*; the arcane rituals of a court of law, the formulae of royal assent to an Act of Parliament, visits of school inspector, all are statements. They define, in great detail, acceptable forms and images of social activity and individual and collective identity; they regulate, in empirically specifiable ways, much ... of social life. Indeed, in this sense, 'the State' never stops talking" (Corrigan and Sayer, *The Great Arch*, 3).

72 Chanda Committee Report 1967.

73 Ibid.

74 Ibid.

75 The commissioning policy of the Films Division replicated the general bureaucratic practice of awarding government contracts to the most "economical" bidder. In the case of the Films Division, this meant the commissioning of filmmakers with the lowest budget, rather than on creative-aesthetic grounds. See Chanda Committee Report 1967.

76 The following example from my own life is illustrative of this "crossed signals" effect. My memory of a family outing to see the Hindi film *Sholay* in Calcutta in the mid-1970s is vividly associated not with images from the film but with black-and-white visions from a pre-film documentary about a *gobar* (cow dung) gas-producing contraption surrounded by smiling farmers. I cannot recall the title, the location, or any other details of the Films Division documentary, the source of these images. However, the imagery of the farmer and the fantastic piece of technology, and the combination of fascination and queasiness that the notion of a cow-dung-powered machine elicited, are strangely easy to relive thirty years later.

77 The Films Division provided only 12,000 free prints, or one print for every group

of 250,000 people. However, since the life of a film print was approximately two hundred screenings (it would wear out after this point), significant numbers of people were left "uncovered" by the distribution scheme.

78 In discussing the limits of the Films Division's linguistic reach, the Chanda committee drew particular attention to its neglect of the (unspecified) "tribals of India": a lapse that it deemed especially problematic given their palpable "need" for modernization.

79 Hansen, "Governance and Myths of the State in Mumbai."

80 Indian Institution of Mass Communications, *Proceedings of the Seminar on the Role of Film in National Development*.

81 Ibid.

82 Scott, *Seeing like a State*, 2–3.

83 Ibid.

84 The considerable revenue-earning potential of such international sales influenced the decision to create a "customer friendly" Web site containing sample clips of documentaries in 2002; see http://www.filmsdivision.org.

85 Elsewhere I have examined these contemporary (nonstate and transnational) reproductions of the diversity imagination, and I argue that there are significant points of convergence with established idioms of official nationalism. See Roy, "Nation and Commemoration."

86 For related discussions about the "misrepresentations" of multiculturalism, see Mackey, *The House of Difference*; Povinelli, *The Cunning of Recognition*; and Hutnyk, *The Critique of Exotica*.

87 Amin, "On Representing the Musalman," 95.

88 For a rich discussion of the calendar art and posters of Nehruvian India, and the popular cultural visualization of "unity in diversity," see Uberoi, "Unity in Diversity?"

89 As Hasan and Menon have documented, the categorical logic that informs discussions about "Muslim women" obscures the host of regional, class, and other differences within this apparently monolithic group. See Hasan and Menon, *Unequal Citizens*.

90 Amin, "On Representing the Musalman."

91 India's "healthy" and "vibrant" democratic tradition has been a staple theme of media discourse, and it has also informed scholarly analyses for the past half century. For a recent reiteration of this argument, see among others, Khilnani, *The Idea of India*; Kohli, *The Success of India's Democracy*; and Linz, Stepan, and Yadav, "Nation-State or State-Nation?"

92 See, for example, *Say It With a Smile* (1960), a film that depicts the ideal civic behavior of "courtesy for others' feelings"; *Vital Records* (1964), on birth and death registration procedures; *With Your Own Hands* (1956), on the dignity of manual labor; and *Withering Flowers* (1963), on the institutional reform and "uplift" of "delinquent children."

CHAPTER 2 *Marching in Time*

1 According to the anthropologist Richard Handler, "nationalism is an ideology of what C. B. Macpherson (1962) called possessive individualism." The representation of the nation as a discrete entity that owns or possesses something (whether a land, a people, a history, or a future) creates an equivalence, and therefore an identification, between the abstract social form of the modern nation and the concrete lived experience of the "possessive individual." See Handler, *Nationalism and the Politics of Culture in Quebec*, 6–8.
2 This is Slavenka Drakulic's succinct phrase describing the transformative impact of Croatian nationalism and the experience of ethnic identification, as cited in Brubaker, *Nationalism Reframed*, 20.
3 Cohn, *An Anthropologist among the Historians and Other Essays*, 632.
4 Anderson, *Imagined Communities*, 7.
5 Slezkine, "The USSR as a Communal Apartment," 207.
6 See Geertz, *Negara*; Handelman, *Models and Mirrors*; and Lane, *The Rites of Rulers*.
7 I take the term "models and mirrors" from Handelman's book by that name.
8 *Times of India* (Bombay), 26 January 1950.
9 For a discussion of national days and commemorative practices, see Spillman, *Nation and Commemoration*; Gillis, *Commemorations*; and Ozouf, *Festivals and the French Revolution*.
10 See Apter, "The Subvention of Tradition"; Cohn, *Colonialism and Its Forms of Knowledge*; Metcalf, *Ideologies of the Raj*; and Ranger, "The Invention of Tradition Revisited."
11 Mitchell, "Society, Economy, and the State Effect."
12 Cannadine, "The Context, Performance and Meaning of Ritual," 103.
13 Cohn, *Colonialism and Its Forms of Knowledge*, 208.
14 Ibid., 209.
15 For a discussion of how January 26 was commemorated between 1931 and 1947, see Masselos, "India's Republic Day: The Other 26 January."
16 Masselos, "India's Republic Day," 194–95.
17 Ibid.
18 The independence day pledge as issued by the Congress Working Committee; cited in Masselos, "India's Republic Day," 188.
19 Masselos, "India's Republic Day," 192.
20 The official national anthem of India is *Jana Gana Mana*, a composition by the Indian poet Rabindranath Tagore. The choice of Tagore's song was the product of a heated debate in the Indian Constituent Assembly, in which several members argued that the popular nationalist song *Bande Mataram* was unsuitable as a national anthem because of its predominantly Hindu imagery. *Jana Gana Mana* is a hymn in praise of Indian diversity—it describes India as a constellation of different cultural communities and different geographical regions.
21 Correspondence between Humayun Kabir, Secretary, Ministry of Education, and

B. N. Kaul, 30.1.1952. Annotated by Ashfaque Husain. Ministry of Education File No. 6–11/52-G, 2(A), National Archives, Government of India, New Delhi.
22 As noted by Ashfaque Husain, in ibid.
23 Letter dated 10.9.1952 from Jawaharlal Nehru to Chief Ministers of States, in ibid.
24 Ibid.
25 Ibid.
26 Ernest Renan's famous discussion of the nation defines it as a "daily plebiscite." See Renan, "What Is a Nation."
27 "Nation Goes Gay on Republic Day," *Times of India* (Bombay), January 28, 1957.
28 For the notion of the state as fetish, see Abrams, "Notes on the Difficulty of Studying the State"; Mitchell, "The Limits of the State"; and Taussig, *The Magic of the State*. For a discussion of the state's multiple faces, see Navaro-Yashin, *Faces of the State*.
29 Malik, "The Snow Maidens," *Times of India* (Bombay), January 27, 1960.
30 Television coverage of the parade was first provided in a limited experimental broadcast in 1960 to twenty All India Radio tele-clubs in and around Delhi. In 1976, national television centers at Amritsar, Bombay, Calcutta, Delhi, Lucknow, Madras, and Srinagar telecast the parade live for the first time.
31 Dirks, "Ritual and Resistance," 499.
32 "No Cultural Pageant," *Times of India* (Bombay), January 27, 1963.
33 As noted in chapter 1, India and China went to war in 1962 over a disputed border. The outbreak of war was seen to take India by surprise, since Indian foreign policy toward China had ostensibly been forged in the name of "Indo-Chinese solidarity" up until this point. For Nehru's critics, the war was decisive proof of the folly of Nehruvian internationalism and its idealist rather than realist stance toward international relations.
34 The National Discipline Scheme was introduced by the Ministry of Education in 1954 as part of the Nehruvian drive to build new subjects and to combat the growing specter of "student indiscipline" in university campuses throughout the nation.
35 *Times of India* (Bombay), January 27, 1963.
36 Césaire's description of colonialism took the form of the equation "Colonization = Thingification." See Césaire, *The Discourse of Colonialism*, 42.
37 "Impressive Republic Day Parade in Delhi," *Times of India* (Bombay), January 27, 1965.
38 "MIGs Steal the Republic Day Show in Capital," *Times of India* (Bombay), January 27, 1967.
39 Among the first group of winners were a boy who had shot an eight-and-a-half-foot-long tigress in mid-attack, and another boy who had rescued an infant from the railway tracks right before a speeding train reached the spot. See "MIGs Steal the Republic Day Show In Capital," *Times of India* (Bombay), January 28, 1967.
40 Bata advertisement for 1955, "Plans and the People," *Times of India* (Bombay), January 26, 1955.

41 Advertisement for Bata, "The Mother of Three Jawans Knows No Fear," *Times of India* (Bombay), January 28, 1963.

42 Advertisement for Punjab National Bank, "The Oldest Name in Modern Indian Banking," *Times of India* (Bombay), January 26, 1964.

43 "Our Unity Should Not Be in the Name of War Only but for Basic Ideals," *Times of India* (Bombay), January 26, 1972.

44 Advertisement for Hindustan Steel, "So Much Depends on India's Men of Steel!" *Times of India* (Bombay), January 26, 1972.

45 In 1975, Indira Gandhi declared a period of national emergency in India, during which many constitutional rights (including fundamental rights of citizens) were suspended, elections were canceled, there was significant press censorship, and political dissidents were imprisoned. Ostensibly declared as a preventive measure against the "lawlessness" that prevailed internally, the emergency has widely been seen as a desperate measure by an increasingly autocratic ruler to thwart challenges to her regime. The emergency lasted until 1977, when national elections swept a new political front, the Janata Party, to power, thereby ending the reign of the Congress Party for the first time since independence.

46 One such example of a combined military-cultural display is from the parade of 1965, where the National Cadet Corps of India organized a "parade of ancient soldiers." Cadets marched past the assembled audience, dressed in the military outfits of the Maurya, the Gupta, the Rajput, and the Mughal periods. In the spirit of historical verisimilitude, some postcolonial subjects gamely donned the military outfits of the East India Company as well. See "Impressive Republic Day Parade in Delhi," *Times of India* (Bombay), January 27, 1965.

47 "Cold Fails to Check R-Day Ardor," *Times of India* (Bombay), January 27, 1964.

48 In 1956, with the passage of the Linguistic Reorganization of States Act, the administrative units of the Indian Union (the states) were reconstituted along the lines of linguistic homogeneity. For a comprehensive discussion of the "language politics" that accompanied this controversial decision, see King, *Nehru and the Language Politics of India*.

49 See Nairn, "The Modern Janus"; and Bhabha, "DissemiNation."

50 Sometimes state floats are absent from the Delhi parade because they have been censured and suspended by the Tableaux Selection Committee. For instance, the state of Karnataka was suspended for a period of three years starting in 2003 because at the last minute it reneged on its commitment to send a float to 2003 parade. This in turn was a product of the patronage politics associated with the granting of float-building commissions—the "business" of culture on Republic Day is lucrative, since the amount of money involved is fairly substantial (about Rs. 400,000) and there is also the possibility of winning awards for creativity.

51 There were only two state floats in the parade: Madhya Pradesh and Sikkim. The other floats represented the work of different state agencies, such as the Department of Industrial Development's tableau on bonded labor. See "Country Celebrates Republic Day with Enthusiasm," *Times of India* (Bombay), January 28, 1976.

52 See Taras, "Making Sense of Matrioshka Nationalism."
53 "Bombay's Contribution to National Pageant," *Times of India* (Bombay), January 26, 1953.
54 The alliance between state and capital that results in the commodification of the nation and the articulation of national identity as a 'lifestyle brand' has been observed in a variety of contexts. See, for instance, Davila, *Sponsored Identities* for a discussion of how multinational corporations such as Bacardi and Budweiser engage with the government-sponsored project of cultural identity formation to produce and disseminate understandings of Puerto Ricanness.
55 Advertisement for Bharath Beedi Works Private Limited, "Jai Hind!" *Times of India* (Bombay), January 26, 1985.
56 The first reports of widespread national protests on Republic Day were noted in 1970. On January 26, members of the Akali Dal party observed a "protest day" over the contested status of the city of Chandigarh (their demand was that it should be a part of Punjab state); there were student demonstrations in Churu, Rajasthan; and there was a strike or *hartal* in the Mandi district of Himachal Pradesh to protest "imposition of property tax and arbitrary assessment of properties." See *Times of India* (Bombay), January 28, 1970.
57 As noted at the beginning of the chapter, the security regulations for each parade become even more formidable each year. Presently cars must be parked at least 500 meters from the parade ground, and all audience members have to pass through three sets of metal detectors before reaching their enclosure. No handbags or packages are allowed, and in the absence of any parcel-check facilities admission is refused to people who even bring a purse with them. If found, pens and pencils are confiscated since they could be potential weapons. Finally, an admission ticket alone is not enough: everyone is required to bring at least one form of photo identification.
58 See Navaro-Yashin, *Faces of the State*, for a discussion of "cynicism" as a subject position in relation to the state.
59 The quotations in this section are drawn from the official commentary scripts of Republic Day parades from previous years, large sections of which were reproduced verbatim in the course of the fiftieth anniversary parade. See Government of India, "Republic Day Parade Commentary."
60 "India parades Kargil success on Republic Day." See Rediff.com at http://www.rediff.com/news/2000/jan/26akd.htm.
61 Sacrifice is an important trope in official nationalist discourse—whether in school textbooks produced and approved by the Ministry of Education, events to inculcate civic consciousness that are organized by the department of youth affairs, or dramatized depictions of the lives of nationalist heroes produced by All India Radio and Doordarshan. Nongovernmental organizations also echo the sacrificial theme in their varied depictions of Indian nationhood, and in their understanding of the state-society/state-citizen relation in postindependence India. For instance, the Indira Gandhi Memorial, a "personalia museum" set up on the grounds of the

former prime minister's residence by the Indira Gandhi Memorial Trust, foregrounds the assassination (and implicit martyrdom) of Indira Gandhi in its museum display. An accompanying exhibit on Rajiv Gandhi also reproduces a similar theme of sacrifice and martyrdom, drawing parallels between the assassinations of Mahatma Gandhi in 1948, Indira Gandhi in 1984, and Rajiv Gandhi in 1991. "Leaders who laid down their lives in the service of their country" are to be emulated by ordinary citizens in their daily lives, urges the museum display—perhaps not literally by facing bullets but symbolically by bearing with quiet fortitude economic hardship, food rationing, and other failures of the state to deliver the goods.

62 It can be argued that the organization of the Indian Army in a regionally territorialized fashion is a purely symbolic gesture—officers can serve in any contingent, regardless of their regional origin. However, the symbolic effect is precisely what is of interest—despite its lack of direct material impact, the regionalized nomenclature of the army's classificatory system draws attention to, and even legitimizes the existence of, a regionally compartmentalized way of being.

63 While this is geographically appropriate in the case of Kashmir (Kargil is a district in the state), the Delhi float's depiction of Kargil martyrs speaks less of the distinct regional identity of the state than of its self-representation as *primus inter pares*—the premier state of the nation that houses its capital city and that can therefore lay claim to national events such as the Kargil war.

CHAPTER 3 *Indian Darkness*

1 "India Shining" was the formal name of the massive publicity campaign that was launched by the BJP coalition government in late 2003 and early 2004 to showcase the significant social, economic, and technological advances made by the Indian nation-state. Unlike the modernizing discourses of nation building, "India Shining" proclaimed modernity as an already-achieved goal in India. I take up the political significance of the "India Shining" campaign in further detail in chapter 5.
2 Brubaker, *Nationalism Reframed*, 25.
3 I borrow the term "need for science" from Fraser, "Talking about Needs."
4 For a discussion of the international institutional and ideational complex of development that emerged in the postwar era, see Escobar, *Encountering Development*; and Cooper and Packard, *International Development and the Social Sciences*.
5 For a discussion of the normative reconfiguration of the postwar international order, and the ways in which these normative shifts facilitated the process of imperial withdrawal in Asia and Africa, see Crawford, "Decolonization as an International Norm."
6 See Hamza Alavi, "State and Class in Peripheral Capitalism," for a classic analysis of the processes and implications of the "internationalization of capital" and its impact on social relations and state structures in decolonizing polities.

7 I borrow this phrase from Sangeeta Kamat's discussion in *Development Hegemony* of the structuring impact of development ideologies on the field of postcolonial politics in India, both during the era of state planning and in the present conjuncture of economic liberalization and the "NGO-ization of civil society."
8 Sivaramakrishnan and Agrawal, "Regional Modernities," 28.
9 See, among others, Ludden, "India's Development Regime"; Mehta, *Liberalism and Empire*; and Chakrabarty, *Provincializing Europe*.
10 According to Partha Chatterjee, colonial power was consolidated through the "preservation of the alienness of the ruling group," or the assertion of an absolute and ineradicable or unbridgeable distance between the colonizer and the colonized. See Chatterjee, *The Nation and Its Fragments*, 10.
11 David Ludden has argued for a longer historical genealogy of development, with the eighteenth century as the period in which the "preconditions" for India's "development regime" emerged as a result of transformed relations and structures of indigenous class formation through "pervasive commercialism." See Ludden, "India's Development Regime," 253–61. For a related discussion, see Cowen and Shenton, "The Invention of Development."
12 See Chakrabarty, *Provincializing Europe*.
13 Strachey, *India: Its Administration and Progress*, cited in Larson, *India's Agony over Religion*, 5.
14 See Mehta, *Liberalism and Empire*; and Chakrabarty, *Provincializing Europe*.
15 In the case of social reform, other colonial presumptions about the "enduring" social hierarchies of caste and the need to respect "natural" religious differences came into play to limit the scope and extent of reform projects. Thus, for instance, the legal reform initiatives that were undertaken by the colonial state included the creation of a uniform Penal Code (1860) and a codification of criminal procedure (1861), but not the codification of "personal law" systems that governed marriages and their dissolution, dowry, adoption, succession, or inheritance. As stated in the Privy Council's explanation in 1871 for the existence of multiple personal law regimes: "The difference of religion pervades and governs all domestic usages and social relations" in India, and legal reform initiatives would accordingly have to be modified in recognition of this social-cultural difference. Cited in Larson, "Introduction," 4.
16 Ludden, "India's Development Regime," 260.
17 The introduction of newer and more coordinated institutions and technologies of "the state information apparatus" in the 1840s and beyond consolidated this process. See Ludden, "India's Development Regime," 259–61.
18 The term "transition narrative" is from Chakrabarty, *Provincializing Europe*, 30.
19 As noted in earlier chapters, Gandhian nationalism upheld a very different vision of state-society relations, envisioning the future of India along the lines of decentralized and self-sufficient village communities.
20 Chakrabarty, *Provincializing Europe*, 30.
21 Ludden, "India's Development Regime," 264.

22   Chatterjee, *The Nation and Its Fragments*.
23   In the effort to delineate a distinctive national essence for India, the "splitting strategies" of anticolonial nationalism had separated the "inner domain" of culture from the "outer domain" of "economy and of statecraft, of science and technology, a domain where the West had proved its superiority and the East had succumbed" (Chatterjee, *The Nation and Its Fragments*, 6).
24   Chakrabarty, *Provincializing Europe*.
25   This fragmentary constitution of the nation as a collection of (differently) inadequate human subjects was only one aspect of postcolonial needs discourse. The subject of needs was also conceptualized in totalized, abstract, and disembodied terms. To use Foucault's description of modern governmental power as the project of ensuring "the right disposition of men and things," not just "men" but "things" as well were the targets of developmentalist technologies in postcolonial India. Thus, alongside the problem-stricken workers, peasants, and youth, "industry," "agriculture," "economy," and "education" also took their place as governmental categories that were invested with problems, backwardness, and needs of their own. Like their human counterparts, they also called for the ameliorative actions of "better and more" state intervention. See Foucault, "The Subject and Power." See also Cruikshank, *The Will to Empower*.
26   See Bhabha, *Nation and Narration*, 139–70.
27   The process of transforming a movement politics of nationalism into an institutional politics of state formation and legitimization was one such dynamic. Another was the effort to constitute nationhood in both universalist and particularist terms—a general problematic of "national modularity" that was given an added edge at a time when the "universal grammar" of nation-statehood and the coordinates of the international system were in flux, and a variety of viable "modular templates" from liberalism to socialism were on offer. For a discussion of the political-ethical pitfalls that attend the transformation of a movement of "national liberation" into a nation-statist project, see Fanon, *The Wretched of the Earth*, and, more recently, the work of Neil Lazarus, who in *Nationalism and Cultural Practice in the Postcolonial World* has drawn upon Fanon to discuss the postcolonial transmutation of internationally solidarist "nationalitarian" consciousness into an insular and exclusivist expression of national identity. For a discussion of the "modularity" of the nation-form, see Anderson, *Imagined Communities*; and Goswami, "Rethinking the Modular Nation Form."
28   Kaviraj, "A Critique of the Passive Revolution." For related but different discussions of class and state formation in postcolonial India, see Vanaik, *The Painful Transition*; and Bardhan, *The Political Economy of Development in India*.
29   For a discussion of the political and social compromises that affected the trajectories of social and economic reform in Nehruvian India, see Corbridge and Harriss, *Reinventing India*; Frankel, *India's Political Economy*; and Rudolph and Rudolph, *In Pursuit of Lakshmi*.

30 See Som, "Jawaharlal Nehru and the Hindu Code Bill"; Galanter, *Law and Society in Modern India*; and Smith, *India as a Secular State*.
31 Krishna, "Cartographic Anxiety."
32 For a discussion of the political effects of India's boundary-making projects, and the unsettled status of borderlands (and those who inhabit these areas), see Van Schendel, "Stateless in South Asia"; Ludden, "Maps in the Mind and the Mobility of Asia"; and Aggarwal, *Beyond Lines of Control*.
33 The central government had to settle "accession issues" with the several hundred independent "princely states" that had remained juridically exterior to the colonial territories of British India immediately following the transfer of power in 1947. For further discussion, see the introduction to this volume.
34 For a witty and incisive account of postcolonial India's fascination with science and technology, and the evolution of the "engineering elite," see Bhaya Nair, *Technobrat*.
35 Ludden, "India's Development Regime."
36 The colonial period was witness to a wide variety of engagements by political leaders such as Nehru, Ambedkar, and Gandhi with the question of how, whether, and what kind of science was relevant to the nationalist cause. Scientific practitioners such as Homi Bhabha, S. S. Bhatnagar, Meghnad Saha, and J. C. Bose, and industrial entrepreneurs such as J. R. D. Tata, also had a significant role to play. Among the numerous biographical accounts of these individuals, the following focus on the social-historical context of colonial science in India: Sur, "Scientism and Social Justice"; Dasgupta, *Jagdish Chandra Bose*; Lala, *For the Love of India*; and Mian, "Homi Bhabha Killed a Crow."
37 Prakash, *Another Reason*.
38 Ibid.
39 For a discussion of how postcolonial science and technology policies reflected the ideologies of nationalism and normative ideals of citizenship and modernity, see Anderson, "Cultivating Science as Cultural Policy"; and Chakravartty, "Telecom, National Development, and the Indian State."
40 Chakrabarty, *Provincializing Europe*.
41 Abraham, *The Making of the Indian Atomic Bomb*, 28.
42 Nehru, "Address at the opening of the National Mettalurgical Laboratory, Jamshedpur, November 26, 1950"; cited in Singh, *Jawaharlal Nehru on Science and Society*, 86.
43 Nehru, "Inaugural Address at the Silver Jubilee Session of the State Medical Conference at Meerut on October 24, 1959"; cited in Singh, *Jawaharlal Nehru on Science and Society*, 204.
44 The difference between the "conservatism," or the "principle of continuity," that characterized Indian society was contrasted with "discovery" as the primary animating principle of science. See Nehru, "Speech delivered at the Central Fuel Research Institute, Jealgoda, April 22, 1950"; cited in Singh, *Jawaharlal Nehru on Science and Society*, 78.

45 Existing accounts of the hegemonic status of official science in postcolonial India paint a one-dimensional picture that ignores these fissures and contradictions. In their linear narratives, science and technology were uncritically "worshipped" by political and cultural elites. Although Meera Nanda's recent discussion of postcolonial science in India criticizes the "anti-modernist" arguments of these writers by arguing that they fail to recognize the emancipatory possibilities of Western science in India and lend support to the ideological-political project of Hindu nationalism, she also subscribes to a similarly one-dimensional understanding of the state-science relationship. Where for Ashis Nandy the alliance between state and science is inherently oppressive, for Meera Nanda it is inherently emancipatory—equally a position that overlooks the contradictions and the multiple institutional locations and actors that shaped the state-science relationship in the postcolonial period. See Nanda, *Prophets Facing Backward*. For the opposing "anti-modernist" viewpoint, see Nandy, *Science, Hegemony and Violence*; Visvanathan, *A Carnival for Science*; Alvares, *Science, Development and Violence*; and Shiva, *The Violence of the Green Revolution*.

46 Government of India, "Report of the Review Committee for the Indian Institute of Sciences," 15.

47 Ibid., 13.

48 Ibid., 9.

49 Nehru, "Address at the Anniversary Meeting Associated with the Silver Jubilee Celebrations of the National Institute of Sciences, New Delhi on December 31, 1960"; cited in Singh, *Jawaharlal Nehru on Science and Society*, 229.

50 Meghnad Saha was among those who argued for a different relationship between laboratories and universities by proposing a fuller integration of the techno-scientific enterprise into the broader mission of higher education in India. However, as in the case of Saha's marginalization during the debates over official secrecy and the Atomic Energy Bill, his views were ignored. See Visvanathan, *Organizing for Science*. For an interesting discussion of the distinctive political-ethical vision of science, social justice, and democracy that Saha endorsed from the early stages of his career as a young physicist in colonial India, see Sur, "Scientism and Social Justice."

51 For instance, in order to gain admission to an engineering college, students were required to take a "Joint Entrance" examination (thus named because the examination qualified students for admission to a range of different engineering institutions, depending on their rank) after completing high school.

52 Haritash and Gupta, "Mapping of S & T issues in the Indian Parliament."

53 For a discussion of how the principle of official secrecy and the reign of democratically unaccountable statist reason—the "state knows best"—was authorized for the development of nuclear science and other techno-scientific enterprises deemed essential for "national security," see Abraham, *The Making of the Indian Atomic Bomb*.

54 See Chatterjee, *The Nation and Its Fragments*, on how the "experts" of the Planning Commission were insulated from the political process.

55 Nehru, "Remarks at the Annual General Meeting of the Association of Scientific Workers of India, New Delhi, January 24, 1959"; cited in Singh, *Jawaharlal Nehru on Science and Society*, 186.

56 Speaking at the tenth council meeting of the Association of Scientific Workers in India, Nehru observed: "I suppose you have done useful work. There are two aspects of your work: firstly, as a trade union, you should protect your rights, and secondly—and this I consider more important—you should *get together and discuss the problems of advancing science in India. Trade union means advancing your own interests, and that is very good provided it is not at the cost of others*" (Nehru, *Bulletin of the Association of Scientific Workers of India*, September 1958; cited in Singh, *Jawaharlal Nehru on Science and Society*, 153. Emphasis added).

57 Ibid.

58 For a discussion of the trade union activities at the National Physical Laboratory, see Visvanathan, *Organizing for Science*.

59 Nehru, "Speech at the Inaugural Meeting of the All-India Scientific Workers' Association, New Delhi, January 7, 1947"; cited in Singh, *Jawaharlal Nehru on Science and Society*, 44. My choice of the pronoun "himself" is deliberate, since the ideal scientist was invariably described as a male.

60 Nehru, "Address on the Occasion of the Opening of the National Chemical Laboratory, Pune on January 3, 1950"; cited in Singh, *Jawaharlal Nehru on Science and Society*, 72.

61 In the anthropormorphized description of the *varna* system of caste from the Rig Veda, the four orders emanated from four parts of the body of Purusha: the Brahmin from the head or the mouth, the Kshatriya from the arm, the Vaishya from the thigh, and the Shudra from the feet.

62 Nehru, untitled writing from December 28, 1948; cited in Singh, *Jawaharlal Nehru on Science and Society*, 69.

63 Nehru, "Irrigation and Power"; cited in Singh, *Jawaharlal Nehru on Science and Society*, 95–96.

64 For a discussion of how science was the site and means for the "fetishization" of the postcolonial state, see Abraham, *The Making of the Indian Atomic Bomb*, chapter 1.

65 According to Foucault, heterotopias, unlike the "non-places" of utopias, are simultaneously real and mythic spaces. Thus, a CSIR industrial laboratory was at once a concrete building with a specified location and an ideological-normative expression of a particular nation-statist ideal. See Foucault, "Of Other Spaces." For a Foucauldian reading of Nehruvian India's heterotopias, see Deshpande, "Hegemonic Spatial Strategies."

66 Nehru, "Religion, Philosophy and Science"; cited in Singh, *Jawaharlal Nehru on Science and Society*, 35. Emphasis added.

67 Jawaharlal Nehru, "Address at the Opening of the National Metallurgical Laboratory, Jamshedpur on November 26, 1950"; cited in Singh, *Jawaharlal Nehru on Science and Society*, 86.

68 Nehru, "Speech at the Foundation-Stone Laying Ceremony for the National Institute of Sciences, Delhi, April 19, 1948"; cited in Singh, *Jawaharlal Nehru on Science and Society*, 64.

69 Nehru, "Speech at the Golden Jubilee Celebrations of the Indian Institute of Science, Bangalore on February 4, 1959"; cited in Singh, *Jawaharlal Nehru on Science and Society*, 189.

70 Addressing the audience at the inaugural ceremony for the National Metallurgical Laboratory in Jamshedpur in November 1950, Nehru described scientific temper as "not only the devoted study of a particular subject, but the devoted search for truth [that] produces a dispassionate mind. It makes a person study objectively. It prevents an individual from being swept away by momentary passions" (cited in Singh, *Jawaharlal Nehru on Science and Society*, 86).

71 "To my mind, complacency is a dangerous thing—the person who is complacent naturally falls out of the race. I want that we should be impatient and dissatisfied with the pace of our progress, so that we always have the desire to increase the tempo of our work. But we must also remember that we have to change this impatience into activity and not froth and foam as many people are tending to do these days. Such people are really stumbling blocks in the nation's path to peace and prosperity." Nehru, "Speech Delivered at the Opening Ceremony of the Central Building Research Institute, Roorkee, April 12, 1953"; cited in Singh, *Jawaharlal Nehru on Science and Society*, 107.

72 The eminent chemist Shanti Swaroop Bhatnagar was one of the key figures of the "state scientific complex" or the elite group of scientists who played a crucial role in the formulation of science and technology policy in the postcolonial period. Bhatnagar's close rapport with Nehru led many contemporary observers to describe the establishment of industrial research laboratories as a product of the "Nehru-Bhatnagar Effect." See Richards, *The Life and Work of Sir S. S. Bhatnagar*.

73 Between 1950 and 1964, a total of twenty-nine national laboratories were established by the CSIR. In addition to those listed above were the following: National Metalurgical Laboratory (Jamshedpur); Central Drug Research Institute (Lucknow); Publications and Information Directorate (New Delhi); Central Road Research Institute (New Delhi); Indian National Scientific Documentation Centre (New Delhi); Central Leather Research Institute (Madras); National Botanical Research Institute (Lucknow); Central Electronics Engineering Research Institute (Pilani); Central Salt and Marine Chemicals Research Institute (Bhavnagar); Central Mining Research Station (Dhanbad); Indian Institute of Chemical Biology (Calcutta); Indian Institute of Chemical Technology (Hyderabad); Regional Research Laboratory (Jammu); Central Mechanical Engineering Research Institute (Durgapur); National Environmental Engineering Research Institute (Nagpur); Central Institute of Medicinal and Aromatic Plants (Lucknow); National Aero-

nautical Laboratory (Bangalore); Regional Research Laboratory (Jorhat); Indian Institute of Petroleum (Dehradun); Central Scientific Instruments Organization (Chandigarh); National Geophysical Research Institute (Hyderabad); and National Research Laboratory (Bhubaneswar). For further details, see Rajagopal, *The CSIR Saga*, 103.

74   Visvanathan, *Organizing for Science*, 143.

75   Like the laying of the foundation stone at the National Physical Laboratory, the opening of the National Chemical Laboratory also coincided with the meeting of the Indian Science Congress. As S. S. Bhatnagar (the director of the CSIR) observed at the opening ceremony for the National Chemical Laboratory, the date for the event was moved forward to take advantage of the fact that the "cream of Indian and Foreign scientists as well as all our young university men are available without any extra expenditure." See Bhatnagar, "Opening of NCL," in *S. S. Bhatnagar on Science, Technology, and Development*, 222.

76   Visvanathan, *Organizing for Science*, 143.

77   Given the diversity of speakers at these events, there were varied accounts of the relevance and meaning of the scientific venture at hand, as scientists and politicians deployed internalist and externalist criteria respectively in their account of the importance of science. Thus Bhatnagar delivered a rousing speech on the intrinsic value of "Big Science" at the opening of the National Physical Laboratory, in which he drew attention to the ways that the laboratory complex would advance the formation of scientific knowledge in India and also contribute to the universal episteme of science. The same event occasioned a very different narrative from the parliamentarian John Mathai. For Mathai, the value of the laboratory was related to its industrial utility and the role it would play in advancing the cause of planned development. See Visvanathan, *Organizing for Science*.

78   Ibid., 146.

79   Bhatnagar, "Opening of NPL," in *S. S. Bhatnagar on Science, Technology, and Development*, 231.

80   For instance, at the inauguration of the National Chemical Laboratory on January 3, 1950, Bhatnagar thanked, in the following order, "our beloved prime minister"; the (former) Viceroy Lord Linlithgow; the eminent scientist Ramaswamy Mudaliar, the first president of the Board of Scientific and Industrial Research (the colonial precursor of the CSIR); other members of the Board (Ardershir Dalal and Akbar Hydari); Governor-General Chakravarty Rajagopalachari; the governor of Bombay, B. G. Kher; the member of parliament and chair of the Planning Committee of the NCL, John Mathai; and the army officers in Pune, "without [whose] bulldozer we could not have held this ceremony today." See Bhatnagar, "Opening of NCL," in *S. S. Bhatnagar on Science, Technology, and Development*, 217–18.

81   Bhatnagar, "On the Opening of NPL," in *S. S. Bhatnagar on Science, Technology, and Development*, 232.

82   Mathur, "How It All Began—NPL in Retrospect," *NPL Silver Jubilee Supplement*; cited in Visvanathan, *Organizing for Science*, 146.

83 The efforts to ensure the presence of international scientists at these events highlights the global orientation of the national science project and the quest to garner international recognition of India's scientific prowess.
84 "It is human beings who make science, not bricks and mortar." Nehru, "Speech delivered at the Central Fuel Research Institute, Jealgoda, April 22, 1950"; cited in Singh, *Jawaharlal Nehru on Science and Society*, 77.
85 This was the thrust of John Mathai's comments at the inauguration of the National Physical Laboratory. See Visvanathan, *Organizing for Science*.
86 Cited in Singh, *Jawaharlal Nehru on Science and Society*, 75.
87 Nehru, "Speech at the Inauguration of the Bhakra Nangal Canal"; cited in Central Board of Irrigation and Power, *Modern Temples of India*.
88 See Chatterjee, *Nationalist Thought and the Colonial World*.
89 See the discussion of Anderson and Gellner in the introduction to this volume.
90 Anderson, *Imagined Communities*.
91 According to Alev Cinar's discussion of the modernization project of Kemalist Turkey, the production of modernity as the ultimate telos of the national-building project was secured through the continual denigration or defamation of the present as a nonmodern and backward time and place. See Cinar, *Modernity, Islam, and Secularism in Turkey*.
92 See Ferguson, *The Anti-Politics Machine*.

CHAPTER 4 *Cities of Hope*

1 For a discussion of the import-substitution industrialization policies of the Nehruvian state that were ushered in by the "Nehru-Mahalanobis" second five-year plan (so named in reference to the shared vision of economic development endorsed by the Indian prime minister and the economist P. K. Mahalanobis, the chair of the Planning Commission), and the considerable state investment in heavy industrialization and the rapid growth of a public sector that followed, see Bhagwati and Desai, *India: Planning for Industrialization*; Chibber, *Locked in Place*; and Bardhan, *The Political Economy of Development in India*.
2 Steel Authority of India, *Tryst with Steel*, 6.
3 Rushdie, *Midnight's Children*, 112.
4 Buck-Morss, *Dreamworld and Catastrophe*.
5 Town and Country Planning Organization, *Durgapur Steel Township*, 2.
6 See Sivaramakrishnan, "Durgapur," for a general overview of postcolonial India's new urban projects. For discussions of Bhubaneswar, see Kalia, *Bhubaneswar*; and for Chandigarh, see Evenson, *Chandigarh*; Prakash, *Chandigarh's Le Corbusier*; and Kalia, *Chandigarh*. For a discussion of the urban planning projects that were undertaken with the specific mandate of housing Partition refugees, see Jain, *City of Hope*. This autobiographical account of the Faridabad "model town" draws attention to the competing imperatives that informed the project, namely the simultaneous commitment to the rehabilitation of refugees or the normalization of their

liminal status and to the continued preservation of their distinction as people in need of special forms of assistance.

7   Government of India, *Durgapur Steel Township*, 2–3.
8   Despite methodological and epistemological differences (for instance, the difference between the "primordialist," "instrumentalist," and "constructivist" scholars of nationalism discussed in the introduction), there is a remarkable convergence around the view of nationalism as a homogenizing ideology and practice, and of nation-formation as a process of "scaling up" from local-level particularities to produce a seamless national "whole."
9   My focus on the centrality of the "new urban" in Nehruvian India goes against the grain of most discussions on the place of the urban in the postcolonial national imagination. For instance, in the Indian context studies of Nehruvian nationalism have argued that the postcolonial moment is marked by a "frugal investment in the urban" and that the legacy of the anticolonial movement and the shadow of the "Great Peasant" Gandhi led to the view of the village rather than the city as the authentic heartland of India. See Sundaram, "The Bazaar and the City"; and Seth, "Nationalism, National Identity and 'History.'" For a notable exception, see the recent essay by Gyan Prakash, "The Urban Turn." Moreover, even when nationalism is seen to entail the valorization of "metropolitan modernity" this has been described in terms of a logic of abstract placelessness—the metropolis figuring as an idea or a symbol rather than a specific place targeted by specific sets of spatial practices. These arguments about the urban lack in the Nehruvian national imagination miss an important part of the picture—namely, the importance accorded to the spatial production of the *new urban*. See Srivastava, *Constructing Post-Colonial India*, 165–89. My argument also addresses general theoretical debates about the relationship between the urban and the national. By locating my discussion of the interrelationship between the urban and the national in the specific space of the steel town, I call into question the historical-metropolitan bias of urban studies—the conflation of the urban with the "big city" and the "old city." As this essay suggests, the category of the urban is not exhausted by Bombay, Delhi, Calcutta, and Madras in the Indian context, or, if we use a broader geopolitical canvas, by Istanbul, Paris, Karachi, New York, London, Mexico City, or Nairobi.
10 In fact in some ways the initial celebration of the steel town as a national dreamworld already prefigured its future condemnation as a national catastrophe, since the actual achievement of promises and targets would have made the call for "nation-building" redundant and removed the "need for the state" that was integral to the Nehruvian understanding of nationhood.
11 Although the terms "communal" and "communalism" are defined in the dictionary as "pertaining to a community," in the Indian context they are used in exclusive reference to hostile relations between religious communities.
12 For a discussion of these colonial steel towns, see Benegal, "Township and Housing Design for Bokaro Steel Project, India," 7.
13 A significant qualifier is necessary here: all of the public-sector steel plants and

townships of postcolonial India were built with financial and technical assistance from other nation-states. The Soviet Union collaborated on Bhilai and Bokaro, the British state on Durgapur, and the Federal Republic of Germany on Rourkela. Significant numbers of foreign nationals lived and worked in the towns, especially during the initial years after their construction, and they were frequently evoked in political debates and discussions unfolding in contexts as far removed from provincial India as the U.S. Congress or the German Bundestag. Consequently, the steel town as both a literal site as well as a symbolic site or "dreamworld" owed its existence to the intersection of national and global desires and efforts. For a fascinating account of the German experience in Rourkela, see *The Human Dimensions of Technical Assistance*, the memoirs of Jan Sperling who served as director of German social, cultural, and medical services in Rourkela from 1958 to 1962. For a discussion of the Soviet experience in Bhilai, see Runyantsev, *Bhilai*; and Dymshits, *How Bhilai Was Built*. For a discussion of the debates in the U.S. Congress about providing foreign aid for the Bokaro project, see Rangnekar, *Bokaro*; and Singh, "An Evaluation of U.S. Economic Assistance to India." The proposal to provide foreign aid to Bokaro had been endorsed by President Kennedy. However, both the House and the Senate voted down the Bokaro clauses in the foreign aid bill presented before them in 1963, on the grounds that providing financial assistance for a "socialist" project (a state-owned steel plant) was an inappropriately "ideological" gesture. As the Clay Committee observed, "The U.S. should not aid a foreign government in projects establishing government owned industrial and commercial enterprises which compete with private endeavors ... Moreover, the observation of countless instances of politically operated, heavily subsidized, and carefully protected inefficient state enterprises in less developed countries makes us gravely doubt the value of such undertakings in the economic life of these nations" (U.S. Department of State, "The Scope and Distribution of United States Military and Economic Programs," in *Report to the President of the U.S. from the Committee to Strengthen the Security of the Free World* (Clay Committee), 1963; cited in Singh, *An Evaluation of U.S. Economic Assistance to India*, 94.

14 Sundaram, "The Bazaar and the City."
15 Government of India, *Rourkela*, 5.
16 "Old Glory, New Achievement: Hindustan Steel," *Times of India* (Bombay), January 26, 1953, 3.
17 Without the state and its concern to secure "balanced regional development," the steel plants wouldn't exist where they did, and consequently neither would the steel towns. Life within the steel town was also structured around the facilities and services provided by the state and its agencies. For instance, the plan for Bokaro was based on a "primary and secondary school district concept"—that is, instead of creating a center based on recreational spaces such as parks or commercial spaces such as markets, a primary school built by the state would serve as the center of activities for each residential sector, which was comprised of approx-

imately 750 families in an area of 40 or 50 acres. See Town and Country Planning Organization, *Town and Country Planning in India*, 90.

18 These particular locations appear to be obvious choices given their abundance of mineral resources. However, factors other than natural endowment were involved in the decision—after all, rich deposits of coal and iron ore could be found in various locations throughout the country. As several scholars have noted, certain non-economic imperatives relating to the project of postcolonial nation building played a significant role. For example, the state's commitment to balanced national development could be showcased through its act of "bringing progress" (in the form of steel plants) to "backward areas." In other instances, the final decisions about the location of steel plants were shaped by the political compromises of the federal bargaining process. These surfaced with particular intensity during the planning process for the Bokaro steel project in the late 1950s, as political elites in several other states of India made the case for building a steel plant in Bokaro rather than in Bihar. If Bokaro was chosen in the end, its selection had more to do with the "politics of steel" and the political skills of the chief minister of Bihar at the time than with the quality of iron ore in Salem, Hospet, or Visakhapatnam (the other proposed locations). For an extended discussion of this issue, see Town and Country Planning Organization, *Town and Country Planning in India*, 67; Desai, *Bokaro Steel Plant*, 8–9; and Sivaramakrishnan, "Durgapur," 144.

19 Town and Country Planning Organization, *Town and Country Planning in India*, 91, 68–69.

20 Ibid., 87. This observation accompanied an account of why the process of building Bokaro was easier than the building of other steel towns, where construction workers had to contend with a less "undulating" environment. In contrast, intensively cultivated land is flat land and therefore easier to build upon.

21 Bose, *Chittaranjan Township*, 3. In the case of the establishment of Rourkela township, the "empty land" narrative was actually set aside to include a consideration of the "local population": "The attitude initially of the local population was one of opposition. Happily however, when they came to understand the benefits of the project, this changed into one of cooperation. Good progress has since been made in the establishment of the township" (Publications Division, *Rourkela*, 15).

22 The lack of educational qualifications was a significant barrier to the employment of Bauris in formal positions on the shop floor, where all positions above the grade of "operator" required education up to the eighth standard. See Sengupta, *Destitutes and Development*.

23 Sengupta's study of the effects of planned development on the lives of the Bauri community establishes that, contrary to the expectations that steel complexes would be "generative engines" of growth and development, the local communities experienced rapid increases in levels of poverty, unemployment, and general social-economic "destitution." See Sengupta, *Destitutes and Development*.

24 Town and Country Planning Organization, *Town and Country Planning in India*, 68.

25 Ibid., 69.
26 The highest-paid employees of the steel plant (the managerial and administrative personnel) earned almost sixty times more than the lowest-paid employee eligible for housing ("casual labour" did not qualify for housing). Of the six grades of housing, Grade A, reserved for those at the highest end of the salary scale (earning approximately 3,500 rupees per month), consisted of a 2,100 square foot house with three bedrooms, "servants' quarters," and a garden. On the other end, Grade F, reserved for those who earned less than sixty rupees per month, consisted of a room with a balcony, a shared bathroom, and a common passage (these rooms were clustered within two- or three-storied dormitory-style buildings). Taking into account a proportionate amount of this common space, each employee living within Grade F housing apparently had exactly 365 square feet of space. Finally, there was also an "extra-special" category above Grade A houses, which Benegal describes simply as "a lavish house." These were reserved for "extra-special" people like the general manager of the steel plant and the general superintendent, and the structures also served as guesthouses for government officials and dignitaries. See Benegal, "Township and Housing Design for Bokaro Steel Project, India," 10, 20.
27 Cited in Prakash, *Chandigarh's Le Corbusier*, 9 n.11.
28 Krishna, *Postcolonial Insecurities*, xix.
29 In Ebenezer Howard's original vision of the garden city, the preservation of such an expanse of agricultural land was what would enable it to realize its role as a "town-country magnet." See Howard, *Garden Cities of To-Morrow*.
30 For a discussion of the different types of urban planning activity undertaken in the postcolonial period, and the varied genealogies of these plans, see Koenigsberger, "New Towns in India."
31 The term "planned hybridity" is from Spivak, "City, Country, Agency," 3; cited in Prakash, *Chandigarh's Le Corbusier*.
32 The memoirs of Bagaram Tulpule, general manager of Durgapur steel plant from 1971 to 1974, illuminate some of the complexities of this situation. See Tulpule, *Amidst Heat and Noise*, 85–94.
33 The "area committees" of Chittaranjan township were charged with these responsibilities. They were also entrusted with undertaking certain kinds of prohibitory activities, such as preventing "acts of vandalism" and discouraging "wild rumour." For a detailed account of the role and responsibilities of the area committees, see Bose, *Chittaranjan Township*, 9.
34 It would take time before this dream of national integration was perfectly realized —before "living together" as empirical description translated into something meaningful and substantive. However, this was in keeping with the "logic of deferrence" that structured the Nehruvian discourse of nation building and its conceptualization of the nation in terms of becoming rather than being. See Krishna, *Postcolonial Insecurities*, and also the discussion of temporal deferral and developmental nationalism in chapter 3.

35 The term "parasitic" is from Sahai, *Urban Complex of an Industrial City*, 233. Sahai had set himself the task of evaluating whether Durgapur was a "generative" or a "parasitic" city, according to the typology developed by the University of Chicago economist Bert Hoselitz, who was an advisor to the Indian government from 1957 to 1958. See Hoselitz, *Sociological Aspects of Economic Growth*.
36 For a discussion of the different categories of representation, see Pitkin, *The Concept of Representation*.
37 For a discussion of the "individualizing" and "totalizing" effects of state power, see Foucault, "Omnes et Singulatim." As he observes, "right from the start, the state is both individualising and totalitarian. Opposing the individual and his interests to it is just as hazardous as opposing it with the community and its requirements. Political rationality has grown and imposed itself all throughout the history of Western societies. It first took its stand on the idea of pastoral power, then on that of reason of state. Its inevitable effects are both individualisation and totalisation. Liberation can only come from attacking, not just one of these two effects, but political rationality's very roots" (85).
38 Sperling, *The Human Dimensions of Technical Assistance*, 120. Within the steel township there were numerous other ways in which "foreign presence" could be discerned: direct encounters with the significant numbers of German and Russian personnel who lived and worked in Rourkela and Bhilai, respectively; the development of residential areas and recreational centers set aside for the exclusive use of "foreigner-residents" of the township; and the growth of a differentiated service economy (specifically, that of domestic service) catering to "specialized" needs. See Sperling, *The Human Dimensions of Technical Assistance*; and Runyantsev, *Bhilai*.
39 For an extended discussion of the macroeconomic reasons for the increases in economic inequality among steel plant workers and, by extension, among steel town residents, see Benegal, "Township and Housing Design for Bokaro Steel Project, India," 15–16.
40 For a discussion of the preponderance of "inside contracting" (the subcontracting of jobs that are then carried out within the premises of the plant itself, in contrast to a "putting out" system of subcontracting) and other forms of informal labor practices in the steel plant, see Sengupta, *Contract Labour in the Rourkela Steel Plant*; and Mohanty, *Collective Bargaining in the Steel Industry in India*.
41 Government of India, *Durgapur Steel Township*, appendix 4.
42 Ibid., 63.
43 Tulpule, *Amidst Heat and Noise*, 14.
44 Benegal, "Township and Housing Design for Bokaro Steel Project, India," 1.
45 Government of India, *Durgapur Steel Township*, 3, 67.
46 The conclusion about the inability of planned urbanism to realize an effective "urbanity" was also invoked during discussions about other planned cities. Ravi Kalia's commentary on Chandigarh is strikingly similar to the observations about the steel towns noted above: "Chandigarh was meant to be something beyond a

new state capital. But it lacks a culture. It lacks the excitement of Indian streets. It lacks bustling, colorful bazaars. It lacks the noise and din of Lahore. It lacks the intimacy of Delhi. It is a stay-at-home city. It is not Indian. It is the anticity" (Kalia, *Chandigarh*, 29).

47 Parry, "Two Cheers for Reservation."
48 Chatterjee, Singh, and Rao, *Riots in Rourkela*, 125.
49 Ibid., 132.
50 These are among the conclusions and recommendations offered by the Town and Country Planning Organization in their 1962 report.
51 Foucault, *Discipline and Punish*.
52 This proposal is developed at length by Benegal in "Township and Housing Design for Bokaro Steel Project, India."
53 Other occlusions and silences were at work as well. For instance, none of the "urban reform" proposals addressed the situation of the displaced *adivasi* communities. Neither the initial proposals on building the steel town nor the subsequent discussions on its rebuilding took cognizance of the founding violence of the nation-state.
54 See "Army Called Out in 3 Orissa Towns: 28 Killed, 59 Hurt in Rourkela Clashes," *Times of India* (Bombay), March 21, 1964, 1.
55 As Brass has observed in his magisterial account of the patterns of collective violence in northern India, narrative "texts" about riots are never neutral observations of objective facts that "actually happened," but rather are interested or situated representations that shape and even produce the "contexts" of violence that they describe. In this sense, each elucidation of the "facts of the case" is already a causal explanation, which highlights confirming evidence at the expense of "anomalous" or "extraneous" details. See Brass, *Theft of an Idol*.
56 *Times of India* (Bombay), March 23, 1964; *Hindustan Times*, March 23, 1964.
57 *Times of India* (Bombay), March 21, 1964, 1. The following discussion is based on articles that appeared in the *Times of India* on a daily basis between March 21 and April 5, 1964.
58 Thus, "the minority community" is understood to be a reference to Muslims, even though there are many other "minority communities" in India, religious and otherwise.
59 There were some additions as well. Thus, in contrast to the media reports, state accounts offered a normative interpretation of the riots, stressing the "gravity," the "unfortunate" nature, and the fact that there was a "serious problem" at hand. Further, although the riots were located within Rourkela and confined within a discrete temporal framework (several days in March 1964) their significance was translocal in the official narrative: for all state actors, Rourkela's riots were India's problem. See "Calling Attention to Matter of Urgent Public Importance," *Lok Sabha Debates*, volume 28, March 23, 1964, 6910–14.
60 *Indian Express* (New Delhi), March 23, 1964, 7; cited in Chatterjee, Singh, and Rao, *Riots in Rourkela*, 11.

61 *Hitavada* (Nagpur), April 4, 1964, 5; cited in Chatterjee, Singh, and Rao, *Riots in Rourkela*.
62 Chatterjee, Singh, and Rao, *Riots in Rourkela*, 125.
63 "Calling Attention to Matter of Urgent Public Importance," *Lok Sabha Debates*, vol. 28, March 23, 1964, 6910–14 (translation from Hindi is mine).
64 While such questions went unanswered, and also unasked, in the dominant narratives, they were central to an inquiry conducted by academics affiliated with the Gandhian Social Institute two years after the riots. Their conclusions regarding the causes of the riots were markedly different from those highlighted by the paradigm of communalism, and in fact entailed an explicit repudiation of its logic: "This study has made it clear that to hold "communalism" as responsible for the entire range and magnitude of the mob violence that took place at Rourkela is to over-simplify and misunderstand a complex social situation." In its place, several specific factors were identified, all of which related the violence to the structures, policies, and practices of postcolonial governance. Thus instead of the broad indictment of "unionism" privileged in official narratives, the inequities of industrial development in the area and the inadequacies of existing labor laws came under scrutiny. Where Pakistani agents had been named as the instigators, and the spontaneity of the violence had been its defining characteristic, the study provided evidence for the involvement of the Rashtriya Swayamsevak Sangh (RSS), the primary Hindu nationalist organization in India, and drew attention to the organized rather than "random" nature of the violence. Finally, the general description of the "gullible" and "impressionable" *adivasis* in the official narratives was replaced by a detailed consideration of how the establishment of the steel town had transformed the social and economic landscape of the Rourkela area. Not surprisingly, the concluding recommendations of the study did not include the call to "combat communalism" by disavowing politics. In fact, the opposite was called for: a commitment to unabashedly *political* forms of struggle. See Chatterjee, Singh, and Rao, *Riots in Rourkela*, 7.
65 See Handelman, *Models and Mirrors*.

CONCLUSION

1 There are several different views on how to date the historical emergence of Indian nationalism. According to Chris Bayly, structures and sentiments of patriotism and a sense of "nationality" in South Asia can be traced to the eighteenth century and the traditions and practices of the precolonial period. According to Manu Goswami, the conventional historiography of the late-nineteenth-century rise of Indian nationalism fails to take into account the transformations in the nature and structure of colonial state power after 1857 as well as the new national imaginings of India (as a particular territorially bound "national space") that emerged at this time. See Bayly, *Origins of Nationality in South Asia*; and Goswami, *Producing India*.

2 Further, as the subaltern school of historical studies has pointed out, even the singular category of a nationalist movement requires revision, since the numerous contestations of state authority that were staged across India in the years before independence in 1947 were motivated by often incommensurable sets of immediate or localized rather than abstract and uniform "national" concerns. To draw upon Rogers Brubaker's useful distinction, the binary "master cleavage" of "nationalism against colonialism" is more a "category of analysis" than a "category of practice" (Brubaker and Cooper, "Beyond Identity," 34; see also the various volumes published by the Subaltern Studies collective).

3 I borrow this term from social movement theory. See Gamson, "The Social Psychology of Collective Action."

4 "Moment of arrival" is the term used by Partha Chatterjee in his discussion of the Nehruvian project of the nation-state in the late 1930s and beyond—the concluding episode in his narrative of the emergence and transformation of anticolonial nationalism in India. See Chatterjee, *Nationalist Thought and the Colonial World*.

5 The involvement of state agencies was similarly varied. As established earlier, different "faces of the state" enabled different kinds of nation-statist encounters (compare, for instance, the spectacular, extraordinary event of Republic Day commemorations with the humdrum rhythms of everyday life in the steel town).

6 As further evidence of the multiplex rather than seamless character of the postcolonial nation-statist project, the form of these encounters and the affective responses that they produced were very different in each case. Photographs of the foundation-laying ceremony render this difference in graphic visual detail: the anonymous mass of workers, farmers, and peasants sit on the floor facing the podium, while the scientists with their prominent name tags share the stage with state officials.

7 Cooper, *Colonialism in Question*, 82 (emphasis in the original).

8 A caveat is necessary here: There was always a "statist" imagination of nationhood that propelled the anticolonial movement and that grew to prominence in the mid 1930s and beyond. Scholarship on Indian nationalism describes this as the "Nehruvian" strand of anticolonialism, which stood in marked opposition to the anti-statist provocations of the Gandhian call for anticolonial struggle. See, for instance, the discussion in Chatterjee, *Nationalist Thought and the Colonial World*.

9 Moreover, as demonstrated earlier, Nehruvian India's diversity displays entailed the juxtaposition of images of cultural diversity with those of identity gone wrong; and specters of "ethnic militancy," "communal politics," and "economic backwardness" were frequently singled out in a variety of different political and institutional settings by state as well as nonstate actors. For instance, even as every year the official commentary at the Republic Day parades and the media coverage of the event hailed the colorful pageantry of the cultural floats and folk dancers on Rajpath, attention also centered on the figure of the ethnic militant and rebel as the negative exemplar that threatened and endangered the nation-state and its citizens.

10 This constitution was endorsed not just by state elites alone. As I noted in chapter 4, a range of social actors of varying ideological persuasions found common ground in this constitutive condemnation of political behavior.
11 For a useful discussion of the different trajectories of decolonization in Asia and Africa, see Duara, Decolonization.
12 For a detailed exploration of the political, economic, and social-cultural transformations in the Indian polity, see Corbridge and Harriss, Reinventing India.
13 For an insightful account of the new national imagination that dominates "globalizing India," see Mazzarella, Shoveling Smoke.
14 Verdery, "Nationalism and National Sentiment in Post-Socialist Romania," 180.
15 Chatterjee, The Politics of the Governed. For a related discussion on the "creative appropriations" of governmental categories and techniques by slum dwellers in Mumbai, see Appadurai, "Deep Democracy."
16 Sen, The Argumentative Indian.
17 For a discussion of the distinctive ideological-political practices of Hindu nationalism, see the collection of essays in Ludden, Making India Hindu, along with Christophe Jaffrelot's recent compilation, The Sangh Parivar: A Reader.
18 These include the assertiveness of subnational movements seeking political autonomy and the wars with China and Pakistan in 1962 and 1965, respectively.
19 Sudipta Kaviraj's pithy description of the postcolonial national imagination is discussed at length in chapter 2.
20 "One of the most remarkable features of . . . Hindu nationalism is the relative ease with which it has fitted into most of the authorized discourses on India and more generally on politics and culture in the postcolonial world" (Hansen, The Saffron Wave, 5).

BIBLIOGRAPHY

: : :

Abraham, Itty. "Landscape and Postcolonial Science." *Contributions to Indian Sociology* 34 (2000): 163–87.

———. *The Making of the Indian Atomic Bomb: Science, Secrecy, and the Postcolonial State.* New Delhi: Orient Longman, 1998.

Abrams, Phillip. "Notes on the Difficulty of Studying the State." *Journal of Historical Sociology* 1.1 (1988): 58–89.

Adams, Julia. "Culture in Rational-Choice Theories of State Formation." In *State/Culture: State Formation after the Cultural Turn*, ed. George Steinmetz. Ithaca, N.Y.: Cornell University Press, 1999. 98–122.

Adeney, Katherine, and Andrew Wyatt. "Democracy in South Asia: Getting beyond the Structure-Agency Dichotomy." *Political Studies* 52.1 (2004): 1–18.

Aggarwal, Ravina. *Beyond Lines of Control: Performance and Politics on the Disputed Borders of Ladakh, India.* Durham, N.C.: Duke University Press, 2004.

Alavi, Hamza. "State and Class in Peripheral Capitalism." In *Introduction to the Sociology of Developing Societies*, ed. Hamza Alavi and Teodor Shanin. London: Macmillan, 1982.

Alvares, Claude. *Science, Development, and Violence.* New Delhi: Oxford University Press, 1992.

Amin, Shahid. "Educational Reforms: What Is Not to Be Done." *Times of India* (Delhi), June 2, 2004. Available online at http://timesofindia.indiatimes.com.

———. "On Representing the Musalman." *Sarai Reader 04: Crisis/Media.* New Delhi: Sarai, 2004.

Anagnost, Ann. *National Past-Times: Narrative, Representation, and Power in Modern China.* Durham, N.C.: Duke University Press, 1997.

Anderson, Benedict. *Imagined Communities: Reflections on the Origins and Spread of Nationalism.* Rev. ed. London: Verso, 1991.

Anderson, Robert. "Cultivating Science as Cultural Policy: A Contrast of Agricultural and Nuclear Science in India." *Pacific Affairs* 56.1 (1983): 38–50.

Appadurai, Arjun. "Deep Democracy: Urban Governmentality and the Horizon of Politics." *Public Culture* 14.1 (2002): 21–47.

———. "Number in the Colonial Imagination." In *Modernity at Large: Cultural Dimensions of Globalization.* Minneapolis: University of Minnesota Press, 1996. 114–35.

Apter, Andrew. "The Subvention of Tradition: A Genealogy of the Nigerian Durbar." In *State/Culture: State Formation after the Cultural Turn*, ed. George Steinmetz. Ithaca, N.Y.: Cornell University Press, 1999. 213–52.

Ashcroft, Bill, Gareth Griffin, and Helen Tiffin, eds. *The Postcolonial Studies Reader*. London: Routledge, 1995.

Austin, Granville. *The Indian Constitution: Cornerstone of a Nation*. New York: Oxford University Press, 2000.

Axel, Brian Keith. *The Nation's Tortured Body: Violence, Representation, and the Formation of a Sikh Diaspora*. Durham, N.C.: Duke University Press, 2001.

Balibar, Étienne, and Immanuel Wallerstein. *Race, Nation, Class: Ambiguous Identities*. London: Verso, 1994.

Bardhan, Pranab. *The Political Economy of Development in India*. Expanded ed. New Delhi: Oxford University Press, 1999.

Barnouw, Erik. *Documentary: A History of the Non-Fiction Film*. Rev. ed. New York: Oxford University Press, 1993.

Barsam, Richard Meran. *Nonfiction Film: A Critical History*. New York: E. P. Dutton, 1973.

Barua, Pradeep. "Inventing Race: The British and India's Martial Races." *Historian: Journal of History* 58 (1995): 107–16.

Basu, Amrita, and Srirupa Roy, eds. *Violence and Democracy in India*. London: Seagull Books, 2006.

Baumann, Zygmunt. *Modernity and the Holocaust*. New York: Polity Press, 1989.

Bayly, Chris. *Origins of Nationality in South Asia*. New Delhi: Oxford University Press, 1998.

Benegal, Niranjan Krishna. "Township and Housing Design for Bokaro Steel Project, India." M.S. thesis, North Dakota State University, 1966.

Berezin, Mabel. "Political Belonging: Emotion, Nation and Identity in Fascist Italy." In *State/Culture: State Formation after the Cultural Turn*, ed. George Steinmetz. Ithaca, N.Y.: Cornell University Press, 1999. 355–77.

Berghahn, Volker. "Philanthropy and Diplomacy in the 'American Century.'" *Diplomatic History* 23.3 (1999): 393–419.

Berlant, Lauren. "The Theory of Infantile Citizenship." *Public Culture* 5.3 (1993): 395–410.

Bhabha, Homi K. "DissemiNation: Time, Narrative, and the Margins of the Modern Nation." In *The Location of Culture*, 1994. 139–70.

Bhagwati, Jagdish, and Padma Desai. *India: Planning for Industrialization*. New York: Oxford University Press, 1970.

Bhatnagar, S. S. S. S. *Bhatnagar on Science, Technology, and Development, 1938–1954*. Delhi: NISTADS, 1993.

Bhaya Nair, Rukmini. *Technobrat: Culture in a Cybernetic Classroom*. New Delhi: Harper Collins, 1997.

Billig, Michael. *Banal Nationalism*. London: Sage Publications, 1995.

Binder, Leonard et al., eds. *Crises and Sequences in Political Development*. Princeton, N.J.: Princeton University Press, 1971.

Bose, S. K. *Chittaranjan Township*. Delhi: UNESCO Research Center; Indian Institute of Public Administration, 1960.
Bourdieu, Pierre, and Loic Wacquant. "On the Cunning of Imperialist Reason." *Theory, Culture and Society* 16.1 (1999): 41–57.
Brass, Paul. "The Gujarat Pogrom of 2002." 2002. Available online at SSRC Contemporary Conflicts, http://www.ssrc.org.
———. *Language, Religion and Politics in North India*. Cambridge: Cambridge University Press, 1974.
———. *Theft of an Idol: Text and Context in the Representation of Collective Violence*. Princeton, N.J.: Princeton University Press, 1997.
Breckenridge, Carol, ed. *Consuming Modernity: Public Culture in a South Asian World*. Minneapolis: University of Minnesota Press, 1995.
Brown, Mark. "Ethnology and Colonial Administration in Nineteenth Century British India: The Question of Native Crime and Criminality." *British Journal for the History of Science* 36.2 (2003): 201–19.
Brubaker, Rogers. *Citizenship and Nationhood in France and Germany*. Cambridge, Mass.: Harvard University Press, 1992.
———. *Nationalism Reframed: Nationhood and the National Question in the New Europe*. Cambridge: Cambridge University Press, 1996.
Brubaker, Rogers, and Frederick Cooper. "Beyond Identity." *Theory and Society* 29 (2000): 1–47.
Buck-Morss, Susan. *Dreamworld and Catastrophe*. Cambridge, Mass.: MIT Press, 2000.
Butalia, Urvashi. *The Other Side of Silence: Voices from the Partition of India*. Delhi: Penguin Books, 1998.
Cannadine, David. "The Context, Performance and Meaning of Ritual: The British Monarchy and the Invention of Tradition, c. 1820–1977." In *The Invention of Tradition*, ed. Eric Hobsbawm and Terence Ranger. Cambridge: Cambridge University Press. 1992.
Cassirer, Ernest. *The Myth of the State*. New Haven, Conn.: Yale University Press, 1946.
Central Board of Irrigation and Power. *Modern Temples of India: Selected Speeches of Jawaharlal Nehru*. New Delhi: Central Board of Irrigation and Power, 1989.
Césaire, Aimé. *The Discourse of Colonialism*. Trans. Joan Pinkham. New York: Monthly Review Press, 2000.
Chakrabarty, Dipesh. "Modernity and Ethnicity in India." In *Multicultural States: Rethinking Difference and Identity*, ed. David Bennett. London: Routledge, 1998.
———. *Provincializing Europe: Postcolonial Thought and Historical Difference*. Princeton, N.J., Princeton University Press, 1998.
Chakravartty, Paula. "Telecom, National Development, and the Indian State: A Postcolonial Critique." *Media Culture and Society* 26 (2004): 227–49.
Chakravarty, Sumita S. "National Identity and the Realist Aesthetic: Indian Cinema of the Fifties." *Quarterly Review of Film and Television* 11 (1989): 31–48.
———. *National Identity in Indian Popular Cinema*. Austin: University of Texas Press, 1993.

Chatterjee, B. B., P. N. Singh, and G. R. S. Rao. *Riots in Rourkela: A Psychological Study.* New Delhi: Popular Book Services, 1967.

Chatterjee, Partha. *Nationalist Thought and the Colonial World: A Derivative Discourse?* Minneapolis: University of Minnesota Press, 1991.

———. *The Nation and Its Fragments.* Princeton, N.J.: Princeton University Press, 1993.

———. *Our Modernity.* Rotterdam and Dakar: SEPHIS-CODESRIA Publications, 1997.

———. *The Politics of the Governed: Reflections on Popular Politics in Most of the World.* New York: Columbia University Press. 2004.

Chibber, Vivek. *Locked in Place: State-Building and Late Industrialization in India.* Princeton, N.J.: Princeton University Press. 2003.

Chow, Rey. *The Protestant Ethnic and the Spirit of Capitalism.* New York: Columbia University Press, 2002.

Cinar, Alev. *Modernity, Islam, and Secularism in Turkey.* Minneapolis: University of Minnesota Press. 2005.

Coakley, John, ed. *The Territorial Management of Ethnic Conflict.* London: Frank Cass, 2003.

Cohen, Jerome Allen, and Shao-Chuan Leng. "The Sino-Indian Dispute over the Internment and Detention of Chinese in India." In *China's Practice of International Law: Some Case Studies,* ed. Jerome Allen Cohen. Cambridge, Mass.: Harvard University Press, 1972. 268–320.

Cohn, Bernard. *An Anthropologist among the Historians and Other Essays.* Delhi: Oxford University Press, 1996.

———. *Colonialism and Its Forms of Knowledge: The British in India.* Princeton, N.J.: Princeton University Press, 1996.

Connolly, William. *The Ethos of Pluralization.* Minneapolis: University of Minnesota Press, 1995.

Cooper, Frederick. *Colonialism in Question.* Berkeley: University of California Press, 2005.

Cooper, Frederick, and Randall Packard, eds. *International Development and the Social Sciences: Essays in the History and Politics of Knowledge.* Berkeley: University of California Press, 1997.

Copland, Ian. *The Princes of India in the Endgame of Empire, 1917–1947.* Cambridge: Cambridge University Press, 1997.

Corbridge, Stuart, and John Harriss. *Reinventing India: Liberalization, Hindu Nationalism, and Popular Democracy.* Cambridge: Polity Press. 2000.

Coronil, Fernando. *The Magical State: Nature, Money, and Modernity in Venezuela.* Chicago: University of Chicago Press. 1997.

Corrigan, Philip, and Derek Sayer. *The Great Arch: English State Formation as Cultural Revolution.* Oxford: Blackwell, 1985.

Cowen, Michael, and Robert Shenton. "The Invention of Development." In *Power of Development,* ed. Jonathan Crush. New York: Routledge, 1995. 27–43.

Crawford, Neta. "Decolonization as an International Norm: The Evolution of Practices, Arguments, and Beliefs." In *Emerging Norms of Justified Intervention,* ed. Laura Reed and Carl Kaysen. Cambridge: American Academy of Arts and Sciences, 1993.

Cruikshank, Barbara. *The Will to Empower: Democratic Citizens and Other Subjects.* Ithaca, N.Y.: Cornell University Press, 1999.

Culler, Jonathan. "Anderson and the Novel." In *Grounds of Comparison: Around the Work of Benedict Anderson,* ed. Jonathan Culler and Pheng Cheah. London: Routledge, 2003.

Culler, Jonathan, and Pheng Cheah, eds. *Grounds of Comparison: Around the Work of Benedict Anderson.* London: Routledge, 2003.

Dasgupta, Jyotirindra. "India's Federal Design and Multicultural National Construction." In *The Success of India's Democracy,* ed. Atul Kohli. Cambridge: Cambridge University Press, 2001.

Dasgupta, Subrata. *Jagdish Chandra Bose: An Indian Response to Western Science.* New Delhi: Oxford University Press, 1999.

Davila, Arlene. *Sponsored Identities: Cultural Politics in Puerto Rico.* Philadelphia: Temple University Press, 1997.

Dean, Mitchell. *Critical and Effective Histories: Foucault's Methods and Historical Sociology.* London: Routledge, 1994.

Desai, Padma. *Bokaro Steel Plant: A Study of Soviet Economic Assistance.* New York: American Elsevier Publishing. 1972.

Deshpande, Satish. "Hegemonic Spatial Strategies: The Nation-Space and Hindu Communalism in Twentieth-Century India." In *Subaltern Studies XI,* ed. Partha Chatterjee and Pradeep Jeganathan. New York: Columbia University Press. 2001.

Devji, Faisal Fatehali. "Hindu/Muslim/Indian." *Public Culture* 5.1 (1992): 1–18.

Dirks, Nicholas. *Castes of Mind: Colonialism and the Making of Modern India.* Princeton, N.J.: Princeton University Press, 2001.

———. "Ritual and Resistance: Subversion as a Social Fact." In *Culture/Power/History,* ed. Nicholas Dirks, Geoff Eley, and Sherry Ortner. Princeton, N.J.: Princeton University Press, 1994. 483–503.

Dobrenko, Evgeny, and Eric Naiman, eds. *The Landscape of Stalinism: The Art and Ideology of Soviet Space.* Seattle: University of Washington Press, 2003.

Duara, Prasenjit. *Decolonization: Perspectives from Now and Then.* London: Routledge Press, 2004.

Dymshits, Veniamin. *How Bhilai Was Built.* Delhi: Soviet Land Booklets, 1980.

Easterly, William. "Can Institutions Resolve Ethnic Conflict?" *Economic Development and Cultural Change* 49.4 (2001): 687–706.

Eley, Geoff, and Ronald Grigor Suny. "Introduction: From the Moment of Social History to the Work of Cultural Reproduction." In *Becoming National: A Reader,* ed. Geoff Eley and Ronald Grigor Suny. New York: Oxford University Press, 1996. 3–37.

Eller, Jack, and Reed Coughlan. "The Poverty of Primordialism." *Ethnic and Rational Studies* 16.2 (1993): 187–201.

Escobar, Arturo. *Encountering Development: The Making and Unmaking of the Third World.* Princeton, N.J.: Princeton University Press, 1994.

Evenson, Norma. *Chandigarh.* Berkeley: University of California Press, 1966.

Fanon, Frantz. *The Wretched of the Earth.* New York: Grove Press, 1967.

Ferguson, James. *The Anti-Politics Machine: "Development," Depoliticization, and Bureaucratic Power in Lesotho*. Minneapolis: University of Minnesota Press, 1994.

Foucault, Michel. *Discipline and Punish*. Trans. Alan Sheridan. New York: Vintage, 1995.

———. "Of Other Spaces." *Diacritics* (spring 1986): 22–27.

———. "Omnes et Singulatim: Towards a Criticism of Political Reason." In *Politics, Philosophy and Culture: Interviews and Other Writings, 1977–1984*. London: Routledge, 1988.

———. "The Subject and Power." In *Michel Foucault: Beyond Structuralism and Hermeneutics*, ed. Hubert Dreyfus and Paul Rabinow. 2nd ed. Chicago: University of Chicago Press, 1983.

Frankel, Francine. *India's Political Economy, 1947–1977: The Gradual Revolution*. Delhi: Oxford University Press, 1978.

Fraser, Nancy. "Talking about Needs: Interpretive Contests as Political Conflicts in Welfare-State Societies." *Ethics* 99.2 (1989): 291–313.

Fuller, C. J., and Veronique Benei, eds. *The Everyday State and Society in Modern India*. New Delhi: Social Science Press, 2000.

Galanter, Marc. *Law and Society in Modern India*. New York: Oxford University Press. 1993.

Gamson, William. "The Social Psychology of Collective Action." In *Frontiers in Social Movement Theory*, ed. Aldon Morris and Carol Mueller. New Haven, Conn.: Yale University Press, 1992. 53–76.

Ganti, Tejaswini. "Casting Culture: The Social Life of Hindi Film Production in Contemporary India." Ph.D. dissertation, New York University, 2000.

Garga, B. D. "Is Anyone Watching?" *Cinema in India* 2.3 (1988): 26–30.

———. "Turbulent Years: The Indian Documentary." *Cinema in India* 2.2 (1988): 32–36.

Geertz, Clifford. "The Integrative Revolution: Primordial Sentiments and Civil Politics in the New States." In *The Interpretation of Cultures: Selected Essays*. New York: Basic Books, 1973.

———. *Negara: The Theatre State in Nineteenth-Century Bali*. Princeton, N.J.: Princeton University Press, 1980.

Gellner, Ernest. *Nations and Nationalism*. Ithaca, N.Y.: Cornell University Press, 1983.

Gillis, John, ed. *Commemorations: The Politics of National Identity*. Princeton, N.J.: Princeton University Press, 1994.

Girard, Augustin. *Cultural Development: Experiences and Policies*. Paris: UNESCO, 1983.

Gleason, Philip. "Identifying Identity: A Semantic History." *Journal of American History* 69.4 (1983): 910–31.

Goldberg, David Theo, ed. *Multiculturalism: A Critical Reader*. London: Blackwell, 1994.

Gopalan, Lalitha. *Cinema of Interruptions: Action Genres in Contemporary Indian Cinema*. London: British Film Institute, 2002.

Goswami, Manu. *Producing India*. Chicago: University of Chicago Press, 2004.

———. "Rethinking the Modular Nation Form: Toward a Sociohistorical Conception of Nationalism." *Comparative Studies in Society and History* 44.4 (2002): 770–99.

Government of India, Ministry of Defense. *Republic Day Parade Commentary*. 2000.
Government of India, Ministry of Education. *Report of the Review Committee for the Indian Institute of Sciences*. 1948.
Government of India, Ministry of Information and Broadcasting. *Symposium on Historical and Biographical Film*. 1956.
——. *Annual Report of the Ministry of Information and Broadcasting*. 1950–51, 1962–63, 1964–65.
Government of India, Publications Division. *Rourkela*. 1959.
Guha, Ramachandra. "What If: History as Entertainment." *Outlook*, August 23, 2004. Available online at http://www.outlookindia.com.
Guibernau, Monserrat, and John Hutchinson. "History and National Destiny: Ethnosymbolism and Its Critics." *Nations and Nationalism* 10.1 (2004): 1–8.
Gupta, Akhil. "Blurred Boundaries: The Discourse of Corruption, the Culture of Politics, and the Imagined State." *American Ethnologist* 22.2 (1995): 375–402.
——. *Postcolonial Developments: Agriculture in the Making of Modern India*. Durham, N.C.: Duke University Press, 1998.
Gupta, Dipankar. *The Context of Ethnicity*. Delhi: Oxford University Press, 1996.
Hacking, Ian. "Making Up People." In *Reconstructing Individualism*, ed. T. C. Helier et al. Stanford, Calif.: Stanford University Press, 1986. 222–36.
Hage, Ghassan. *White Nation: Fantasies of White Supremacy in a Multicultural Society*. London: Routledge, 2000
Hale, Henry. "Explaining Ethnicity." *Comparative Political Studies* 37.4 (2004): 458–85.
Handelman, Donald. *Models and Mirrors: Toward an Anthropology of Public Events*. Cambridge: Cambridge University Press, 1990.
Handler, Richard. "Is 'Identity' a Useful Cross-Cultural Concept?" In *Commemorations: The Politics of National Identity*, ed. John Gillis. Princeton, N.J.: Princeton University Press, 1994. 27–40.
——. *Nationalism and the Politics of Culture in Quebec*. Madison: University of Wisconsin Press, 1988.
Hansen, Thomas. "Governance and State Mythologies in Mumbai." In *States of Imagination: Ethnographic Explorations of the Postcolonial State*, ed. Thomas Hansen and Finn Stepputat. Durham, N.C.: Duke University Press, 2002.
——. *The Saffron Wave: Democracy and Hindu Nationalism in Modern India*. Princeton, N.J.: Princeton University Press, 1999.
——. *Wages of Violence: Naming and Identity in Postcolonial Bombay*. Princeton, N.J.: Princeton University Press, 2001.
Hansen, Thomas, and Finn Stepputat, eds. *States of Imagination: Ethnographic Explorations of the Postcolonial State*. Durham, N.C.: Duke University Press, 2002.
Harding, Sandra. *Is Science Multicultural? Postcolonialisms, Feminisms, and Epistemologies*. Bloomington: Indiana University Press, 1998.
Haritash, Nirmal, and B. M. Gupta. "Mapping of Science and Technology Issues in the Indian Parliament." *Scientometrics* 54 (2000): 91–102.

Hasan, Mushirul. "The Myth of Unity: Colonial and National Narratives." In *Contesting the Nation: Religion, Community and the Politics of Democracy in India*, ed. David Ludden. Philadelphia: University of Pennsylvania Press, 1996.

———, ed. *Will Secular India Survive?* New Delhi: Imprint One, 2004.

Hasan, Zoya, and Ritu Menon. *Unequal Citizens: A Study of Muslim Women in India*. New Delhi: Oxford University Press, 2004.

Haynes, John. *New Soviet Man: Gender and Masculinity in Stalinist Soviet Cinema*. Manchester: Manchester University Press, 2003.

Hechter, Michael. *Internal Colonialism*. London: Routledge and Kegan Paul, 1975.

Herzfeld, Michael. *The Social Production of Indifference: Exploring the Symbolic Roots of Western Bureaucracy*. Chicago: University of Chicago Press, 1993.

Hindess, Barry. *Discourses of Power: From Hobbes to Foucault*. Oxford: Blackwell, 1996.

Hoffmann, Steven. *India and the China Crisis*. Berkeley: University of California Press, 1990.

Hopf, Ted. *Social Construction of International Politics: Identities and Foreign Policies, Moscow, 1955 and 1999*. Ithaca, N.Y.: Cornell University Press, 2002.

Horowitz, Donald, *Ethnic Groups in Conflict*. Berkeley: University of California Press, 1985.

Hoselitz, Bert. *Sociological Aspects of Economic Growth*. New York: Free Press, 1962.

Howard, Ebenezer. *Garden Cities of To-Morrow*. London: Faber and Faber, 1946.

Hroch, Miroslav. "From National Movement to the Fully-Formed Nation: The Nation-Building Process in Europe." In *Becoming National: A Reader*, ed. Geoff Eley and Ronald Grigor Suny. New York: Oxford University Press, 1996. 60–77.

Human Rights Watch. "We Have No Orders to Save You: State Participation and Complicity in Communal Violence in Gujarat." *Human Rights Watch* 14.3 (2002).

Hunt, Lynn. *The Family Romance of the French Revolution*. Berkeley: University of California Press, 1992.

Hutnyk, John. *The Critique of Exotica: Music, Politics, and the Culture Industry*. London: Pluto Press, 2000.

Indian Institution of Mass Communications. *Proceedings of the Seminar on the Role of Film in National Development*. New Delhi: Indian Institute of Mass Communications, 1976.

Jaffrelot, Christophe. *Dr. Ambedkar and Untouchability: Analyzing and Fighting Caste*. London: C. Hurst, 2005.

———, ed. *The Sangh Parivar: A Reader*. Delhi: Oxford University Press, 2005.

Jain, L. C. *The City of Hope: The Faridabad Story*. Delhi: Concept Publishing, 1998.

Jalal, Ayesha. "Exploding Communalism: The Politics of Muslim Identity in South Asia." In *Nationalism, Democracy and Development: State and Politics in India*, ed. Sugata Bose and Ayesha Jalal. Delhi: Oxford University Press, 1999. 76–103.

Jenkins, Rob. "Turning Princes into Subjects." *Journal of Commonwealth and Comparative Politics* 38.1 (2002): 103–11.

Jha, Shefali. "Representation and Its Epiphanies: A Reading of Constituent Assembly Debates." *Economic and Political Weekly* 39 (September 25, 2004): 4357–60.

Johnson, Gary. "The Architecture of Ethnic Identity." *Politics and the Life Sciences* 16.2 (1997): 257–62.
Jones, Kenneth. "Religious Identity and the Indian Census." In *The Census in British India*, ed. Gerald Barrier. Delhi: Manohar, 1981. 73–101.
———, ed. *Religious Controversy in British India*. Buffalo: State University of New York Press, 1992.
Joseph, Gilbert, and Daniel Nugent. *Everyday Forms of State Formation*. Durham, N.C.: Duke University Press, 1994.
Kalia, Ravi. *Bhubaneswar: From a Temple Town to a Capital City*. New Delhi: Oxford University Press, 1994.
———. *Chandigarh: In Search of an Identity*. Carbondale: Southern Illinois University Press, 1987.
———. *Chandigarh: The Making of an Indian City*. New Delhi: Oxford University Press, 2000.
Kamat, Sangeeta. *Development Hegemony: NGOs and the State in India*. New Delhi: Oxford University Press, 2002.
Kapur, Geeta. "Cultural Creativity in the First Decade." *Journal of Arts and Ideas* 23–24 (1993): 17–49.
Kaviraj, Sudipta. "A Critique of the Passive Revolution." *Economic and Political Weekly* 33 (1988): 45–47.
———. "The Imaginary Institution of India." In *Subaltern Studies VII: Writings on South Asian History and Society*, ed. Partha Chatterjee and Gyanendra Pandey. Delhi: Oxford University Press, 1993. 1–39.
Kelly, John, and Martha Kaplan. *Represented Communities: Fiji and World Decolonization*. Chicago: University of Chicago Press, 2001.
Khilnani, Sunil. "Branding India." *Seminar* 533 (2004). Available online at http://www.india-seminar.com/2004/533/.
———. *The Idea of India*. London: Hamish Hamilton, 1997.
King, Robert. *Nehru and the Language Politics of India*. Delhi: Oxford University Press, 1997.
Koenigsberger, Otto. "New Towns in India." *Town Planning Review* 23.2 (1952): 94–132.
Kohli, Atul. "Can Democracies Accommodate Ethnic Nationalism? Rise and Decline of Self-Determination Movements in India." *Journal of Asian Studies* 56.2 (1997): 325–44.
———, ed. *The Success of India's Democracy*. Cambridge: Cambridge University Press, 2001.
Kohn, Hans. "Western and Eastern Nationalisms." In *Nationalism*, ed. John Hutchinson and Anthony Smith. Oxford: Oxford University Press, 1994 [1945]. 162–65.
Krishna, Sankaran. "Cartographic Anxiety: Mapping the Body Politic in India." In *Challenging Boundaries: Global Flows, Territorial Identities*, ed. Michael Shapiro and Hayward Alker. Minneapolis: University of Minnesota Press, 1996. 193–216.
———. *Postcolonial Insecurities: India, Sri Lanka and the Question of Nationhood*. Minneapolis: University of Minnesota Press, 1999.
Lakatos, Imre. "Falsification and the Methodology of Scientific Research Pro-

grammes." In *Criticism and the Growth of Knowledge*, ed. Imre Lakatos and A. Musgrave. Cambridge: Cambridge University Press, 1970. 91–196.

Lal, Vinay. "Black Cat Commandos, Gunmen and Other Terrors." *South Asia* 20.2 (1997): 103–38.

———. *The History of History: Politics and Scholarship in Modern India*. Delhi: Oxford University Press, 2003.

———. *Of Cricket, Guiness and Gandhi: Essays on Indian History and Culture*. Calcutta: Seagull Books, 2003.

Lala, R. M. *For the Love of India: The Life and Times of Jamshetji Tata*. New Delhi: Penguin-Viking, 2004.

Lane, Christal. *The Rites of Rulers: Ritual in Industrial Society—the Soviet Case*. Cambridge: Cambridge University Press, 1981.

Larson, Gerald James. *India's Agony over Religion*. Albany: State University of New York Press, 1995.

———. "Introduction: The Secular State in a Religious Society." In *Religion and Personal Law in Secular India: A Call to Judgment*, ed. Gerald James Larson. Bloomington: Indiana University Press, 2001.

Lazarus, Neil. *Nationalism and Cultural Practice in the Postcolonial World*. Cambridge: Cambridge University Press, 1999.

Lijphart, Arendt. *Democracy in Plural Societies: A Comparative Perspective*. New Haven, Conn.: Yale University Press, 1980.

Linz, Juan, Alfred Stepan, and Yogendra Yadav. "Nation-State or State-Nation? Conceptual Reflections and Some Spanish, Belgian and Indian Data." *Human Development Report Background Paper*. New York: United Nations Development Program, 2004. 20–21.

Ludden, David. "India's Development Regime." In *Colonialism and Culture*, ed. Nicholas Dirks. Ann Arbor: University of Michigan Press, 1992.

———, ed. *Making India Hindu*. 2nd ed. Delhi: Oxford University Press, 2005.

———. "Presidential Address: Maps in the Mind and the Mobility of Asia." *Journal of Asian Studies* 62.4 (2003): 1057–78.

———, ed. *Reading Subaltern Studies: Critical History, Contested Meaning, and the Globalization of South Asia*. London: Anthem, 2002.

Lustick, Ian. "Stability in Deeply Divided Societies." *World Politics* 31.3 (1979): 325–44.

MacCann, Richard Dyer. *The People's Films: A Political History of U.S. Government Motion Pictures*. New York: Hastings House, 1973.

Mackey, Eva. *The House of Difference: Cultural Politics and National Identity in Canada*. London: Routledge, 2000.

Mahmood, Cynthia Keppley. *Fighting for Faith and Nation: Dialogues with Sikh Militants*. Philadelphia: University of Pennsylvania Press, 1996.

Makiya, Kanan. *Republic of Fear: The Politics of Modern Iraq*. Updated edition. Berkeley: University of California Press, 1998.

Mamdani, Mahmood. *Citizen and Subject: Contemporary Africa and the Legacy of Late Colonialism*. Princeton, N.J.: Princeton University Press, 1996.

Marx, Anthony. *Faith in Nation: Exclusionary Origins of Nationalism.* New York: Oxford University Press, 2003.

———. *Making Race and Nation: A Comparison of the United States, South Africa, and Brazil.* Cambridge: Cambridge University Press, 1998.

Masselos, Jim. "India's Republic Day: The Other 26 January." *South Asia* 19 (1996): 183–203.

Maxwell, Neville. *India's China War.* Garden City, N.Y.: Anchor Books, 1972.

Mazzarella, William. *Shoveling Smoke: Advertising and Globalization in Contemporary India.* Durham, N.C.: Duke University Press, 2003.

Mbembe, Achille. *On the Postcolony.* Berkeley: University of California Press, 2001.

Mehta, Uday Singh. *Liberalism and Empire: A Study in Nineteenth-Century British Liberal Thought.* Chicago: University of Chicago Press, 1999.

Menon, Ritu, and Kamala Bhasin. *Borders and Boundaries: Women in India's Partition.* Delhi: Kali for Women, 1998.

Metcalf, Thomas. *Ideologies of the Raj.* Cambridge: Cambridge University Press, 1997.

Mian, Zia. "Homi Bhabha Killed a Crow." In *The Nuclear Debate: Ironies and Immoralities,* ed. Zia Mian and Ashis Nandy. Colombo: Regional Centre for Strategic Studies, 1998.

Migdal, Joel, Atul Kohli, and Vivienne Shue, eds. *State Power and Social Forces: Domination and Transformation in the Third World.* Cambridge: Cambridge University Press, 1994.

Miliband, Ralph. "The Capitalist State: Reply to Nicos Poulantzas." *New Left Review* 59 (1970): 53–60.

Miller, Toby. *The Well-Tempered Self: Citizenship, Culture, and the Postmodern Subject.* Baltimore: Johns Hopkins University Press, 1994.

Mitchell, Timothy. "The Limits of the State: Beyond Statist Approaches and Their Critics." *American Political Science Review* 85.1 (1991): 77–94.

———. "Society, Economy, and the State Effect." In *State/Culture: State Formation after the Cultural Turn,* ed. George Steinmetz. Ithaca, N.Y.: Cornell University Press, 1999. 76–97.

Mohan, Jag. *Documentary Films and National Awakening.* New Delhi: Publications Division, 1990.

———. *Dr. P. V. Pathy, Documentary Film Maker (1906–1961).* Poona: National Film Archive of India, Ministry of Information and Broadcasting, 1972.

———. *Two Decades of the Films Division.* New Delhi: Ministry of Information and Broadcasting, 1969.

Mohanty, P. K. *Collective Bargaining in the Steel Industry in India.* New Delhi: Discovery Publishing House, n.d.

Mosse, George. *The Nationalization of the Masses: Political Symbolism and Mass Movements in Germany from the Napoleonic Wars through the Third Reich.* New York: New American Library, 1975.

Mukherjee, Rudrangshu, ed. *The Penguin Gandhi Reader.* New Delhi: Penguin Books, 1995.

Nairn, Tom. *The Break-Up of Britain*. London: New Left Books, 1977.
———. "The Modern Janus." *New Left Review* 94 (1975): 3–29.
Nanda, Meera. *Prophets Facing Backward: Postmodern Critiques of Science and Hindu Nationalism in India*. New Brunswick: Rutgers University Press, 2003.
Nandy, Ashis. "The Invisible Holocaust and the Journey as an Exodus." *Postcolonial Studies* 2.3 (1999): 305–29.
———. *The Romance of the State and the Fate of Dissent in the Tropics*. New York: Oxford University Press, 2003.
———. *Science, Hegemony and Violence: A Requiem for Modernity*. Tokyo: United Nations University Press, 1998.
Narwekar, Sanjit. *Films Division and the Indian Documentary*. New Delhi: Publications Division, 1992.
Navaro-Yashin, Yael. *Faces of the State: Secularism and Public Life in Turkey*. Princeton, N.J.: Princeton University Press, 2002.
Nehru, Jawaharlal. *An Autobiography*. New Delhi: Penguin Books, 2004 [1927].
———. *A Bunch of Old Letters*. New York: Asia Publishing House, 1958.
———. *The Discovery of India*. New Delhi: Penguin Books, 2004 [1946].
———. *Essential Writings of Jawaharlal Nehru*, ed. S. Gopal and Uma Iyengar. New Delhi: Oxford University Press, 2003.
———. *Glimpses of World History*. New Delhi: Penguin Books, 2004 [1939].
———. *Letters to Chief Ministers, 1948–1964*. New Delhi: Oxford University Press, 1988.
———. "A Tryst with Destiny." *Constituent Assembly of India Debates*, August 14–15, 1947. Available online at http://parliamentofindia.nic.in/.
Okamura, John. "Situational Ethnicity." *Ethnic and Racial Studies* 4.4 (1981): 452–65.
Olick, Jeffrey, ed. *States of Memory: Continuities, Conflicts, and Transformations in National Retrospection*. Durham, N.C.: Duke University Press, 2003.
Oliver, Pamela, and Hank Johnston. "What a Good Idea: Frames and Ideologies in Social Movement Research." *Mobilization* 5 (2000): 37, 54.
Omvedt, Gail. *Dalits and the Democratic Revolution: Dr. Ambedkar and the Dalit Movement in Colonial India*. New Delhi: Sage Publications, 1993.
Oxfeld, Ellen. *Blood, Sweat, and Mahjong: Family and Enterprise in an Overseas Chinese Community*. Ithaca, N.Y.: Cornell University Press, 1993.
Ozouf, Mona. *Festivals and the French Revolution*. Trans. Alan Sheridan. Cambridge, Mass.: Harvard University Press, 1988.
Pandey, Gyanendra. *The Construction of Communalism in Colonial North India*. New York: Oxford University Press, 1998.
Parekh, Bhikhu. *Colonialism, Tradition and Reform: An Analysis of Gandhi's Political Discourse*. New Delhi: Sage Publications, 1989.
———. "Making Sense of Gujarat." *Seminar* 513 (2002). Available online at http://www.india-seminar.com/2002/513/.
Parry, Jonathan. "Lords of Labour: Working and Shirking in Bhilai." In *The Worlds of Indian Industrial Labour*, ed. Jonathan Parry, Jan Breman, and Karin Kapadia. New Delhi: Sage Publications, 1999.

———. "Two Cheers for Reservation: The Satnamis and the Steel Plant." In *Institutions and Inequalities: Essays in Honour of André Béteille*. New Delhi: Oxford University Press, 1999.

Pathy, P. V. "A Document on Indian Documentary." *The People* (July 2, 1950): n.p.

Pati, Biswamoy. "BJP's 'Stumbling Blocks': The Voter, Pluralism and Democracy." *Economic and Political Weekly* (May 22, 2004).

Pati, Pramod. *Films Division Catalogue of Films, 1948–1972*. Bombay: Films Division, 1974.

Pitkin, Hanna. *The Concept of Representation*. Berkeley: University of California Press, 1967.

Poulantzas, Nicos. "The Problem of the Capitalist State." *New Left Review* 58 (1969): 67–78.

Povinelli, Elizabeth. *The Cunning of Recognition: Indigenous Alterities and the Making of Australian Multiculturalism*. Durham, N.C.: Duke University Press, 2002.

Prakash, Gyan. *Another Reason: Science and the Imagination of Modern India*. Princeton, N.J.: Princeton University Press, 1999.

———. "The Urban Turn." n.d. Available online at http://www.sarai.net.

Prakash, Vikramaditya. *Chandigarh's Le Corbusier: The Struggle for Modernity in Postcolonial India*. Seattle: University of Washington Press, 2002.

Prasad, M. Madhava. *Ideology of the Hindi Film: An Historical Construction*. New Delhi: Oxford University Press, 1998.

Rajagopal, N. R. *The CSIR Saga: A Concise History of Its Evolution*. Delhi: Council of Scientific and Industrial Research, 1991.

Ramaswamy, Sumathi, ed. *Beyond Appearances: Visual Practices and Ideologies in Modern India*. Delhi: Sage Publications, 2003.

———. "Maps and Mother Goddesses in Modern India." *Imago Mundi* 53 (July 2001): 97–114.

———. *Passions of the Tongue: Language Devotion in Tamil India, 1891–1970*. Berkeley: University of California Press, 1997.

Ranger, Terence. "The Invention of Tradition Revisited: The Case of Colonial Africa." In *Legitimacy and the State in Twentieth-Century Africa*, ed. Terence Ranger and Olefumi Vaughan. London: Macmillan Press, 1993.

Rangnekar, D. K. *Bokaro: A Story of Bungling*. New Delhi: National Institute of Public Affairs, 1963.

Renan, Ernest. "What Is a Nation." In *Nation and Narration*, ed. Homi Bhabha. London: Routledge, 1990 [1882].

Richards, Norah. *The Life and Work of Sir S. S. Bhatnagar*. Rev. ed. New Delhi: NISTADS, 2004.

Roberts, Graham. *Forward Soviet: History and Non-Fiction Film in the USSR*. New York: St. Martin's Press, 1999.

Roy, Srirupa. "Nation and Commemoration: Celebrating the Fiftieth Anniversary of Indian Independence." *Interventions: The International Journal of Post-Colonial Studies* 3.2 (2002): 251–65.

———. "Seeing a State: National Commemorations and the Public Sphere in India and Turkey." *Comparative Studies in Society and History* 48.1 (2006): 200–32.

———. "A Symbol of Freedom: The Indian Flag and the Transformations of Nationalism, 1906–2002." *Journal of Asian Studies* 65.3 (2006): 459–527.

Rudolph, Lloyd, and Susanne Hoeber Rudolph. *In Pursuit of Lakshmi: The Political Economy of the Indian State*. Chicago: University of Chicago Press, 1987.

Runyantsev, Yevgeny. *Bhilai: Youth and Maturity*. Delhi: Soviet Land Booklets, 1975.

Rushdie, Salman. *Midnight's Children*. London: Picador, 1982.

Ruud, Arild Engelsen. "Talking Dirty about Politics: A View from a Bengali Village." In *The Everyday State and Society in Modern India*, ed. C. J. Fuller and Veronique Benei. New Delhi: Social Science Press, 2000. 115–36.

Sahai, Jugendra. *Urban Complex of an Industrial City*. Allahabad: Chugh Publications, 1980.

Sangeet Natak Akademi. *Seminar on Film in India*. New Delhi: Sangeet Natak Akademi.

Savarkar, Vinayak. *Hindutva*. 2nd ed. Delhi: World Book Centre, 1942.

Scott, David. *Refashioning Futures: Criticism after Postcoloniality*. Princeton, N.J.: Princeton University Press, 1999.

Scott, James. *Seeing like a State: How Certain Schemes to Improve the Human Condition Have Failed*. New Haven, Conn.: Yale University Press, 1998.

Sen, Amartya. *The Argumentative Indian*. Delhi: Penguin Books, 2005.

Sengupta, Nirmal. *Contract Labour in the Rourkela Steel Plant*. Mimeo, 1980.

———. *Destitutes and Development: A Study of the Bauri Community in the Bokaro Region*. New Delhi: Concept Publishing, 1979.

Seth, Sanjay. "Nationalism, National Identity, and 'History': Nehru's Search for India." *Thesis Eleven* 32 (1992) 37–54.

Sewell, James. "UNESCO: Pluralism Rampant." In *The Anatomy of Influence: Decision-Making in International Organization*, ed. Robert Cox and Harold Jacobson. New Haven, Conn.: Yale University Press, 1974. 139–74.

Shiva, Vandana. *The Violence of the Green Revolution: Third World Agriculture, Ecology, and Politics*. London: Palgrave Macmillan, 1992.

Singh, B. P. *India's Culture: The State, the Arts and Beyond*. New Delhi: Oxford University Press, 1998.

Singh, Baldev, ed. *Jawaharlal Nehru on Science and Society: A Collection of his Writings and Speeches*. Delhi: Nehru Memorial Museum and Library, 1988.

Singh, Dayal. "An Evaluation of U.S. Economic Assistance to India: With Particular Reference to the Proposed Public Sector Bokaro Steel Plant in India." Ph.D. dissertation, Indiana University, 1965.

Sinha, Aseema. *The Regional Roots of Developmental Politics in India: A Divided Leviathan*. Bloomington: Indiana University Press, 2005.

Sinha, Subir. "Development Counter-Narratives: Taking Social Movements Seriously." In *Regional Modernities: The Cultural Politics of Development in India*, ed. K. Sivaramakrishnan and Arun Agrawal. New Delhi: Oxford University Press, 2003.

Sivaramakrishnan, K. C. "Durgapur: Case Study of an Indian New Town." In *Urban Planning Practice in Developing Countries*, ed. John Taylor and David Williams. Oxford: Pergamon Press, 1982.

Sivaramakrishnan, K., and Arun Agrawal. "Regional Modernities in Stories and Practices of Development." In *Regional Modernities: The Cultural Politics of Development in India*, ed. K. Sivaramakrishnan and Arun Agrawal. Delhi: Oxford University Press, 2003. 1–61.

Skocpol, Theda. "Bringing the State Back In: Strategies of Analysis in Current Research." In *Bringing the State Back In*, ed. Peter Evans et al. Cambridge: Cambridge University Press, 1985.

Slezkine, Yuri. "The USSR as a Communal Apartment, or How a Socialist State Promoted Ethnic Particularism." In *Becoming National: A Reader*, ed. Geoff Eley and Ronald Suny. Oxford: Oxford University Press, 1996. 203–38.

Smith, Anthony. *The Ethnic Origins of Nations*. Oxford: Blackwell, 1986.

Smith, Donald. *India as a Secular State*. Princeton, N.J.: Princeton University Press, 1963.

Som, Reba. "Jawaharlal Nehru and the Hindu Code Bill: A Victory of Symbol over Substance?" *Modern Asian Studies* 28 (1994): 165–94.

Sperling, Jan. *The Human Dimensions of Technical Assistance: The German Experience at Rourkela, India*. Trans. Gerald Onn. Ithaca, N.Y.: Cornell University Press, 1969.

Spillman, Lynn. *Nation and Commemoration: Creating National Identities in the United States and Australia*. Cambridge: Cambridge University Press, 1997.

Srivastava, Sanjay. *Constructing Postcolonial India: National Character and the Doon School*. London: Routledge, 1998.

———. "Voice, Gender and Space in Time of Five Year Plans." *Economic and Political Weekly* (May 15, 2004).

Steel Authority of India. *Tryst with Steel: Nehru and the Public Sector Steel Industry*. Delhi: Steel Authority of India, 1988.

Stepan, Alfred. "Federalism and Democracy: Beyond the U.S. Model." *Journal of Democracy* 10.4 (1999): 19–34.

Strachey, John. *India: Its Administration and Progress*. 4th ed. London: Macmillan and Company, 1911 [1888].

Sundaram, Ravi. "The Bazaar and the City: History and the Contemporary in Urban Electronic Culture." 1999. Available online at http://www.monoculartimes.co.uk/architexts/bazaarandcity_1.shtml.

Sur, Abha. "Scientism and Social Justice: Meghnad Saha's Critique of the State of Science in India." *Historical Studies in the Physical and Biological Sciences* 33.1 (2002): 87–106.

Swann, Paul. *The British Documentary Film Movement, 1926–1946*. Cambridge: Cambridge University Press, 1989.

Taras, Raymond. "Making Sense of Matrioshka Nationalism." In *Nations and Politics in the Soviet Successor States*, ed. Ian Bremmer and Raymond Taras. Cambridge: Cambridge University Press, 1993. 513–38.

Taussig, Michael. *The Magic of the State*. London: Routledge, 1996.

———. "Maleficium: State Fetishism." In *The Nervous System*. New York: Routledge Press, 1993.

Taylor, Richard. *Film Propaganda: Soviet Russia and Nazi Germany*. 2nd ed. London: I. B. Tauris, 1998.

———. "Now That the Party's Over: Soviet Cinema and Its Legacy." In *Russia on Reels: The Russian Idea in Post-Soviet Cinema*, ed. Birgit Beumers. London: I. B. Tauris, 1999. 34–42.

Thapar, Raj. *All These Years: A Memoir*. New Delhi: Seminar Publications, 1991.

Town and Country Planning Organization. *Durgapur Steel Township General Development Plan*. New Delhi: Town and Country Planning Organization, 1971.

———. *Town and Country Planning in India*. New Delhi: Town and Country Planning Organization, 1962.

Tulpule, Bagaram. *Amidst Heat and Noise: Durgapur Recalled*. New Delhi: All India Management Association, 1977.

Uberoi, Patricia. "Unity in Diversity? Dilemmas of Nationhood in Indian Calendar Art." In *Beyond Appearances: Visual Practices and Ideologies in Modern India*, ed. Sumathi Ramaswamy. Delhi: Sage Publications, 2003.

Upadhyaya, Prakash. "The Politics of Indian Secularism." *Modern Asian Studies* 26 (1992): 815–23.

Vanaik, Achin. *The Painful Transition: Bourgeois Democracy in India*. London: Verso, 1990.

Van der Berghe, Pierre. *The Ethnic Phenomenon*. London: Praeger, 1987.

Van der Veer, Peter. *Imperial Encounters: Religion and Modernity in India and Britain*. Princeton, N.J.: Princeton University Press, 200.

Van Schendel, Willem. "Stateless in South Asia: The Making of the India-Bangladesh Enclaves." *Journal of Asian Studies* 61.1 (2002): 115–47.

Varadarajan, Siddharth ed. *Gujarat: The Making of a Tragedy*. New Delhi: Penguin Books, 2002.

Varshney, Ashutosh. *Ethnic Conflict and Civic Life: Hindus and Muslims in India*. New Haven, Conn.: Yale University Press, 2002.

———. "Explaining Gujarat Violence." 2002. SSRC Contemporary Conflicts, available online at http://www.ssrc.org.

Vasudev, Aruna. *Liberty and License in the Indian Cinema*. New Delhi: Manohar, 1978.

Vasudevan, Ravi. "Addressing the Spectator of a 'Third World' National Cinema: The Bombay 'Social' Film of the 1940s and 1950s." *Screen* 36.4 (1995): 305–24.

Verdery, Katherine. *National Ideology under Socialism: Identity and Cultural Politics in Ceausescu's Romania*. Berkeley: University of California Press, 1991.

———. "Nationalism and National Sentiment in Post-Socialist Romania." *Slavic Review* 52 (1993): 179–203.

———. "Whither 'Nation' and "Nationalism." *Daedalus* 122.3 (1993): 45.

Visvanathan, Shiv. *A Carnival for Science*. New Delhi: Oxford University Press, 1998.

———. *Organizing for Science: The Making of an Industrial Research Laboratory*. Delhi: Oxford University Press, 1985.

Weber, Eugen. *Peasants into Frenchmen: Modernization of Rural France, 1870–1914.* Stanford, Calif.: Stanford University Press, 1976.

Wedeen, Lisa. *Ambiguities of Domination: Politics, Rhetoric, and Symbols in Contemporary Syria.* Chicago: University of Chicago Press, 1999.

Weldes, Jutta, and Mark Laffey. "Beyond Belief: Ideas and Symbolic Technologies in the Study of International Relations." *European Journal of International Relations* 3.2 (1997): 193–237.

Wilkinson, Steven. "Putting Gujarat in Perspective." *Economic and Political Weekly* (April 27 2002): 1579–83.

Wolpert, Stanley, *Nehru: A Tryst with Destiny.* New York: Oxford University Press, 1996.

Woods, Philip. "Chappatis by Parachute: The Use of Newsreels in British Propaganda in India." *South Asia* 23.2 (2000): 89–109.

———. "From Shaw to Shantaram: The Film Advisory Board and the Making of British Propaganda Films in India, 1940–1943." *Historical Journal of Radio, Film and Television* 21.3 (2001): 293–308.

Yadav, Yogendra. "Radical Shift in the Social Basis of Political Power." *The Hindu,* May 20, 2004. Available online at http://www.hinduonnet.com/elections2004/verdict2004/stories/.

Yang, Anand, ed. *Crime and Criminology in British India.* Tucson: University of Arizona Press, 1985.

Young, Robert J. C. *Postcolonialism: An Historical Introduction.* Oxford: Blackwell, 2001.

Zelinsky, Wilbur. *Nation into State: The Shifting Symbolic Foundations of American Nationalism.* Chapel Hill: University of North Carolina Press, 1988.

INDEX

: : :

Abbas, K. A., 159
Abraham, Itty, 116
Abrams, Philip, 15
Advertising: of Hindu Nationalist BJP, 163; of "India Shining" campaign, 163–165; patriotism and, 85, 93; Republic Day and, 69, 85, 86, 93; role of, in nation-state formation, 159; visual, 85–86
Agni-II missile, 98–99
Agriculture: films about, 47, 60
All India Radio, 44; broadcast of Republic Day on, 82; national anthem and, 51; state publicity and, 55
Amar Jawan Jyoti, 96–97
Ambedkar, Bhimrao, 25
Amin, Shahid, 64
Anagnost, Ann, 56, 193 n.69
Anderson, Benedict, 10–12, 95, 130, 175 n.24
Ansari, Qutubuddin, 2
Anticolonial nationalist movement, 13–14, 16, 67, 111, 130, 157, 161–162; Asian and African nation-state formation and, 11, 13; *Discovery of India* and, 50; lack of films about, in the 1950s, 49–50; rejection of state-led development by, 108; Republic Day and, 70–74, 96
Arboreal pluralism, 161, 176 n.31
Army Film Centre (AFC), 37
Asansol Township, 138. See also Steel townships

Assam, 90, 100
Association of Scientific Workers, 120–121
Atomic Energy Bill (1948), 116
Azad, Maulana, 26, 105, 131, 163

Backwardness, 17, 21, 48–49, 107, 109–111, 117; steel towns and, 136
Balibar, Étienne, 8
Bangalore, 118
Bangladesh, 167
Bata (shoemaking company), 85–86
Baumann, Zygmunt, 3
Belief: explanatory inadequacy of, 14–15; theories of nationalism and, 11–12; versus encounters and practice, 14–15; versus recognition and identification, 18–19
Benegal, Niranjan, 141
Bengal: labor unrest among Bengalis in Durgapur, 147; Rabindranath Tagore and, 46, 196 n.20
Berkeley-Hill, Sam, 57
Bharatiya Janata Party (BJP), 95, 163, 166, 168; advertising campaign of, 163; national security under, 167; violence against Muslims and, 1. See also Hindu nationalism
Bhatnagar, S. S., 125, 128, 159, 206 n.72
Bhilai Township, 134, 141, 144, 148, 150. See also Steel townships
Bihar, 123

BJP. *See* Bharatiya Janata Party
Black Gold, The (film), 47
Bokaro Township, 134, 139–141, 144, 150; Bauri community at, 140. *See also* Steel townships
Bollywood, 34
Bound for Haj (film), 53
Brazil, ethnic diversity in, 7
Brubaker, Rogers, 15, 33, 160, 182 n.89, 216 n.2

Calcutta: slum dwellers in, 165
Case of Mr. Critic, The (film), 45
Caste, 25, 49, 146, 163; colonial policies on, 24; in steel towns, 147–148
Césaire, Aimé, 84
Chacha Nehru (comic book), 113
Chakrabarty, Dipesh, 108, 116
Chanda committee, 58–61
Chatterjee, Partha, 23, 109, 130, 165, 178 n.61
China, war with, 27, 50–51, 86–87, 186 n.116; Republic Day and, 82–84, 87–88
Chittaranjan Township, 139. *See also* Steel townships
Citizenship: citizen-soldier and, 27, 86, 99; citizen-workers in steel towns and, 136–137, 143, 145, 149–150, 156; Films Division of India and, 44–46, 64; Hindu nationalism versus Nehruvian conceptions of, 167; ideal, 27, 44–46, 51, 64, 99, 104, 132, 156, 161, 167, 181 n.79; "infantile," 20, 22; Muslims and, 53; spectatorship and, 104; during war, 86
Civil disobedience, 70
Cohn, Bernard, 71
Colonial India, 201 n.15; census of, 24–25; development and, 36, 107–111; discourses on Indian national identity in, 157; diversity and, 24–25, 27; documentary film and, 35–38, 158; imperial assemblage and, 71–73; Indian nation-state formation and, 24–27, 158–159; Muslims and, 24; needs discourse and, 107–110; religious identity and, 24, 155; Republic Day and, 67, 69, 71–76, 99, 158; ritual idioms of, 71–72, 74, 80; science and, 115; spatial practices of, 134; spectacle and, 67, 71–72; steel towns and, 137–138; transition period from, 25–26
Committee for Emergency Publicity, 51
Communalism, 2, 167; combating "virus" of, in Rourkela riots, 137, 150–156; evils of, 49; master narrative of, 150–155, 215 n.64; naturalizing of diversity and, 137, 155
Constituent Assembly, 25–26, 69
Cooper, Frederick, 160
Coronil, Fernando, 22
Council of Scientific and Industrial Research (CSIR), 125
Creole nationalism, 11, 13
Cultural floats, 77; national security and, 88
Culture, 4; dispensability of, by the state, 81–82, 103; Films Division documentaries and, 43–44, 57–58, 63; folk, 43–44; national security and, 87–88; Nehruvian era and, 76–78, 83–84; Republic Day and, 76–78, 82–84, 87–92, 100, 102–103; the state and, 13, 44, 57–58, 76, 90, 102–103, 109; as unchanging resource, 90–91

Dams, 17, 19, 39, 110, 114, 123, 129; films on, 47; as visual representation, 62
Decolonization: development and, 109, 111–112; Films Division and, 38–39, 45; Gandhi's versus Nehru's vision of, 45, 131; Indian nation-state formation and, 111–112; national identity and, 112, 114; nation-state formation and, 131; needs discourse and, 111–112, 114,

130–131; "passive revolutionary" nature of, 111–112. *See also* Colonial India; Indian independence; Indian nation-state formation; Postcolonial culture and politics
Defence of India Rules, film and, 38
Destination India (film), 56–57
Development, 17; agency and, 48; colonial films and, 36; colonialism and, 36, 107–111, 158; decolonization and, 109, 111–112; economic, 133; endorsement of state-led, 38–39, 107–110, 138, 158; Films Division documentaries and, 47–49, 61; five-year plan for, 110, 133; global, hegemony, 107; Indian people as agents of, 48, 110–111; nationalist movements and, 108–109; postcolonial, 38–39, 109, 142; Republic Day and, 88, 96; territorial ambiguity and, 112. *See also* Science and technology; Steel townships
Dilly Dallying (film), 45
Dirks, Nicholas, 82
Disavowal of politics. *See* Fear of politics
Discovery of India (Nehru), 50, 123
Disenchantment and nonresonance, 21, 29, 33, 35, 56, 58–61, 160
Dissent, 14–15, 17–18, 106, 154, 161–162; at Republic Day, 93–94
Diversity: arboreal pluralism and, 161; colonial policies on, 24–25, 27; communalism and, 155; endurance of idea of, 2–8; Films Division and, 7, 161; versus homogeneity, 77, 161; inconsistent embrace of, 147–148; Indian nation-state formation and, 2–8, 112, 114; national identity and, 112, 114; naturalizing of, 7, 155, 169; Republic Day and, 7, 69, 73–74, 76, 161; Soviet displays of, 69; state as representative of, 69; state authority and, 7, 24–25; state embrace of, 161–162; in steel towns, 147–148. *See also* Culture; Ethnic diversity; Regional diversity; "Unity in diversity"
Documentary films, 28–29; authoritative, 37; citizenship and, 44–46; colonial state and, 36–38, 158; debates on educational value of, 39–40; distribution scheme of, 34, 41, 43, 59–61; Indian documentary movement and, 36; origins of the term, 35; reception of, 34; reinvention of, in postcolonial India, 38; review committees on, 58–61; state identification and, 38–40; state simplification and, 62; table of Films Division categories of, 42, 43; WWII propaganda films, 36–38. *See also* Films Division of India
Dowry system, 47–48
Dry Leaves (film), 47–48
Durgapur Township, 133–135, 139, 141, 143–144, 150; housing at, 146; labor unrest among Bengalis in, 147; quality of life in, 148. *See also* Steel townships

Economic policy, 49, 69, 109, 133, 163
Emergency years, 87, 91, 198 n.45
Ethnic diversity, 24–25, 173 n.15; colonial policies on, 24; communalism and, 155; durability of nation and, 5–7; Films Division and, 63; institutional pluralist imagination and, 7–8; institutional safeguards for, 4–5; naturalization of, 7, 155; "unity in diversity" and, 2–3, 24–25; U.S. versus Brazilian, 5–6. *See also* Caste; Diversity; "Unity in diversity"
Ethnonationalist movements, 3
Ethno-religious conflict, 49; Hindu nationalists and, 1–2, after partition, 5

Failure discourses, 61; "exemplary Indians" theme and, 46; Films Division and, 61; of Indian citizens, 110; obstacles, 48; state, 61; state dis-

Failure discourses (*continued*)
courses of, 17, 21, 27, 105–106, 110–111, 117, 137; of steel towns, 135–137, 144–150, 155–156
Faith, The (film), 53
Fear of politics, 22, 106, 130–132, 154, 158, 161–162, 167, 215 n.64; Films Division of India and, 64; Rourkela riots and, 137, 154; steel towns and, 29, 148, 156
Fight the Floods (film), 47
Film Advisory Board (FABR), 37–38
Films Division of India, 19, 21, 29, 33–34, 136; anticolonial movement and, 49–50; architectural films and, 44; audience strength of, 34; "biography and personality" films of, 46; boring content of, 34–35, 58–61, 63; censorship and, 54; Chanda committee recommendations for, 58–61; citizenship and, 44–46, 64; cultural diversity films and, 43–44, 57–58; decolonization and, 38–39, 45; "defence" films of, 46–47; development and modernization films of, 47–49, 61; "disenchanted imaginary" of, 34–35, 58–61; distribution scheme of, 34, 41, 43, 59–61; dowry system film of, 47–48; ethnic diversity and, 63–64; "exemplary Indians" theme and, 46; fear of politics and, 64; "festivals of India" films, 44; filmmakers and, 35–36, 39–41, 159; folk cultural diversity films and, 43–44, 63–64; futurist tilt in first decade, 49–51; Indian nation-state formation and, 159; "international scene" films of, 46–47; languages dubbed in, 60; Muslims and, 51, 52, 53, 64; narrative style of films of, 56, 63; national security discourses and, 51; organizational structure of, 40–41, 59; post-1960 shift in, 50–51; propaganda and, 34, 158; rationing of film stock by, 54; regional diversity films, 43, 46, 63–64; rural distribution of, 60; state formation and, 46, 48–51, 53–55, 58, 62–64; state identification and, 19, 29, 34–40, 55–58, 62–63; state officials in, 46–47; state publicity and, 53–55; table of documentary film categories, 42, 43; war with China and, 50–51. *See also* Documentary films; Ministry of Information and Broadcasting

Flag: Republic Day and, 73, 75; as visual symbol, 127
Flag Code of India, 6
Flaherty, Robert, 35–36
Floods: films about, 47, 60
Foucault, Michel, 149
Fragmenting, 46, 69, 137, 147, 161; of culture, 90; diversity and, 53; nature of Indianness and, 102–103; state vision, 48
France, national identity projects of, 6, 14

Gandhi, 6; mass mobilization strategies of, 72; versus Nehru's vision of decolonization, 45; salt march of, 70
Gandhi, Indira, 86–87, 180 n.76, 198 n.45
Gellner, Ernest, 9–10, 13, 130
Government of India Act (1935), 26
Grierson, John, 35–36
Gujarat, violence against Muslims in, 1–3, 166, 171 n.1, 172 nn.5–6

Handelman, Donald, 155
Hansen, Thomas, 55, 169, 179 n.73, 180 n.74, 181 n.81, 217 n.20
Haryana, 92
Hechter, Michael, 10
Herzfeld, Michael, 12
Hindi: in films, 57
Hindu nationalism, 2, 4, 16, 100, 166–

169, 171 n.4, 217 n.20; advertising campaign of, 163; Bharatiya Janata Party and, 166; dissemination efforts of, 16; halting of, 1–2; ideal citizen under, 167; India as *punyabhumi* and *pitrubhumi* (holy land and fatherland) and, 157; religious identity under, 166–167; Republic Day and, 69, 94–95, 100–101; supplanting of Nehruvian secularism by, 69, 94, 166; Swarna Jayatri Rath Yatra procession of, 168, 169; "unity in diversity" and, 168, 169; violence against Muslims and, 1. *See also* Bharatiya Janata Party (BJP)

Hindus: colonial policies on, 24; India as Hindu nation and, 166, 168; India as *punyabhumi* and *pitrubhumi* (holy land and fatherland) and, 157; Rourkela riots and, 152

Hindustan Steel, 86, 138, 143

Hindustan Times (newspaper): on Rourkela riots, 151

Hirlekar, K. S., 36

Hroch, Mrioslav, 10

Husain, Ashfaque, 76

Hussain, Zakir, 53

Hyderabad, 26

Illiteracy, 6, 39

Imagination of institutions, 28, 160

Imperial Department of Information, 37

Independence pledge, 74–75; Republic Day and, 70–71

India, 74; "backwardness" of, 17, 21, 48–49, 107, 109–111, 117, 136; communalism and, 137; consumer goods and, 93; events in shaping understandings of, 27–28; exemplary, 46, 54; Films Division documentaries and, 43–44, 46, 54; as Hindu nation, 166, 168; Indian darkness and, 105–106, 164–165; militarism and, 27, 87–88; as "needy nation," 106–107, 111, 116–117, 129, 131, 165; People of, chart, 19–20, 68; regional identity and, 89–93; Republic Day and, 67, 87–89, 93; statist configuration of, 160–161; "universalizing," 116; in "waiting room of history," 48, 165. *See also* Partition

India Gate, 96

Indian Air Force: Republic Day. and, 75, 83

Indian constitution, 25, 45, 69–70, 96, 192 n.60. *See also* Republic Day

Indian darkness, 104–106, 131, 164–165

Indian flag, 51

Indian Flag Code, 6–7

Indian independence, 25, 69–71, 186 n.113; development and, 39; global development hegemony and, 107; nationalism after, 157

Indian Institute of Mass Communication, 61

Indian Institute of Science (IIS), 118–119, 122, 124

Indian National Congress, 16, 24; adoption of *purna swaraj* (Indian independence) and, 70; Republic Day and, 72; secular-pluralist nationhood and, 157; state-led economic development and, 109

Indian national identity, 16–18, 32–33, 73–75; colonial discourses on, 157; consolidation of, 33; decolonization and, 112, 114; diversity and, 6, 112, 114; Films Division documentaries and, 34, 46–47; national identity card and, 167; versus nation-statist identity, 8; needs discourse and, 112, 114; political discourses and, 16; statist configuration of, 33, 45–47, 160–161; territorial nature of, 89–90

Indian nation-state formation: actors

Indian nation-state formation (continued)
and, 18, 159; authoritative institutional form of, 155, 158, 160; "banal" mode of, 22; colonialism and, 23–27, 111–112, 158–159; contemporary changes in, 163–169; contending visions of, 157; disenchantment and nonresonance and, 21, 29, 33, 35, 56, 58–61, 160; diversity and, 2–8, 24–25; documentary films and, 38–40, 43–45, 62; durability despite diversity and, 4–8; encountering versus believing in, 14–20, 159–160; encounters with, 28; failure discourses and, 17; as field of political discourse, 14–18, 50; Films Division of India and, 19, 159; Gandhian versus Nehruvian visions of, 45–46; Hindu nationalists and, 69, 94, 166–169, 171 n.4, 217 n.20; as historicized field of social and political relations, 21, 27–28, 69, 130–131, 158; homogeneous cultural community and, 112, 114, 155; inconsistent embrace of diversity and, 147–148; Indian independence and, 70–71; "monumental" style of, 38–39; national identity and, 16–17, 112, 114; neoliberalism and, 163–165; "passive revolutionary" nature of, 111–112; postcolonial anxiety and, 38–39; postcolonialism and, 22–23, 38–39, 158; publicity and, 54–55; Republic Day and, 18, 76–82; science and, 38–39, 45–46, 122–132, 158–159; scientific expertise and, 106, 117–123; secular-pluralism of Indian National Congress and, 157; shifts in, over time, 69; spatial practices of, 72, 122–123, 126, 134–136, 139–140, 155–156, 158; steel towns and, 28–29, 30–31, 135–137, 139–140, 155–156, 158; territorial ambiguity of, 25–26, 92, 112, 131; transition from colonial rule and, 25–27, 111–112; uniqueness of, 5–6, 23–25, 106, 111–112, 131, 162; "unity in diversity" and, 25, 158; varied imperatives of, 53–58; war with China and, 27. *See also* Citizenship; Development; Dissent; Fear of politics; "Nation-building" discourse; Nehruvian era; Postcolonial culture and politics; State; Visual representations

Indian News Parade (INP), 37, 158
Indian Tourism Board, 164
"India Shining," 163–165, 200 n.1; appropriation of Nehruvian needs discourse and, 165; versus Indian darkness, 105–106, 165; Nehruvian imagination compared with, 164–165
Industrial India (film), 37
Industrial townships. *See* Steel townships
Infantile citizen, 22
Information Films of India (IFI), 37–38, 158
Institutional pluralist imagination, 7–8

Jammu, 88, 90, 100
Jamshedpur, 137–138
Junagadh, 26

Kaplan, Martha, 13
Kargil war, 97–100
Kashmir, 26, 88, 90–91, 100, 103
Kaviraj, Sudipta, 111
Kelly, John, 13
Khalistan movement, 3, 172 n.8, 180 n.76
Krishna, Sankaran, 38, 142, 176 n.32, 212 n.34

Ladakh, 88
Language, 49, 89, 112, 114, 168, 184 n.102; films and, 49, 60; recognition of linguistic diversity, 7, 25, 161; struggles of the 1950s, 27, 49

Liberation of Lord Rama's Birthplace campaign, 168–169
Linz, Juan, 6

Magical State, The (Coronil), 22
Magic of the State, The (Taussig), 22
Malik, Amita, 81
"Mapping," of state power, 62
March of Time, The (film), 37
Masselos, Jim, 72–75
Media coverage: on Republic Day, 78, 80–82, 103; of Rourkela riots, 150–154
Military: films, 50–51; Republic Day and, 76, 78, 82–85, 87–90, 97–103. See also National security; War
Ministry of Defence, 76, 82; Republic Day and, 95, 103
Ministry of Education, 118
Ministry of Information and Broadcasting, 29, 34, 40–41, 54; Chanda committee of, 58–61; on decorum during National Anthem, 51. See also Films Division of India
Mir, Ezra, 37
Mitchell, Timothy, 18
Moana (film), 35
Mohan, Jag, 32
Mosaic nationalism, 3–4, 92, 147
Muslim Festival in Secular India, A (film), 53
Muslim League, 24
Muslims, 31, 166, 184 n.101; colonial policies on, 24; Films Divisions documentaries and, 51, 52, 53, 64; "good," 53, 64; as ideal citizens, 53; Rourkela riots and, 152; violence against in Gujarat, 1–3, 166, 171 n.1, 172 nn.5–6
Mysore Township, 123, 138. See also Steel townships

Nairn, Tom, 10
Narwekar, Sanjit, 38
National anthem, 51, 196 n.20
National Anthem-cum-Flag (film), 51
National Chemical Laboratory, 80, 126–128, 207 n.75
National commemoration rituals, 28, 104, 158; nation-state production and, 65–66, 158; as performance of nationhood, 66–67, 104. See also Republic Day; Ritual idioms
National Cultural Trust, 109
National Defense Council, 51
National Discipline Scheme, 83, 197 n.34
Nationalist movements, 16; anticolonial, 16; development and, 108–109; January 26th and, 69–71
National Physical Laboratory, 77, 126–128, 207 n.75
National security, 120; under BJP government, 167; discourses, 51; films and, 51; nuclear energy and, 120; Republic Day and, 84–88, 97, 100–102. See also Military; War
"Nation building" discourse, 26, 105–106, 110–111, 113; cultural floats on Republic Day and, 77; failures and problems of, 26, 105–107, 110; impact of, on real lives, 17; inauguration of scientific laboratories and, 127–130; industrial development and, 30–31; Nehruvian vision of culture and, 76–78, 83–84; steel towns and, 133
Nation-state formation, 175 n.24; in Africa, 11, 13, 162; anti-colonialism and, 11, 13; in Asia, 11, 13, 162; as byproduct of structural transformations, 9–10, 12, 130; "coercive" mode of, in Syria, 22; definition of, 15; dual orientation toward time of, 90–91; European, 8, 10, 182 n.89; as field of political discourse, 15–18, 50; as historicized field of social and political relations, 32–33, 69, 130–131, 162;

INDEX : 243

Nation-state formation (continued)
"imagined communities" and, 10–15, 95, 130; "magical" mode of, in Venezuela, 22; in mid-twentieth century versus eighteenth and nineteenth, 13–14; modular transfer of, 13, 22–23, 130, 162, 202 n.27; mytho-pscyhic nation and, 9, 11–12; national commemorations and, 65–66; national identity and, 33; postcolonial, 13–14; premodern *ethnies* and, 9; religious belief and, 11; situated versus modular, 162; socio-biological theory of, 9, 12, 32; steel towns and, 134; theories of, 8–9, 32–33, 130, 162; uniqueness of Indian, 162; variations in postcolonial, 162; Venezuelan, 22. See also Indian nation-state formation

Nation-statist identity, 158–161; versus national identity, 8

Needs discourse, 106–107, 130–131, 159, 202 n.25; decolonization and, 111–112, 114, 130–131; extranational and colonial origins of, 107–110; inauguration of scientific laboratories and, 117, 129; Indian participation and, 110–111, 117, 129; national identity and, 112, 114; nuclear energy and, 116; science and, 106, 114–117, 159, 165; scientific expertise and, 117–125; "scientific temper" and, 123–125; "Shining India" appropriation of, 165; state as figure of need and, 110–111; state as problem solver and, 117

Needy nation discourses, 106, 111, 131, 165; inauguration of scientific laboratories and, 129; science and, 116–117; state as problem solver for, 117

Nehru, Jawaharlal, 32, 50, 126, 133, 141, 180 n.78; adoption of *purna swaraj* (Indian independence) and, 70; decolonization vision versus Gandhi's, 45; on folk dancing, 76–77; on Indians as problems, 105, 109; on New Delhi, 122; on problems in Indian villages, 116–117; on Republic Day, 76–77; on science, 116, 119–122; "scientific temper" and, 123–125; on steel towns, 133–134, 141–142; "universalizing India" and, 116

Nehruvian era, 180 n.78, 185 n.108; colonialism and, 26–28, 158; criticism of democratic practices, 20, 45–46, 161–162; culture and, 76–78, 83–84; development discourses of, 48–49, 110–111, 158; Films Division documentaries and, 50–65; Gandhi and, 45–46; inauguration of scientific laboratories in, 28, 125–130; "India Shining" imagination compared with, 164–165; "infantile" citizenship and, 20, 22; nation-state encounters in, 19–22, 28, 81, 158–161; nation-state formation in, 27–28; needs discourse in, 106–107, 110–111, 114–117, 159, 165; nuclear energy and, 116; politics in, versus contemporary politics, 163; science and, 114–132, 159, 165; secular-pluralism in, 1–3, 53, 69, 166–167; state-centrism of, 19–22, 45–47, 130–131, 154, 158, 160–162, 164; steel townships and, 134–135, 138, 209 n.9; "unity in diversity" encounters, 19–20, 77, 169; war with China and, 86. See also Indian nation-state formation; "Nation building" discourses; Newness and difference; Postcolonial culture and politics; Republic Day

New Delhi, 26, 136; Nehru on, 122; Republic Day in, 75–76. See also Rajpath

New middle classes, 94, 163

Newness and difference, 67, 90–91, 94; Films Division documentaries and, 50; steel towns and, 135, 138, 141–143

New Pastures (film), 50

Nigeria, 25, 96

244 : INDEX

Nuclear energy: national security and, 120; Nehru and, 116; reactors, 114; secrecy surrounding, 120; tests, 66, 94, 100, 167; weapons, 100

Orissa, 139. *See also* Rourkela Township
Our Regulated Markets (film), 47

Padyatras (marches), 72
Pakistan, 84, 87, 94; in "India Shining" campaign, 164; Kargil war and, 95, 97–99; partition and, 5; Republic Day and, 99; Rourkela riots and, 153–154
Parry, Jonathan, 148
Partition, 5, 26, 87, 174 n.18; religious conflict following, 49; territorial ambiguity of, 112, 131
Partners for Plenty (film), 47
Patel, Sardar, 70, 128
Pathy, P. V., 36
Patnaik, Biju, 153
Patriotism, 85, 93
People of India chart, 19–20, 68
"People's science movement," 165
Planning Commission, 110, 120
Politics: discourses of, and Indian nation-state formation, 14–18; Nehruvian versus contemporary, 163; separation of science from, 120–123, 132; steel towns and, 161. *See also* Fear of politics; Hindu nationalism; Postcolonial culture and politics
Postcolonial anxiety, 38–39
Postcolonial culture and politics, 183 nn.92–95; continuities with colonial past and, 23–28, 67–69, 107–111; cultural reform and, 109; development and, 38–39, 107–111, 131, 142, 145; diversity and, 3–4; documentary films and, 38, 51; fear of politics, 64, 106, 154; Gandhi and, 45–46; militarism and, 87; modular transfer of, 22–23, 38; nation-state formation and, 22–25, 157, 162; "passive revolutionary" nature of, 111–112; principal themes of, 22; science and, 114–117; spatial practices, 133–135; state-centrism of, 20, 54, 102, 145; steel towns and, 138–139, 142, 145; urban areas and, 133–135. *See also* Citizenship; Diversity; Fear of politics; Indian nation-state formation; "Nation building" discourse; Needs discourse; Nehruvian era; Newness and difference; State, the
Prakash, Gyan, 115
Prevention of Terrorism Act (2002), 167
"Print capitalism," 10–11, 130, 175 n.24
Prithvi missile, 98–99
Publications Division, 113
Publicity, state, 54–55
Punjab, 90–92
Punjab National Bank, 86
Purna swaraj (Indian independence), 70

Rajpath, 76, 78, 79, 82, 89. *See also* New Delhi; Republic Day
Ram Janmabhoomi campaign, 168–169
Regional conflict, 91–92
Regional diversity: Films Division documentaries and, 43–46, 63–64; Republic Day and, 89–93
Religious belief: nation-state formation and, 11
Religious conflict, 49. *See also* Gujarat, violence against Muslims in; Rourkela riots
Religious diversity, 2; communalism and, 155; Films Division and, 63; naturalization of, 155
Religious identity: Colonial census and, 24; colonialism and, 24, 155; under Hindu Nationalists, 166–167
Renan, Ernest, 50, 174 n.17
Republic Day, 19, 21, 28–30, 44, 64, 79–80, 93, 136; advertisements placed during, 69, 85, 93; changing configura-

INDEX : 245

Republic Day (continued)
tions of, 82–88, 95–96; colonialism and, 67, 69, 71–76, 99, 158; cultural diversity displays and, 76–78, 82–84, 87–92, 100, 102–103; culture as unchanging resource, 90–91; development and, 88, 96; Hindu nationalism and, 69, 94–95, 100–101; imperial assemblage (1878) and, 71–73, 102; independence pledge and, 70–71, 74–75, 96; Indian constitution and, 96; Indian National Congress and, 72; Kargil war and, 97–99; marches and, 72; media commentaries on, 78, 80–82, 103; military and, 76, 78, 82–85, 87–90, 97–103; national identity and, 73–75, 88–90, 93, 100; Nationalist movements and, 70–75, 96; national security and, 84–88, 97, 100–102; national solidarity and, 75, 83; national sovereignty and, 77, 102; as nation-state encounter, 81, 104; Nehruvian vision of culture for, 76–78, 83–84; newness and disjuncture in, 88, 90–91, 94–102; new states and, 89–93, 100, 103; from 1951–1952, 75–78; in 1953, 78, 79, 80–81; in 1963, 83; from 1930–1947, 70–75; opposition and challenge and, 93–94; Pakistan and, 99; patriotism and, 85, 93; regional identity displays and, 89–93, 99–100, 102–103; rhetoric of sacrifice and, 84–86, 96, 98–99; schoolchildren in, 82–84, 99; significance of January 26th and, 69–75, 96; the state and, 18, 75, 78, 80, 101–102; Swarna Jayatri Rath Yatra procession and, 168, 169; in 2000, 95–102; "unity in diversity" and, 69, 73–74, 77, 89–94, 99–104, 168–169; war and, 82–87, 97–100. *See also* National commemoration rituals

Review commissions, 118–119; Chanda committee (on film), 58–61

Ritual idioms, 67, 69, 158; of colonial India, 71–72, 74; diversity and, 71–72; Indian nationalists and, 72, 74; marches and, 72; of Nehruvian India, 125–130; from 1930–1947, 70–75; postcolonial nation-state and, 72; postcolonial versus colonial, 80; science and, 123, 126; spatial practices of Indian nationalists and, 72. *See also* National commemoration rituals; Republic Day

Road to Freedom, The (film), 56
Rotha, Paul, 36
Rourkela riots: connection made to Pakistan in, 153–154; media coverage of, 150–154
Rourkela Township, 31, 134, 139, 141, 144, 150; combating "virus of communalism" in, 151–156; Hindu and Muslim violence at, 148; riots at, 150–155; road layout of, 141; violence at, 137
Rwanda, 25

Sangeet Natak Akademi, 40
Sangh Parivar, 167–168
Sarvarkar, Vinayak, 157
Science and technology, 38–39, 204 n.45; cartography of, 122–123, 126; colonial, 115; education, 114, 118–119; exclusion of masses from, 124–125, 132; films on, 47; inauguration of scientific laboratories and, 28, 110, 117, 125–130, 206 n.73; Indian Institute of Science and, 118–119, 122, 124; nation-state formation and, 122–130, 158–159; needs discourse and, 106–107, 114–125, 131–132, 159, 165; Nehru's "universalizing India" and, 116; in New Delhi, 122; nuclear energy and, 116, 120; parliamentary questions on, 120; Republic Day and, 88, 96; scientific expertise and, 106, 117–125,

131–132; "scientific temper" and, 106, 123–125, 131–132; scientist as Brahmin, 121; separation of from politics, 120–123, 130–132. *See also* Development
Scott, David, 23
Scott, James, 48, 62
Secretariat, 96
Secular-pluralism, 1–4, 7–8, 53, 69, 167, 192 n.60; eroding of, under Hindu nationalists, 69, 96, 166; Indian National Congress and, 157
Shoemaking, 85–86
Slum dwellers, political agency of, 165
Smith, Anthony, 9
Soviet Union, 69, 131, 133; national policy, 92
State, the: culture and cultural diversity and, 13, 44, 76–77, 90, 102–103, 109; development and, 107–110, 138, 158; documentary films and, 38–39, 62; encounters with, 18–21, 28–29, 103, 150, 159; failure discourses of, 17, 21, 27, 105–106, 110–111, 117, 137; Films Division of India and, 19, 29, 34–40, 55–58, 62–63; identification versus national identity, 18; Indian independence and, 70–71; Indian national identity and, 33, 45–47, 160–161; multiple faces of, 21, 48, 78; nation-statism and, 8, 158–161; needs discourse and, 110–111, 117; political discourses structured around, 19–20; publicity and, 54–55; recognition of, as authoritative representation of nation, 14–19, 27, 29, 33–40, 55–58, 62–63, 75, 157; recognition of, and steel towns, 136, 140, 145, 147; Republic Day and, 75–77; science needs discourse and, 115–117; significance of January 26th and, 70–71; simplifications of complex social realities by, 62; speech idiom of, 57; -centrism of Nehruvian era, 19–22, 45–47, 130–131, 154, 158, 160–162, 164; stated and statist nation, 21, 102, 114, 156; transcendent, 55, 158–159; transformation from nation to nation-state, 157–162; "unity in diversity" as central idiom of, 3, 24–25, 69, 102–104, 158. *See also* Dissent; Indian nation-state formation; Visual representations
Steel Authority of India (SAIL), 133–134
Steel plants, 114
Steel townships, 28–31, 133–136, 209 n.13, 210 n.17, 211 n.18; Asansol, 138; backwardness and, 136; Bhilai, 134, 141, 144, 148, 150; Bokaro, 134, 139–141, 144, 150; caste in, 147–148; as catastrophes, 135–136, 144; Chittaranjan, 139; during colonial period, 137–138; community life in, 143–144, 148; contradictions in, 145–148; dislocation of indigenous peoples at, 139–140; Durgapur, 133–135, 139, 141, 143–144, 146–148, 150; economic and ethno-religious segregation at, 141, 145–148, 150, 212 n.26; as exemplary national spaces, 29, 132, 134–136, 140–144, 147, 150, 158–159; labor unrest at, 147–148; Mysore, 123, 138; nation-state formation and, 28–31, 135–137, 156, 158; planning of, 140–143; postcolonialism and, 138–139, 142; reform programs for, 149–150, 156; state encounters in, 28–29, 150; state visibility and, 138–139, 145, 155; structure of political participation in, 143; "unity in diversity" in, 136, 143–144, 147–148; urban planning and, 134, 139–143, 145, 148–149, 209 n.9; workers at, 140, 143, 145–147, 149–150; worker's housing in, 133, 140–141, 145–147, 150, 212 n.26. *See also* Development; Rourkela Township

Stepan, Alfred, 6, 172 n.7
Strachey, John, 108
Swarna Jayatri Rath Yatra, 168, 169
Syria, 14–15; "coercive" mode of nation-state formation in, 22

Tagore, Rabindranath, 46, 196 n.20
Taussig, Michael, 22
Tendulkar, D. G., 36
Terrorist and Disruptive Activities Prevention Act (1987), 19, 180 n.76
Thapar, Romesh, 57
Times of India (newspaper), 83, 105; on Republic Day, 83–84; on Rourkela riots, 151
Town and Country Planning Organization, 133–134, 140; housing at Durgapur Township and, 146
Transcendent state, 55, 61, 158–159
Tulpule, Bagaram, 147
Turkey, nationalism in, 6
Two Decades of the Films Division (Mohan), 32

United Progressive Alliance, 2
United States, 131; "banal nationalism" of, 6, 175 n.25; ethnic diversity in, 7
"Unity in diversity," 2–3, 24–25, 29, 158; as central state idiom, 3, 24–25, 69, 102–104, 158; colonial legacy of, 24–25; encounters with, in Nehruvian era, 19–20, 77, 169; Hindu nationalism and, 168, 169; Republic Day and, 69, 73–74, 77, 89–91, 93–94, 101–104, 168–169; in steel towns, 136, 143–144, 147–148
Urban planning. *See under* Steel townships
Uttar Pradesh, 166

Van der Veer, Peter, 15
Venezuela, 22
Verdery, Katherine, 15
Visual representations, 28; of Muslims, 51, 52; of nation and state, 19, 28–29, 34–35, 50–51, 56–58, 62–67, 104, 127, 139, 158; science and, 127. *See also* Documentary films; Films Division of India; Republic Day

War: with China, 27, 50–51, 82–84, 86–88, 186 n.116; Kargil war, 97–100; Republic Day and, 82–87, 97–100. *See also* Military; National security
Weeden, Lisa, 14–15, 22
Where the Desert Blooms (film), 47
Women of India (film), 37
World War II: films produced during, 36–38

Young, Desmond, 37

SRIRUPA ROY is an associate professor of political science at the University of Massachusetts, Amherst. She is the co-editor, with Amrita Basu, of *Violence and Democracy in India*.

∷ ∷

Library of Congress Cataloging-in-Publication Data
Roy, Srirupa.
Beyond belief : India and the politics of postcolonial nationalism / Srirupa Roy.
p. cm.—(Politics, history, and culture)
Includes bibliographical references and index.
ISBN-13: 978-0-8223-3984-7 (cloth : alk. paper)
ISBN-13: 978-0-8223-4001-0 (pbk. : alk. paper)
1. Nationalism—India—History. 2. National state—India. 3. Nehru, Jawaharlal, 1889-1964.
4. India—Politics and government—1947- I. Title.
JQ231.R695 2007
320.540954—dc22   2006034057

www.ingramcontent.com/pod-product-compliance
Lightning Source LLC
Chambersburg PA
CBHW070758230426
43665CB00017B/2406